In the Name of Wild

IN THE NAME

of

WILD

*One Family, Five Years,
Ten Countries, and a New Vision
of Wildness*

PHILLIP AND
APRIL VANNINI

with Autumn Vannini

a UBC Press imprint
Vancouver. Toronto

31 30 29 28 27 26 25 24 23 22   5 4 3 2 1

Printed in Canada on FSC-certified ancient-forest free paper (100%, post-consumer recycled) that is processed chlorine- and acid-free, with vegetable-based inks.

Library and Archives Canada Cataloguing in Publication

Title: In the name of wild : one family, five years, ten countries, and a new vision of wildness / Phillip and April Vannini ; with Autumn Vannini.
Names: Vannini, Phillip, author. | Vannini, April, author. | Vannini, Autumn, author.
Identifiers: Canadiana (print) 20220249334 | Canadiana (ebook) 20220249385 | ISBN 9780774890403 (softcover) | ISBN 9780774890564 (PDF) | ISBN 9780774890441 (EPUB)
Subjects: LCSH: World Heritage areas. | LCSH: Natural areas. | LCSH: National parks and reserves.
Classification: LCC G140.5 .V36 2022 | DDC 363.6/9—dc23

Canadä

UBC Press gratefully acknowledges the financial support for our publishing program of the Government of Canada (through the Canada Book Fund), the Canada Council for the Arts, and the British Columbia Arts Council.

Printed and bound in Canada by Friesens
Set in Garamond and Meta by Michel Vrana
Substantive and copy editor: Lesley Erickson
Proofreader: Caitlin Gordon-Walker
Cover designer: Michel Vrana

On Point, an imprint of UBC Press
The University of British Columbia
2029 West Mall
Vancouver, BC V6T 1Z2

www.ubcpress.ca

Contents

Prologue

THEY TOLD US WE'D FIND the carnival train ride at the corner of Avenida Baltra and Avenida Charles Darwin. We strolled down Avenida Baltra in the early evening sun, past ice cream parlours with names like 9 Eleven Bazar, Rolls and Pops, and the Corner Sweet Shop. On the corner, two small diving shops, one next to the other, stood beside a bar that advertised happy hour specials on a sandwich board placed on the sidewalk.

We'd been warned that the train had no set schedule. Every evening, it shuttled up and down Avenida Baltra, Avenida Charles Darwin, and Avenida Indefatigable to the tune of its own circus-like jingle. Travelling in a slow loop, it picked up tourists from various hotels along the route and dropped them off on demand at restaurants and shops in downtown Puerto Ayora.

Hotels, gift stands, and pizza parlours along Avenida Charles Darwin, Puerto Ayora

Riding trackless on rubber tires, the train was made of a half dozen wagons, each large enough to accommodate a family in three rows of seats. Each wagon, brightly coloured and covered by a thick plastic canopy, was shaped like a cartoonish animal – a green mouse, a red dog, a yellow duck. At the front, the locomotive looked like a converted VW bug made to look like a pink elephant adorned with flashing lights. When it finally arrived, our nine-year-old daughter, Autumn, was unimpressed. "Maybe after dinner," she said.

If Puerto Ayora were on mainland Ecuador, the carnival train ride would hardly be book material. But Puerto Ayora is not on the mainland. A town of twelve thousand residents located on the small island of Santa Cruz, a staggering 975 kilometres away from the Pacific coast of South America, Puerto Ayora is on an archipelago that most people around the world would never expect to have hotels, resorts, shops, or restaurants, let alone a tacky shuttle train. The name of the archipelago is Galápagos.

It was there, in the Galápagos Islands, in the late summer of 2014, that our journey began. We had long fantasized about travelling to the Galápagos. Inspired by wildlife documentaries and evolutionary biology textbooks, we imagined the place to be the home of world-renowned endemic species and curiously sociable wildlife. We didn't expect a carnival train. Or ice cream parlours. We had no clue the islands would be teeming with cruise ships filled with affluent tourists, a modern and fully developed ecotourism infrastructure, and no fewer than thirty thousand full-time residents of whose existence the outside world seemed to be largely unaware.

There were also scores of other people around the archipelago: scientists, ecologists, and conservationists. Stationed mostly at the research facility at the far end of Avenida Charles Darwin, these people work to make and keep the islands wild. "Wild" might mean pristine or unadulterated, but in today's world – we soon realized – it means something else. Wildness is both an ideal and a specific goal of environmental policy, a criterion that is regularly measured through precise indicators and pursued through the application of regulations and established practices. Not simply an untouched place, a wild environment is often one that is closely guarded and managed.

Though spectacular and enchanting, the wild nature of the Galápagos soon revealed itself to us to be a carefully managed social product: a landscape governed through a complex alliance of environmental NGOs,

UNESCO, the World Heritage program, business interests, and local and national governments. The word "wild" may denote something primitive, undomesticated, uninhabited, or undeveloped, but it is much more. Wildness can be a feeling or an atmosphere. It can be pursued as an ideal. It can be managed as an environmental condition. It can even work as an ideology for the marketing of places and experiences.

When we understand wildness as something that emerges from the way humans interact with a place, we can recognize that different societies informed by different cultures and languages will interact with places in different ways. Different people practise and experience wildness differently. Fascinated by this realization, we dedicated the next six years to learning more about wildness around the world. Over time – through our travels to ten countries in five continents, our own experiences of wildness and wilderness, and about three hundred interviews with residents – we came to understand wildness in a new light that goes against common knowledge.

Wildness is often something that is experienced and defined by visitors, explorers, adventurers, and other people who do not live permanently in the places they label "wild." Wildness, however, is different for residents of so-called wild places. Whereas visitors see absences – of history, of culture, of development, of social relations – inhabitants see presence. Speaking with inhabitants led us to re-envisage wildness as an idea rooted in connection and relation between human and nonhuman lives. It is a vision based on kinship, relationality, and care. It is a dramatically different perspective from the visitors' vision of wild nature as something untouched, remote, and unpeopled.

This book is based on local people's perspectives of wildness. The people we met came from all walks of life. We spoke with business owners, tour guides, environmental activists, local historians, heritage managers, park rangers, farmers, fishers, students, teachers, photographers, adventurers, writers, guards, artists, surfers, climbers, geologists, biologists, pensioners, politicians, and anyone who had something to teach us about the places they call home, the same places visitors call wild.

Though we interviewed over three hundred people in twenty UNESCO World Heritage Sites, we can only feature some of their perspectives. But all of them – regardless of their presence on the printed page – taught us and allowed us to learn about wildness. They taught us what wildness might be, how it feels and, most of all, what it can become: how it can be reimagined as something other than the separation of nature from culture.

Nearly everyone we met lived or worked inside a protected area or in communities next to the site we were visiting. We met people in convenient spaces such as their homes or a nearby park or establishment. Other times, as often as we could, we met people in the sites we were learning about. As people invited us to experience places with them first hand, we learned from their knowledge of that place, saw their perspectives, and endeavoured to understand their viewpoints. We walked much and listened even more.

Early on, we realized that wildness has no borders. It can be experienced atop the highest of peaks or in the valley or town below, deep in the bush, on the edge of town, or in a farmer's field. It can be experienced while staring dangerous wildlife in the eye or heard in the melody of a cowbell. Our experiences of wildness were unlike many found in wilderness books. They pushed us to imagine what else wildness could be if we understood it as something more inclusive and relational and less conventional, confined, colonial, ethnocentric, and anthropocentric.

Wild, unfortunately, is often the exclusive business of explorers and adventurers. Many writers who leave home on a quest to experience the wild are solitary male explorers and adventurers keen on conquering and taming it. In displaying their prowess, strength, and resilience, they reveal, first and foremost, what is wild about them. We, in contrast, were a family who planned our work, travelled, met people, and reflected on our experiences together. Travelling and doing work as a family, especially a family with a young girl, changed not only how we did our work but also how people saw and received us as researchers.

We tried to listen to people and put ourselves in their shoes by asking them what they thought wild was, what it meant to them, where they had experienced wildness, and whether wildness and wilderness were different ideas. By listening to them, we learned and came up with a different, more diverse understanding of wildness than the one bestowed upon us by colonists, explorers, survivalists, or adrenalin junkies. We are merely vessels for their ideas, stories, perspectives, and experiences. As vessels, we hold more doubt and questions than discoveries or answers.

Throughout this book, we refer to ourselves using the first-person plural, "we." "We" most often refers to the principal writers, Phillip and April. But "we" sometimes refers to the three of us, Autumn included. Autumn's experiences, different from those of her parents, are captured in diary-like recollections. In addition to reading the stories we gathered here, you can virtually meet the tellers and visit their homes through our feature documentary film *In the Name of Wild,* available through a variety of video-on-demand platforms. In addition, you can visit most of the sites, and choose your own adventure along the way, through an interactive web documentary (see https://www.inthenameofwild.com/).

We are fully cognizant that our work has a notable carbon footprint. We flew in airplanes, drove rental cars, and contributed our share of waste to the communities we visited. We did this, however, not for the sake of leisure but to learn lessons not available otherwise. Challenging what we take for granted and generating new understandings requires fieldwork – experiencing social and natural worlds, travelling to meet people where they live, and learning from them first-hand. Ultimately, we did it to share original knowledge that we hope will make a difference, knowledge that may encourage you to re-envisage your place in this wild world. This is how we, as ethnographers, learned, and we want to share our learnings with you.

As we travelled, we also abided by the principles of "Leave No Trace." We travelled as a family of three, without a film crew. This book is not about physically going to wild places but rather redefining how we come to understand and experience wildness and wilderness. We learned that people don't need to travel to understand what wildness is – they can look in their own communities and backyards.

Early in our project, as we were driving on the roads of Canada's Yukon territory, we decided to call our project *In the Name of Wild.* When we say "in the name of ..." we invoke a moral authority to speak and act on behalf of a force greater than ourselves. When we say "in the name of the law," "in the name of God," "in the name of justice, or truth, or whatever else," we bear the name of someone or something greater than ourselves, something of great value whose sake we should protect. By saying "in the name of wild," we want to show how wildness isn't just a raw natural force but an institution: a subject of governance, environmental policy, scientific knowledge, local and national politics, global geopolitical dynamics, and complex social histories.

The expression "in the name of wild" reminds us that wildness is, indeed, a name, an idea, a value, and not a natural state that transcends the social world. When we realize this, we become attuned to the fact that, in the name of wild, different cultures indicate different ideas, values, and understandings of nature. So this book's title is *In the Name of Wild* and not "In the name of the wild." There is no such thing as "the wild" as a discrete, tangible entity. "Wild," without a definite article, is an indefinite idea, a possibility, a potential, and a multitude. And that is a good thing. By opening up what "wild" can be, we can reimagine what we can do in the name of it.

"Wild" Can Be a Challenging Word
GALÁPAGOS

"DO YOU HAVE YOUR Galápagos National Park permits?" the stern-faced, blue-jacketed airport agent asked.

We hadn't had a chance to pay the fee yet because we weren't part of an organized tour. "No."

"No problem. You can pay here. It's $250 – $100 for adults and $50 for the girl."

We moved to the side. The passengers behind us, clearly more prepared, cleared customs and flagged the few taxis outside of the small San Cristóbal arrivals lounge.

We dug a small pile of cash out of our suitcases and handed it to the agent.

"Thank you. Enjoy the Galápagos."

There was no airport shuttle to pick us up, and all the taxis were gone. We resorted to our only option – walking. Our travel guidebook suggested it wouldn't be prohibitively long. Quietly, we rolled our suitcases 1.2 kilometres on the dishevelled asphalt of Avenida Alsacio Northia to the heart of Puerto Baquerizo Moreno, San Cristóbal Island's main town.

The time-worn 1992 edition of Lonely Planet's *Ecuador and the Galápagos Islands* had sat at the bottom of a bookshelf since 2004, the year we moved in together. As the price sketched in pencil on the inside cover showed, April had picked it up in 1999 for three dollars at a second-hand bookstore in downtown Nanaimo, British Columbia. A red-billed Tropicbird captured in mid-flight graced its crumpled-up cover. The back cover featured a curious-looking Sally Lightfoot crab. Only a few other images from the Galápagos made it into the book. A cactus. An empty, sandy beach. A distant panoramic view of an unpeopled bay on Isla Bartolomé. A waterscape view of three lonely boats near Islas Plazas. A wooden boat undergoing repair, by no one in particular, in Puerto Ayora. And, finally, in the Appendix, a visual legend for the quick identification of fish and birds.

It had made no sense to pack that guidebook into a moving box in 2004 and hang on to it until 2014, and yet we had. It had ceased being a guidebook long ago. It had become something else – a promised land of sorts. We still thumbed through it every now and then, closing our eyes to add pictures to it, images photographed by nothing but our imagination. We visualized our sailboat – the one we didn't own – docking at a solitary pier under a summer sky. We saw that red-billed Tropicbird gliding over our heads as our feet touched the unpaved ground. When we closed our eyes, we saw a penguin waddling toward us as if to welcome us to the archipelago. We could hear blue-footed boobies squawking, free and unafraid.

Reality was another matter. Earth's "last Eden" – one of the many hyperbolic monikers for the Galápagos – had as much litter as an old port town. Empty water bottles and chip bags had collected against rusty fences that encircled weed-ridden empty lots, among other signs of humankind's fall from grace: the whir and roar of rambunctious scooters and motor-bike engines and a gloomy-looking military base that loomed over the waterfront. Yet the sun stood high and warm in a pollution-free sky, and low-tide scents carried on the breeze. With its souvenir shops and eateries that promised inexpensive ceviche and fruit batidos, Puerto Baquerizo Moreno may not have been pristine, but it was at least approachable and unpretentious.

The Galápagos are a hazy dream in the minds of many wildlife lovers around the world. Once we'd started telling people about our family trip, they'd ask us how we planned to get there without an expedition team and provisions for two weeks, whether we needed a sailboat, whether we had to join groups of scientists working in the wild, and where we'd sleep. Not one friend had a clue that Puerto Baquerizo Moreno had a creperie and a sushi place. Nor did we, really. Our 1992 Lonely Planet guide contained no evidence of such services.

The Galápagos Islands aren't known for getaway travel. They are synonymous with biodiversity, fascinating endemic species, and unusually friendly wildlife. Thanks to Charles Darwin and the generations of evolutionary biologists who followed in his footsteps, people consider the "enchanted islands" a "lost paradise" in the global quest for modernization and industrial development. They are a "natural laboratory" in which to observe nature supposedly living on its own will, untrammelled by the trappings of humankind. This vision makes documentary films, scientific treatises, and travel accounts about the Galápagos so popular and compelling. If you visit the archipelago, the story goes, you'll step back in time, to a time when life was harsher but simpler, purer and wilder.

Wildlife documentaries gloss over the strong social organization at work in this lost paradise. The Galápagos are cleanly parcelled out into two subdivisions. The one that covers 97 percent of the land is how most people envisage the archipelago. It's the stuff of the BBC and Discovery Channel, the stuff that makes wildlife lovers and wanderlust souls tremble with desire. The 3 percent, the area not set aside as a National Park, is where airplanes and plastic water bottles land. It's also where roughly thirty thousand human beings live, work, and marinate ceviche.

Just like rare wildlife species, these thirty thousand legal and illegal human residents are nearly invisible to the rest of the world. Unlike rare wildlife, these beings are not nocturnal, evasive, or endangered. They are simply camouflaged, so to speak, by media accounts that paint the "enchanted islands" as an unpeopled environment.

These people are not Indigenous. A few are descendants of early twentieth-century settlers, others are long-term residents, and most are recent immigrants attracted by a booming economy fuelled by the growing ecotourism industry. They call the islands of San Cristóbal, Isabela, Floreana, Baltra, and Santa Cruz home and welcome the comings and goings of nearly 185,000 visitors per year, most of whom arrive, as we did, by way of a convenient flight from mainland Ecuador and, unlike us, a taxi ride downtown.

After unpacking our bags at the Lonely Planet–endorsed Casa Blanca B & B, we sought out guides to accompany us into the National Park. The park ranges over eighteen major islands and dozens of islets and rocks that straddle the Equator line. Guides are not a luxury, they are mandatory. The Galápagos National Park and the Galápagos Marine Reserve strictly restrict travel. It is illegal to venture inside the park without a licensed guide.

To go anywhere within the park, visitors must be part of either a land-based tour or an expedition ship tour. The land-based tours typically take one day and depart regularly from the main towns. They may stick to land or sail on waters close to the shoreline, but they must return to home base by nightfall. Expedition ship tours can last between five and ten days. During that time, they can sail to the farther reaches of the archipelago and reach nearly all islands, with the sole exceptions of those islands and bays restricted to natural scientists.

We booked our first land-based tour for the next day, then we reminded Autumn, our nine-year-old daughter, that this trip could get rough. Few parents bring young children to the Galápagos. Cost plays a role (then again, places such as the Galápagos are as affordable as an all-inclusive four-star vacation to Disney World), but the challenges of the environment are a primary concern.

We had been backpackers in our younger years. On our first trip together in 2001, we explored India and Nepal on just a few rupees. Each day, we slashed our food and accommodation budget to see and experience more. Now, in our early forties, we believed our responsibility as parents required us to stimulate that same thirst for experience in Autumn, regardless of the challenges. To leave our daughter at home, or to postpone our travels until she was in college, "because it's hard to travel with kids" or "because they might not remember" felt like a terrible excuse. Besides, unlike the leisure trips of our earlier years, this was work travel. Autumn had no choice but to come with us.

We also understood how fortunate our family was to have this opportunity. As ethnographers, we knew we'd meet local people, learn from their perspectives, and eventually see the world from their point of view. As ethnographers, we knew we'd learn about the places we intended to visit in a much deeper way than even the more informed travellers. Unlike packaged tourism or even independent travel, fieldwork opens doors into people's lives and cultures.

Of course, that also meant challenges. Autumn would have to find ways to entertain herself during long interviews, for example. And it meant dealing with occasional difficulties and finding ways to save money that other travelling families, or other researchers, seldom encountered, like catching ferries on choppy high seas instead of flying to save money. Adaptable by nature, Autumn seemed to understand and readily accepted the challenge.

The following morning, we rose early and boarded a small speed boat for our day-trip up the southwestern coast of San Cristóbal and into the National Park. An errant layer of white clouds shrouded the early September sun and provided occasional respite from an otherwise skin-charring sun. As Puerto Baquerizo Moreno receded in the distance, we could finally see the broader contours of San Cristóbal. The island laid low, but a verdant hump rose from its centre into the clouds, a grey, barren shroud. We had heard that the archipelago was no tropical swamp, but no one had managed to convey the sharp contrast between its sparse trees and volcanic shadows, between the browns and blacks of its lava rocks and dirt and its oversaturated aquamarine waters. It was as though a painter had forgotten to colour in the upper half of the landscape.

The two-dozen people on the boat vibrated with excitement. Fresh arrivals and backpackers, their attention focused on their cameras and the wildlife. We had already spotted sea lions sleeping, groaning, wrestling, playing, and shitting throughout the streets of Puerto Baquerizo Moreno. The first appearance of wildlife here, away from town, was a distant family of blue-footed boobies. Half a dozen frigates, happy to display their famous red collar appeared next, yet too far away to be fully appreciated. As the boat swung and cradled us from port to starboard, we struggled to find the best vantage to take photos free of elbows or the back of people's heads in the frame.

When we landed on Isla Lobos, just a few acres in size, paradise broke loose. We stepped off the boat onto dark ashen rocks that guarded access to the red dirt trails. A lizard camouflaged as an ochre-coloured rock cheekily stuck its tongue out at April and recoiled it. A blue-footed boobie sprung its eyes and beak wide in a seeming expression of surprise and concern that we might snatch the brownish egg that found lee under her warm belly. A marine iguana lay prostrate on the warm ground, its scaly skin absorbing the sun's midday heat. Three Sally Lightfoot crabs, their plum and orange shells dotted with beady popeyes glancing forward and backward jostled for position on the edge of their diving platform to the sea.

Our first sighting of wildlife outside the parameters of Puerto Baquerizo Moreno, the blue-footed booby

Galápagos animals truly seemed – as the hype had us believe – unafraid of our predatory human instincts. Never before had we felt such a deep affinity, communion, and harmony with the animal kingdom of which we are part. A quest for authentic, unadulterated, unrestrained wildness had brought us here, and here it appeared in all its glory.

Awed by what lay on the surface, we felt a child-like giddiness at the prospect of diving below. But Autumn, the only child on the boat, had mixed feelings. A decent swimmer in normal conditions, she had never donned a snorkelling mask or fins. Visibly worried, she shared with us her reservations about dipping free of restraints in wavy waters dotted with darting fish, sea lions, and iguanas. These are the moments when, as a parent, you know that making light of a sketchy situation is probably not the most prudent course of action, but it might be the most rewarding option in the long run.

"Don't worry about them," we said. "The sea lions will get out of your way." What parent doesn't say that to his child at least once every summer?

Half-convinced, off Autumn went, aided by a member of our guiding crew. Once she trusted the mechanics of the breathing tube, she ducked her head underwater and made eye contact with a sea lion who had patiently been swimming around her. We had fibbed, she realized. The sea lions didn't get out of the way – they came by to check out what she was all about. Autumn exploded out of the water. She found our faces and beamed a smile more radiant than the sky. She wasn't angry or scared anymore. She was hooked. Over the next half hour, she tried to catch up to sea lions, marine turtles, iguanas, and more fish than our Ecuadorian guide had English words for.

We found the water warm yet refreshing. The floor of the ocean, ten or fifteen feet below us, reflected the light captured by the waves above, forming a strobe-like meshwork of odd shapes on the white sand below. Incapable of speaking through the snorkel in her mouth, Autumn gave the friendly guide a thumbs up. Speechless for deeper reasons, we thought no comment about our circumstances could have been more fitting.

Nevertheless, a different sentiment began to take form. We had no words for it at the time, and as much as we academics like to cultivate our cynicism, we both tried to repress it to enjoy the moment. Yet it was impossible not to feel the tip of that feeling poking up higher and higher in our consciousness with the passing of the hours. There was something domesticated about our experience. We weren't sure if "domesticated" was the right word, but that was the only way we could articulate it at the time.

It wasn't so much that the animals were docile and seemingly pet-like – we found that novel and amusing – but that the experience of being escorted along a well-marked trail, educated by a well-prepared guide, and shown animals as familiar with photograph-posing as celebrities with an Instagram account rubbed us the wrong way. The place seemed as wild as any place is or has ever been on this planet. But was it? Or was it kept that way – gorgeous but planned, safe, and predictable, more like a garden than a wilderness. Had it been gingerly protected from evolving in ways deemed untoward by its wilderness-loving keepers?

Or were our thoughts less about the place and more about the circumstances in which we experienced it? Were we simply peeved because we had to share it with people other than our family; people with cameras, like ours; people with a love of nature, like ours; people who respected the environment, as we did; people who were friendly and kind toward us, as we were toward them; people who were simply too darn nice to dislike and yet, well, just people, like us; people who were there, as we were, and at the same time; people whose presence reminded us that perhaps it was wrong for us to be there as well? Did people, ahem, other people belong in the wild?

We mumbled our sentiments to one another. We noticed that our travel companions, like us, took photos of boobies, iguanas, crabs – all that bounty of wildlife – and tried to keep people out of their frames, just like producers and directors did in the documentaries we watched on TV. Our travel mates, too, had realized that to experience and convey wildness you somehow have to bracket extraneous material out. Wildness resulted from artifice. It was something you had to manufacture, to re-create. "Wild" was everything humanity wasn't, and yet, by glossing over humanity, wildness itself was nothing but a human product.

"Wild" is a challenging word.

"Wild" is used to describe a misbehaving child, a kick-ass party, a city with traffic congestion problems, a piece of salmon that hasn't been designed in a chemical lab, a backyard overgrown with too many weeds. In the same breath, wild is a parcel of land or sea that seems to resist human control. "Wild" – its etymology tells us – signifies something that is self-willed. Relatedly, "wilderness" – arising from a combination of "wild," "deor" (deer or beast), and "ness" (promontory or cape) – is a place that abides by nothing but its own will, a nonhuman will. But if things were that simple, we would be remiss in calling "wild" challenging. What makes the word "wild" semantically treacherous is its lack of formal policing.

If you google "wild Galápagos," *National Geographic,* the Travel Channel, a 3-D IMAX movie come up. They all call the Galápagos "wild." No surprise there. But so does a company called "Wild Planet Adventures," which has a vested interest in selling its cruise package. Others do the same. If they want to sell us a well-kept resort town, they call it "wild." It doesn't end there. The world is full of places that seem wild on the surface.

Wild Dolomiti is the name of a book promising to reveal the Italian Alps' most "pristine" trails. "Wild" is a playground in New York City's Central Park. "Wild Adventures" is a theme park in Georgia, in the United States. "Wild and Natural" is the name of a Cosmetics company that operates on the island of Ibiza, Spain. How can a word be so loose that it can be coupled with anything or anyone? How can it be so generous and so undiscriminating, so cheap and yet still so enticing? Sure, lexical law enforcement is not exactly a thriving business, yet the word "wild" seems more promiscuous than most.

In response to this semantic anarchy, we could establish some clearly demarcated boundaries to protect a true and objective meaning of wild. American legislators attempted to do this when they passed the US Wilderness Act in 1964. For them, "wild" was a land that had a distinctly wild "character" – that is, "untrammelled" land that appeared "to have been affected primarily by the forces of nature, with the imprint of man substantially unnoticeable;" land that had "outstanding opportunities for solitude or a primitive and unconfined type of recreation"; land that was "at least 5,000 acres" or was "of sufficient size" to make its "preservation" practical; land that contained "ecological, geological, or other features of scientific, educational, scenic, or historical value."

Alternatively, we could choose to do what many governments around the world have done: heed the specifications of the world's most influential environmental NGO, the International Union for Conservation of Nature (better known as IUCN). In doing so, we could define "wilderness" as "protected areas" that are "usually large unmodified or slightly modified areas which retain their natural character and influence without permanent or significant human habitation and which are protected and managed so as to preserve their natural condition."

Problem solved, right? Well, only if we are willing to ignore that these two definitions offer no clarity whatsoever on their most important qualifiers. Who determines whether a place is truly unmodified, only slightly modified, or sufficiently modified? What is a "natural character"? When is human habitation "significant"? Above what threshold is the impact of humankind "substantially noticeable"? What constitutes "primitive" recreation? And who has the power to consider something recreational? Hunters? Landscape photographers? Ski resort developers? Hikers? Does a place have to be protected to be considered a true wilderness? If so, isn't the very management that ensures protection a violation of a place's natural (i.e., nonhuman) character? How can something be wild when it has fences around it and surveillance cameras installed at its gates? Above all, whose opinion and perspectives on all this counts?

Things get even worse if we go deeper. More than challenging, the idea behind "wild" can be downright dangerous if you consider that to preserve their natural character – so valuable from a human-defined ecological, geological, historical, educational, or scenic point of view – wild places must be protected from human interference. This ideology has historically been the perfect justification for eviction and resettlement programs that have displaced thousands of residents, turning Indigenous people into conservation refugees.

When used superficially, "wild" is purely rhetorical. It's the Hollywood "wild" of Chris McCandless, played by Emile Hirsch, venturing into the Alaskan bush in *Into the Wild*. It's the "wild" of Reese Witherspoon retracing the steps of Cheryl Strayed along the Pacific Crest Trail. It's the "wild," youthful imagination of *Call of the Wild* and *Where the Wild Things Are*. It's the lawless "wild, wild, West" and the people-less landscapes of "Wild Africa" or India or Antarctica or whatever continent the BBC flies to tonight. It's the pseudo-reality of *Man vs. Wild* and *Out of the Wild: The Alaska Experience* or whatever reality show the Discovery Channel produced last week.

Used politically, "wild" can be divisive, militant. It's the "wild" of fortress-style conservation schemes around the world, schemes that end up separating people from their land in the name of tearing culture from nature. It's the "wild" of first-class ecotourism, which puts an economic premium on luxury ecolodges and turns third-world residents into guides, cooks, dishwashers, and maids. It's the short-sighted "wild" of neat border-lines and environmental zoning, which permits only trail maintenance on one side of a fence and slash-and-burn logging on the other.

The more we reflect on it, the more "wild" begins to feel not only promiscuous and polysemic but also shallow and arbitrary. It's a vacuous brand. Exchanged like cash, "wild" is a dirty, anonymous, and spiritless currency that has more value here, less there. In this capitalist environ-ment, remote fishing and hunting lodges, green eco-resorts, guided paddling adventures, and entire countries are marketed and sold in the name of wild.

We are not the first to notice this. Throughout modern and contem-porary history, wild, wildness, and wilderness have fed the book-publishing industry as much as they have the business of TV and film production. From Thoreau and Goethe to Snyder and Turner, from Strayed and Bryson to MacFarlane and Griffiths, scores of writers before us have answered the call of the wild from places wild in their minds and their hearts. But "wild" continues to evade cognitive capture; its affective notional slipperiness mimics its remarkable semantic agility.

The idea of wild is elusive, but so, too, are its geographical referents. When you seek wildness, where, precisely, do you go? Logically, to a place where you expect to find it, to a place that you deem wild. That is what most writers and adventurers do. But when you do, a problem emerges. If you look for wildness where you expect to find it, what you see mirrors your mental images. Wild places become a mere test of your ideologies, a manifestation of your fantasies, aspirations, and fears. Wilderness areas become fantasies of well-cultivated minds and well-trained bodies keen on putting their Instagram flag on the next highest peak.

We faced the same challenge at the beginning of this project. Keen on researching wildness and wishing to better understand it, we kept asking ourselves where we should go for our fieldwork. Our family loves small islands. We live on one, and we have travelled for leisure and for work to a handful of small islands around the world. Left to our own devices, we would have uncritically dragged Autumn to countless small islands across the world in search of wildness. But to what advantage? Wouldn't those travels, in the end, simply confirm our initial hypothesis about the insular nature of wildness and wilderness? Wouldn't the wildness we'd stumble upon simply confirm our notion of what constitutes wildness in the first place?

Having realized that day tours would lead us to a limited number of destinations, we booked a last-minute discount deal on a multiday cruise expedition. Having never been on a cruise before, the word evoked goofy imagery from *The Love Boat*, a TV show that ran in the late 1970s and early '80s: well-manicured captains, overly accommodating crew with plastic smiles, white-linen-covered tables, five-course dinners, and Bermuda shirt-wearing passengers indulging in lounge music dances at night.

Reality wasn't much different, even though our ship's chief guide vehemently insisted three times a day over five days that ours was "not a cruise" but rather an "expedition ship." We still had a Jacuzzi on the sundeck, a breakfast buffet, and plenty of 1980's-style cocktails and Bermuda shirts.

Unlike *The Love Boat*, our cruise was small, educational, and focused on a prepackaged notion of adventure that had been negotiated with the National Park authorities. Their guidelines allow nearly two hundred ships to sail around the Galápagos in two categories: small yachts and larger vessels. Small yachts accommodate sixteen passengers, larger vessels nearly one hundred. Both options focus on ecotravel and wildlife encounters.

Small yachts are more intimate (which sounds nice until you come to terms with the fact that you have nowhere to hide from those fifteen other people). Small yachts can also be slightly more luxurious and may be structured to cater to niche interests. Larger vessels provide more generic services and are typically better suited for families who wish to share a larger cabin and for people who are prone to experiencing motion sickness.

Galápagos National Park regulations also stipulate that large vessels must take people ashore in shifts, in numbers no higher than sixteen. So, as much as we bemoaned having to sail around the archipelago with nearly seventy people, we knew that we could learn from their experiences as well. Moreover, we'd be taken to places chosen by distant authorities with a clear, official vision of what constituted wildness and wildlife. By going to places we had not quite chosen, we could learn something new and discover something unexpected. We went to bed the first evening and wrote notes to this effect in our journal. The first half day had gone by without much to whine about, and we looked forward to sailing to the farther reaches of the archipelago overnight.

The next morning after breakfast, before the excursion, the chief guide, a young man, warned us that the water would be quite cold. Fortunately, our package included wetsuit rental, and all sizes were available, "even children's," he announced while looking at Autumn. "However," he added, "I'm sure that our one child on board will find that in comparison to her Canadian waters our sea will feel as warm as a swimming pool, and I doubt she'll need a wetsuit."

Autumn offered a groggy smile in return. She wasn't feeling like herself. The constant rocking motion of the top-heavy ship throughout the night had resulted in poor sleep, little appetite, and an unnatural craving for motion-sickness pills.

"Come on, Autumn, you'll feel better once you're in the water snorkelling," we said.

She smiled, softly and unconvincingly, without making eye contact with either of us.

We couldn't wait to get off the ship either. The day before, we had spent only a half hour in the water after two hours of jostling for unencumbered views of pink flamingos and terrestrial iguanas. The chief's briefing, however, went on and on. He advised us about strict park regulations, restrictions on our movements and activities, and the need for our earnest collaboration in keeping the park "pristine." The islands had zero facilities, so our short excursions had to be planned in detail. He underlined that the only sign of human presence on these islands would be a few "dry landings." We had to listen to the warning three times a day for five days in a row. It went something like this:

Remember! There are two kinds of landings. They are different from one another. Very different. Who can tell me what they are? Anyone? Yes, Tim? That's right! Good remembering: dry landings and wet landings. And what's the difference? Does anyone remember? Yes, Fenfang? Good job! Wet landings mean that we pull our Zodiac on the beach. Dry landings mean there is a rocky shore, and so we walk off the boat onto steps carved on the rock. So, this morning's landing is wet. Which is okay, because ours is an e-x-p-e-d-i-t-i-o-n ship, right? Not a cruise. We're here for adventure. Anyway, a wet landing means what? Yes, Gabriela? Good job! No sneakers, only sandals. Did everyone pack their sneakers? Muy bien! You guys are terrific. Everybody gets artisanal gelato and a glass of 1992 Malbec tonight for doing such a good job!

Though the "adventure" wasn't real, the restrictions were. Upon landing – either wet or dry – we had to march in step with our small group's naturalist guide, listen to his interpretive lectures, take nothing but photos, and leave nothing but footprints. And since we had to keep pace behind the group of sixteen in front of us, and ahead of the clan behind us, minor schedule deviations were unthinkable. And so were off-trail detours. Outing after outing, bay after promontory, island after islet, our ship anchored punctually, Zodiacs departed and returned on schedule, and the captain reliably got us back on course before another vessel arrived on site, all as planned by the itinerary gods of Galápagos National Park.

Our guide – an approachable university-educated local man in his early thirties – explained to us that the ships' schedules were even more complex than they seemed. Restrictions dictated how many yachts and ships could operate in the archipelago, which kinds of boats could travel to certain destinations and, of course, how many visitors could set foot on each island, on any specific day or month, and at what hour of the day. This meant that larger ships, smaller yachts, and day-tour boats needed to adhere to rigid timetables put together during painstaking planning sessions held months in advance in the name of sustainable ecotourism.

With a tight schedule in place, we settled into a quotidian routine. Eat breakfast. Receive a daily briefing. Take part in the first excursion. Return to the boat for lunch while the captain sails to the next destination. Alight for another excursion. Mind the gap between the ship and the platform. Return for supper. Sleep while the crew sails on. Repeat the process the following day.

On the third day of our journey, we anchored off Rábida, a small island known for its bright maroon sand. As usual, our guides helped us step onto and off the Zodiacs. As usual, we were guided around the short trail. As usual, we were told about the wildlife that called Rábida home and about the park's sustained historical efforts to exterminate invasive species such as rats. As usual, we were given options to choose from: after our short walk, we could either board a glass-bottom Zodiac and motor along the shore or snorkel around the beach on our own. As usual, we returned to the boat on time for our meal. It felt as though wildness, just like dinner, came à la carte.

Gentrification is not simply an urban phenomenon; it happens in wild places too. Whereas development drives urban gentrification, ecotourism drives the gentrification of wild places. The comfort of visitors, convenience of access, control of behaviour, the education of travellers, and the beautification and rewilding of nature in light of existing environmental standards are the cornerstones of the gentrification of wilderness.

Unlike urban gentrification, the gentrification of the wild works in subtle and nearly invisible ways. Our cabins were cleaned punctually every morning. Our three meals a day were healthy, tasty, and abundant. An onboard doctor looked after us any time we desired her attention. A waiter poured us a stiff drink every time we provided a credit card. The crew laid out fruits, treats, tea, coffee, and juice every time we returned from an off-ship excursion. All this comfort and convenience did not affect the wildness of the places we visited, but it engendered a systematic loss of self-responsibility on our part as travellers.

Like children, we were constantly taught and educated. Our guides' constant interpretation of the natural history around us rendered our world certain, secure, sensible, firm, and real. In this pre-interpreted world, iguanas spat, male sea lions acted out, and frigates showed off in predictable ways. Like parents, our guides knew best. Science knew best. Official interpretation triumphed over our naive curiosity. There was no room for surprise in this gentrified wilderness, no patience for our imagination. There was no enchantment, no wild wonder.

The education we received gave us a sense of control over the situation. The guides' constant interpretation informed our perception of the world and reinforced the need for careful planning. Just as architecture works together with urban planning, here, conservation was working together with science education to make our experience positive and free of doubts and unpredictable encounters with danger. In this neighbourhood, we were all subjects of science and international environmental governance. We were schoolchildren on a field trip. We were ecotourists.

As you would expect from a gentrified neighbourhood, our little ecotourist bubble was clean, beautiful, and camera-ready. No litter on the ground. No one carried prohibited goods. No unwanted residents. No loiterers. No one carried firearms; the only thing you could shoot were photographs. In a beautified urban neighbourhood, you need to worry about nothing but enjoying yourself and consuming sights. In this wild neighbourhood, there was nothing but sights, nothing to be done but sightsee.

Days before our excursion to Isla Lobos, we had struggled to label our experience. It felt domesticated, but we knew that wasn't the right word. We had now found a better qualifier – "gentrified." Like a gentrified urban neighbourhood, the national park had a much higher economic value when its wildness was thoroughly planned, tamed, and controlled for the sake of ecotourist sustainable development.

Whether tourism is sustainable in the Galápagos is a matter of perspective. In 2014, the Galápagos received an annual average of 185,000 visitors, a mind-blowing growth from the few thousands who had travelled to the remote archipelago as recently as thirty years before. This spike in arrivals came with problems serious enough that Ecuador resigned itself, in 2007, to labelling the islands "at risk," and UNESCO added it to its blacklist of World Heritage Sites "in danger."

The trouble laid not so much in tourists' well-regulated bodily presence in the park but in the logistical challenges that tourism brought to the archipelago. Most notably, the expansion of the tourist industry fuelled massive increases in labour-driven migration to the Galápagos from the Ecuadorean mainland, which has resulted in both a serious infrastructural crisis and restructuring of the island economy, politics, and way of life.

Presented as a naturally unpeopled landscape, the Galápagos are allegedly a place for nature only. People are threats to the fragile environment, they are strangers who do not fit in, and they are simply an invasive species. Humans are not part of nature, this argument goes, and without people meddling with self-willed nature, the Galápagos are and will always be a pristine, untouched wilderness.

Try stepping out of this cognitive box, however, and you realize that the Galápagos are not a pristine natural laboratory for the study of evolution. It is only because the islands have been imagined and idealized that way, and only because that deeply ingrained idealization has resulted in the careful manufacturing of a seemingly pristine landscape, that they look so untouched and feel so wild.

The separation of people and nature in the Galápagos depends on clearly demarcated borders between the land and marine reserve and the area where local people work and live. And while the latter has remained constant in terms of space at 3 percent, over the last fifteen years, the resident population has more than doubled as mainland Ecuadoreans have come to the archipelago in search of better-paying jobs.

As people continue to move, tensions mount. Despite the government's strict regulations on domestic immigration, resources and infrastructures have stretched thinner and thinner. The availability of clean water and sewage disposal are grave concerns for residents, and the arrival of new invasive species along with immigrants and tourists has become the biggest threat to endemic biodiversity.

Wilderness areas around the world are "fragile" and "threatened" environments. But the words "fragility" and "danger" often obfuscate other issues: social and cultural dynamics that are easy to forget because we often think of wild places as empty of people. Scores of anthropologists, environmental historians, and geographers have been trying for the last three decades to correct our ignorance; unfortunately, they've had limited success.

In 1996, for example, a provocative volume edited by American historian William Cronon, *Uncommon Ground*, pronounced that pristine wilderness is not quite what it seems. Wilderness, Cronon and colleagues argued, lives first and foremost in our collective imagination and is rooted in the idea that humankind is somehow not part of nature. When we separate people and nature to keep nature safe, untouched, and pristine, we ignore that people are nature, that they have lived and altered every single environment in the world, and that by excluding our species from fragile areas deserving of wilderness protection, we humans essentially give our species the licence to destroy the unprotected rest of the world. The myth of an independent nature ignores the interconnections between our species and all others on this planet we call home, and it hides the notion that nature – as we understand it, imagine it, conceptualize it, defend it, legislate it, experience it, exploit it, study it, enjoy it, and protect it – is very much an idea that our species has created.

The Galápagos may be thought to be wild, but history shows us that they are not people-free. A human presence in the islands was documented as early as 1535. Throughout the seventeenth, eighteenth, and nineteenth centuries, whalers and pirates regularly stopped in the archipelago, mainly to stock up on giant tortoises. The word is that they taste very good. The pirates found that they also kept well and could survive up to one hundred days without food or water. Reports dating nearly a century ago state that whalers took and ate as many as one hundred thousand Galápagos tortoises in the 1800s alone.

Keen on legitimating its sovereignty claims over the islands, the government of Ecuador facilitated a progressive colonization of the Galápagos throughout the nineteenth and twentieth centuries, when many people came in search of guano and coal. Salt mines, sugar cane plantations, small agriculture, a mill, a tortoise oil industry, livestock raising, and fishing were also undertaken – all with a mixed bag of fortune and misfortune. Curiously, the Ecuadorean government even went so far as to advertise settlement opportunities in European newspapers, and more than a few families made the journey across the Atlantic in search of Eden (a subject well-portrayed in *The Galapagos Affair: Satan Came to Eden,* one of very few documentaries to focus on local social and cultural issues instead of wildlife).

By the 1960s, as many as two thousand people lived in the archipelago. Life wasn't easy. An arid climate, difficult terrain to cultivate, and dramatic isolation from the rest of the world meant that people had to be content with subsisting on hunting feral animals and growing fruits and vegetables in the humid highlands of Santa Cruz, San Cristóbal, and Isabela. Oral histories detailing memories of those days depict tightly knit communities and a simple life punctuated by intermittent arrivals of ships from the mainland carrying mail, goods, returning relatives, occasional scientists, and handfuls of new migrants.

Nature in the islands has not been pristine or untouched for at least half a millennium. People have been just as much part of the fabric of life in the Galápagos as wildlife. Yet it was the wildlife, thanks to the diffusion of Darwin's theories, that attracted evolutionary biologists to the islands. Starting in the early 1950s in particular, a few groups of scientists began to actively lobby the Ecuadorean government for active protection of the Galápagos. Subsequently, in 1957 UNESCO asked a German ethnologist, Irenäus Eibl-Eibesfeldt, and an American ornithologist, Robert Bowman, to travel to the archipelago to explore the possibility of establishing a permanent base for visiting scientists. Two years later, the recently formed Charles Darwin Foundation (CDF) managed to persuade the Ecuadorean government to create an officially protected area, paving the way for a biological research station. Today, the CDF's sprawling compound lies just outside of Puerto Ayora's town centre, and it draws most of the cruise-ship passengers given a few hours to spend in town at the end of their journey. The CDF is also a powerful lobby, just as it was in its early days.

A few decades ago, representatives from the Charles Darwin Foundation and the Galápagos National Park sat down together to discuss what types of tourism would best serve the dual goal of conservation and economic development. Rather than exploiting the local environment and its scarce resources with land-based tourism and the related infrastructure it would require, it was determined that floating hotels (expedition ships) would simultaneously assist in land conservation and in attracting well-to-do visitors.

Floating hotels would cruise around the archipelago without requiring any infrastructural development other than the occasional dry landing. Nature-loving tourists could simply fly in and out of Baltra Island – where the American military had previously built an airport during the Second World War. From there, they could easily board a ship, take a tour, sleep and eat on board, and finally return to their home base in the mainland.

This all seemed like a brilliant idea.

Given the alleged environmental soundness of the floating hotel model, we had several ethical qualms about seeking bedroom space in town. By eating imported food, we feared we'd contribute to the environmental costs associated with shipping goods from the mainland and we'd end up giving local fishing folk and farmers more reasons to seek expansion of their business into park and marine reserve land. By showering at a bed and breakfast in town, we knew we'd consume precious water. And by flushing down the toilet everything we ate, we'd clearly pile on the sewage disposal problem affecting the communities. Little did we know when we made our reservations back in Canada that advocates of land-based tourism in the Galápagos had recently been making increasingly compelling arguments for the ethics of their business.

One morning, we told our bed-and-breakfast host, Sofia, that we had given a great deal of thought to our choice of accommodation. We were satisfied with our choice, we told her. She couldn't have been happier to hear that conclusion. By visiting the towns, we could get a glimpse of local culture and understand the uniqueness of social life in the archipelago. "These islands are not only 'a paradise,'" she said. "When you're a tourist, you can see that side. But when you live here as a resident, you can feel the social problems we have."

Highly educated, progressive, supportive of conservation principles, and adamant about the need to protect the unique environment and culture of the islands, Sofia was particularly upset with the local institutions. "I never liked the little attention that social problems get. Nature gets attention, but humans don't. I have been here for twenty-five years, and I am still not able to drink potable water from the tap here. If you are talking about an equilibrium between animals and people, here, we should have good education, good hospitals."

Politically involved and of strong voice, Sofia was critical of local politics, and she sensed we related to her feelings. "The Galápagos are a *marca,* we say in Spanish, a brand." Her voice rose over a cacophony of chanting birds and roaring motorbikes outside the breezy breakfast room.

And a successful brand they are. In 2007, for example, tourists spent US$419 million in the Galápagos. However, only US$62.9 million entered the island economy. As it happens, most cruise ship tourists reserve their cabin space from abroad or through large travel agencies based in the mainland, and cruise ships are owned largely by foreign interests and a small number of mainland Ecuadorean families. Because cruise ship tourists spend hardly any time in the main towns, very little of their money lands in the hands of small and medium-sized local businesses. To compound the problem, cruise ship operators are not obligated to hire their crew locally and often end up employing workers from the mainland who are willing to take in lower wages than islanders.

Small independent businesses such as Sofia's B & B and the many locally owned restaurants and shops operating in Puerto Ayora and Puerto Baquerizo Moreno are starting to change these trends by promoting the advantages of land-based tourism for the sake of social and economic justice. However, the inequalities coursing through the Galápagos economy still run deep, and many locals perceive the politics to be unfair.

"I was recently in Germany," Sofia said, "and I told a woman I was from the Galápagos. She tilted her head in disbelief and stared at me for a while. 'You are human,' she said to me, as if she had discovered a new species. 'I didn't know there were actual humans living there!'"

We laughed and told her some of our fellow cruise passengers did not believe us when we told them there were thirty thousand people living on the islands. Most of the cruises skirted towns and inhabited areas.

"As residents, we are fourth-class citizens here," she said. "The animals are first, the scientists and conservationists are second, the tourists are third and, finally, there are the residents." In fact, a handful of researchers interested in the social conditions of the islands have recorded similar sentiments over the last few years. In survey after survey, residents lament that much more attention is given to the health of various wildlife species – tortoises in particular – than to people.

For example, during a 2012 tsunami warning, the Ecuadorean military and park officials organized a large-scale aircraft and naval evacuation of tortoises, whereas humans largely had to fend for themselves. One stinging outcome of this process was that Lonesome George – the last known surviving member of the Pinta Island tortoise subspecies – was taken to a luxury hotel in the highlands whereas a group of less-mobile senior citizens remained behind.

Sofia told us that many galapagueños have for some time been frustrated with the disparities between the amounts of money channelled into conservation at the expense of social well-being. Their discontent isn't unfounded; the CDF itself has argued that improving social conditions too much could result in larger numbers of immigrants coming to the islands in search of higher standards of living. Compounded by inefficient governmental administration, slow bureaucracy, and corruption, this attitude has played a crucial role in making residents of the archipelago unhappy. So, while cable TV, high-speed internet access, and the frequency of air connections with the mainland have improved considerably over the last few years and now rank among the best in the continent, acute diarrheal diseases, fungal infections, and intestinal parasites resulting from contact with contaminated water continue to plague residents.

Over the last twenty-five years, conflicts have also erupted over restrictions placed on fishing in the archipelago. Sea cucumber fishermen have been particularly aggravated by policies imposed by Galápagos National Park without prior consultation. Following a total ban on sea cucumber collection – largely seen as a punitive response to illegal overfishing – angry fishermen retaliated in 1994 by exterminating tortoises, sharks, and sea lions.

Tensions continued for years. In 2000, Isabela Island fishermen burned park offices and threatened to kill the park director, who escaped only by hiding in the mangroves. More violent strikes erupted in 2003 and 2004 when machete-wielding fishermen took over some visitor sites and went after park officials and scientists, who again just escaped. The indiscriminate killing of animals continued. In 2007, eight tortoises were destroyed on Isabela Island. In 2008, 53 sea lions were decapitated. In 2009, another 18 tortoises were found dead. And in 2011, fishermen turned their murderous anger toward 357 sharks.

Invasive species-control and removal programs have also been a controversial issue. In 1971, scientists estimated that 77 introduced species existed in the archipelago. In 2008, the number had reached 888, of which 31 were considered invasive. In response, between 2001 and 2007, US$43 million were spent in various projects aimed at eradicating introduced species such as goats, whose eating habits make survival difficult for tortoises.

Notably, one of the most controversial eradication programs involved an elaborate plan to employ specially trained sharpshooters to fire at goats from advanced-warfare helicopters. To find as many goats as possible, a few captured female goats were equipped with signal-transmitting GPS and given hormones to attract unsuspecting male goats. The two-year long program was funded to the tune of US$18 million by the national park and CDF together with the USAID, the World Bank, and the Global Environment Facility, as well as a few other smaller donors. The snipers took down 140,000 goats, and nearly all the meat was left to rot, when it could have instead fed many families.

As these histories of discontent and conflict make obvious, views of the Galápagos as wild and pristine are not just abstract attitudes existing in people's minds. Rather, these ideologies have manifested themselves in policies that have resulted in isolating wildlife from people's communities, in separating park management from the political administration of the islands, and in striving to restore park landscapes to supposedly pristine conditions without paying sufficient attention to the social and economic consequences of environmental protection. Recent improvements in both environmental and political relations have resulted in UNESCO taking the Galápagos off the list of World Heritage Sites in danger, but a lot of work remains to improve conditions of life for both humans and wildlife.

We are ethnographers. Ethnography is the study of culture as practised by researchers in anthropology, sociology, geography, education, and countless other social sciences. First and foremost, ethnographers learn from people, people with whom they interact as part of their research over days, weeks, months, and at times even years of extended relationship building, observation, dialogue, and shared participation in daily activities and practices of all sorts.

Contemporary ethnographers learn the same way early anthropological ethnographers did. They learn first and foremost by virtue of people's generosity, their kindness and openness, and their willingness to teach them. As ethnographers, our work often entails travelling, meeting strangers, gathering the lessons they teach us, making sense of that knowledge by putting it in a broader context, and drawing insights from those lessons, often by referring to whatever teachings other researchers have shared before. Guiding our work is a simple principle that asks us to put ourselves in the shoes of others, to see the world from their eyes.

Like journalists, ethnographers tend to write stories, but our purpose is neither investigating culprits nor exposing "the truth." Our work focuses on understanding, on learning from what people can teach us, on accumulating experiences and perspectives to arrive at insights into lifeworlds often distant from our own. Unlike journalists who are driven by agendas, or perhaps by the need to get to the bottom of something, ethnographers are often driven by curiosity and wonder.

We had travelled for research to many other fascinating places before, but the Galápagos had long captured our wonder and that of the people around us. Before departing for Ecuador, we noticed that our friends and families looked toward our little adventure with vicarious excitement, anticipation, and admiration. More than any other travel we had undertaken before, the Galápagos seemed truly remote, wild, the last frontier of modernity and civilization.

So it was hard for us to be cynical, as academic types often are. We hated the idea of going back home with stories of environmental threats, short-sighted conservation policies, social problems, and economic injustice. We loathed our newly found conviction that visitors to the Galápagos could only find some kind of paradise there so long as they did not realize they were in an ecotourist bubble. And most of all, we dreaded the notion that an expensive and systematic conservation plan had managed to maintain 90 to 99 percent of the historical biodiversity of the islands at the obvious expense of the islands' true wilderness. For if "wilderness" signifies a self-willed land, then most certainly the Galápagos – with their fenced park borders, their advanced-warfare helicopters, their reintroduced species, and their "Keep on Trails!" signs – were nothing but the most gentrified natural environment on the planet.

The trouble with wilderness, observes environmental historian William Cronon in *Uncommon Ground*, is that it hides the fact that the entire surface of the planet has been modified in one way or another by humans. There are no pristine places left, anywhere. And to think there are some, somewhere, only leads to ignoring, hiding, and sometimes purging people's presence from the places we somehow disillusion ourselves into deeming wild. So instead of looking for wilderness in the earth's most iconic landscapes, Cronon concludes that we might as well seek a wild closer to us: in our backyards, in city parks, or even in abandoned industrial sites where nature is making an unexpected comeback on its own.

As academics, we could relate to this argument intellectually. But as lovers of wild nature and at a sentimental level it simply turned us off. And as parents, we did not want to tell Autumn that we would spend two weeks the next summer looking for wildlife in a place such as Vancouver's Stanley Park or a former industrial site by the airport. As lovers of the wild, we did not want to surrender our faith in wildness because of our disenchanted belief that no self-willed places are left in the world. As citizens of this planet, we did not want to throw away the baby (conservation) with the bathwater (our society's limited understanding of nature). Like our friends and families, we had been attracted to the Galápagos in the first place because of a sense of hope – hope that wildness would still exist. But had we found it? It was doubtful.

Our short trip to the Galápagos had clearly sparked a crisis in our minds and our hearts. We knew that protected areas were necessary for the sake of biodiversity conservation, but we had also discovered that the dualisms and the speciesism that conservation policies rely on could at times be noxiously arrogant, blind, and unjust. We knew that wilderness was a myth and that the very notion of pristine nature was just an empty ideology and a business brand, but we were unwilling to accept that places such as the Galápagos are no wilder than that patch of grass in our garden overgrown with dandelions.

What now?

"Wild" Can Be an Adjective

TASMANIA

AFTER OUR RETURN HOME to British Columbia, we struggled for months with the meanings of "wilderness" and "wildness." Dictionary definitions, theoretical discussions, and historical writings only seemed to make things muddier. We felt the need to ask people what wild meant to them, to learn from their perspectives, and to experience wild places in person. As ethnographers, we simply wanted to travel to places, meet people, and learn from them.

Phillip's research grants at the university allowed for some fieldwork travel, but more funds were needed to expand the project. So we drew up a new grant proposal and submitted it to the Social Sciences and Humanities Research Council of Canada. The research design was simple: find out what wild meant to people who lived in wild places. A few months went by, and then the response letter arrived in the mail.

Rejected. Too ambitious, too vague, the reviewers thought. And they were right. The problem wasn't so much the idea, but the plan. In our grant proposal, we'd essentially argued that wildness could be found anywhere. But if it could be found anywhere, the reviewers argued, where, precisely, would we go to seek it? Where would we spend research council money, exactly? We had no real answers in our plan.

The trouble with both wilderness and wildness is not so much that they are not clearly defined and catalogued but that they can't be, and perhaps shouldn't be. Once you recognize what's wild – name it, file it, gazette it, put it on a list, and monitor it – it doesn't feel so wild anymore. It feels like its will has succumbed to the administrative prerogatives of state bureaucrats. Moreover, once you define it and measure it, you immediately realize that what you're measuring is nothing but your idea of what wild means. But without authorities, whose words do you take as truth? Do you listen to the definitions of hard-core adventurers, with their quests to penetrate and tame the wild? Ardent conservationists, with their political agendas to prioritize fragility? Marketers, ready to package wilderness as a five-star ecoresort getaway? Whose wilderness areas do you add to your list, whose idea of the wild do you embrace, and whose do you exclude?

We had other funding that allowed for a limited amount of research, so we turned to the UNESCO World Heritage List to generate a temporary list of destinations. Since 165 states around the world have signed the UNESCO Convention on World Heritage, we figured the list had some degree of international authority and recognition. This was a place to start. The solution would present itself when the time was right, we hoped. Existent research funds would suffice to cover Phillip's travel, and our savings and Aeroplan points would have to cover April's and Autumn's. We purchased a new Lonely Planet guide, and the planning began.

First target: the Overland Track. Considered one of Australia's most famous multiday hikes, the Overland Track criss-crosses Cradle Mountain–Lake St. Clair National Park, right in the heart of the Tasmania Wilderness World Heritage Area. Typically completed in five or six days, the track is considered almost a rite of passage among Aussie outdoors lovers. At eighty-two kilometres, the track was long enough and undeveloped enough to be meaningful but not prohibitively exhausting. Beautiful, diverse, and teeming with wildlife, it seemed challenging but not dangerous. We wouldn't have to bushwhack, and there would be no encounters with threatening species. The Overland Track, in short, would allow us to get a sense of wilderness down under.

Because about eight thousand walkers complete the track each year, the government has created a reservation system during summertime to prevent crowding on the trails and shelters along the way. Hikers pay an AUS$100 fee, choose a departure day, and make a promise to not loiter along the way and to end their hike on time – five or six days later. Before departure, permits are validated and attached to backpacks, and off you go. It seemed straightforward enough. The online system showed that December 18, 2015, was still available. We liked the idea of being off the trail by Christmas, so we secured our spot.

Soon enough, we had two more dates and two more bookings. On December 18, early in the morning, a shuttle would pick us up from our hotel in Launceston and drop us off at the park's headquarters. And on December 23, another shuttle would meet us at the ferry landing on Lake St. Clair's shore and deliver us back to Launceston, where our leftover luggage would be waiting.

Then it was time to book airplane tickets and buy new, reliable trekking and camping gear. Sitting at our computers and doing background research wouldn't get us in shape for the trip, so we decided to start hiking the trails around our island. To get our bodies accustomed to carrying heavy loads, we hiked with heavy backpacks. It was fall, and the trails were often muddy from the West Coast rains; that too, we thought, would be a key terrain challenge to get used to.

In addition to the physical preparation, we made a conscientious effort to prepare Autumn psychologically. She was a good walker for her age – she was then ten years old – but walking for six consecutive days would require tremendous effort. We coached her about pacing herself, listening to her body, expressing her feelings clearly and promptly when she was tired or sore, and learning how to enjoy the pleasures of fatigue and the feeling of achievement. In her typically easygoing and upbeat way, she seemed keen and optimistic, which in turn made us feel calm and confident.

By the time we landed in Tasmania, the antipodal spring had started to give way to summer. Launceston's city centre streets were lined with locals enjoying beer outside pubs and restaurants. Shops sold beach toys and advertised swimwear specials. Cafés attracted passersby with their smoothies and ice creams. Among all this – in a profoundly incongruous manner to our Northern Hemisphere minds – pictures of Santa and the elves adorned shop windows promoting gift deals on anything from barbecue grills to surfboards. Unlike mainland Australia, the island of Tasmania enjoys a taste of four seasons. Launcestonians seemed visibly excited about the return of the warm season and couldn't wait to spend

Christmas Day on the beach. Every day after 4 p.m., the whole town appeared to shut down as people headed outdoors to play and relax.

In all, Tassie (Tasmania) seemed pretty awesome. Other than the annoyance of having to decipher the meanings of odd adjectives and unduly abbreviated nouns, life down under felt entirely, er, cruisy. After we filmed two interviews with trekking guides in Lonnie (Launceston), Tassielink showed up at our hotel doors on December 18, loaded our meticulously packed rucksacks, and drove us off to Cradle Mountain. The time had finally come.

Of all the World English expressions for walking outdoors, Australian English has the most adventurous-sounding. North Americans hike, which sounds too much like a chore. In England and Ireland, people either walk (which to North American ears is generic and somewhat urbanized) or ramble (which sounds unfocused, drunken, and weird). Kiwis, on the other hand, go tramping, which to Canadian and American speakers connotes something off-topic, like jumping rides on steamers or freight trains. Aussies, ideally, bushwalk. Though bushwalking is no different from any other form of recreational countryside, mountain, or wilderness walking, the notion sounds something quintessentially Australian with its emphasis on undeveloped, somewhat scruffy backcountry.

Countless volumes have been written on the culture of walking, trekking, rambling, fellwalking, hillwalking, tramping, hiking, and bush-walking – each of which has important historical, geographical, and social dimensions. But the literature all boils down to this: walking in the open country strengthens the body and the soul, and it teaches the walker the virtues of effort, planning, self-sacrifice, achievement, and dedication. A hike allows the walker to learn about the self through contemplation and reflection. Walking also teaches its practitioners about the land through direct exposure and observation. The slow but sustained pace of walking allows ramblers to dedicate their attention to the uniqueness of local ecologies and the beauty of the landscape, drawing historical lines of connection with our predecessors. Tramping around the backcountry can educate walkers about basic survival skills, affirming self-reliance and self-confidence. Walkers, it can be safely concluded, are good for society and good for the environment. Arguably, walking is one of the prime ways to experience wildness, but you have to get to the trailhead first.

After a smooth highway drive from Launceston, the Tassielink shuttle van climbed the steep, narrow, and windy road to Cradle Mountain. Turn after turn, the van swung side to side and jostled over bumps and dips. As it did, Autumn got sick. She spilled the beans on the side of the road not once but twice. Motion sickness wasn't a first for her. In Quito, Ecuador, she had barfed at least four times, and we knew the heat and the twisty road were the cause. We didn't worry much.

After the van dropped us off, we decided to loiter by the park's headquarters to give her a little time to recover. Ethnographically speaking, the break was advantageous in that it gave us time to observe how the park entrance so neatly encapsulated all that was unique to Cradle Mountain. Large buses, vans, and cars spilled day visitors from nearby towns and cities into tourist traps located steps from the parking lot. There were helicopter rides, whitewater rafts, Tassie devil tours, and whatever else loafer-donning day trippers from the city were willing to throw money at. This commercial circus surrounded the bureaucratic park machine, which included rangers' offices, an interpretive centre, historical and ecological displays, and systematic entry-fee processing.

By the time we laced up our boots and snapped a photo of ourselves by the large, metallic sculpture that marked the start of the Overland Track, it was thirty-three degrees Celsius. Hanging around to give Autumn a chance to regain her colour meant we started later than we desired. It was eleven o'clock, and though she was nowhere near her best form, we could not afford to further delay our departure.

The first part of the trail, when our backpacks were heaviest, featured the highest elevation gain. We absolutely had to get started before lunchtime. Our permit and reservation specified that we had to leave that day to reach Waterfall Valley, 10.7 kilometres away, to sleep overnight. Because of the uphill climbs, that journey could take up to six hours, arguably more at our unhurried pace.

The start of the track crossed over a large buttongrass valley with gentle-rising hills covered in Gondwana-type vegetation. Farther afield lay rocky Cradle Mountain, only 1,545 metres in altitude but much

mightier in character. This was no real bushwalking, though. One kilometre in, our boots had yet to touch the soft tussock that lay beneath the
long, wide, wooden boardwalk, covered in metallic mesh to prevent slip-
ping. Boardwalk hiking was a luxury for the feet and hardly any effort at
all.

"I don't feel good," Autumn said. Her face had lost its colour. She
was sweating and she shook.

We paused. We spoke to her calmly, gave her some water, and
reassured her that she could do this. We relieved her of most of the content of her backpack to give her a boost. After a few minutes, she stood
up and smiled softly. We started walking again.

A few minutes later, the duckboard gave way to a compact surface.
After a few hundred metres, when the track entered low-ceiling forest
that wove around a fast-moving creek, the boardwalk began again, and
we walked on actual stairs.

"Can we stop?"

This time, Autumn's tone frightened us. She was scared, and as her
words echoed into our ears, we began to fear this could be the end, fifteen minutes into the beginning. Had we overestimated what our ten-
year-old could do? Was our entire project based on an impractical
assumption that we could do this as a family?

We told her not to worry and asked her if she wanted to stop for
lunch. She agreed. She grabbed a water bottle while we opened the backpack to make sandwiches. We realized we had another problem. We'd
left the salami we'd bought to make lunches for the next six days in the
mini bar in our room at the Launceston Best Western.

"No worries, guys. We have wraps and nuts and bars and dried fruits.
We can still have a great time without salami in our wraps, right?" Phillip
said. We smiled awkwardly at one another.

Twenty minutes of mixed nuts later, we tackled the stairs.

"Guys, I can't do this. I feel so sick." Only ten steps in, tears streamed
down Autumn's face.

Added to the World Heritage List in 1982 as a mixed cultural and natural
site, the Tasmanian World Heritage Wilderness Area encompasses 1.5

million hectares, approximately a fifth of the state. The UNESCO World Heritage List was founded in 1972 and it is currently comprised of 1,154 sites, 897 of which are cultural, 218 natural, and 39 mixed natural and cultural. World Heritage Sites are considered significant to humanity based on their historical, cultural, sociopolitical, biological, or geological value. The sites lie in all seven continents and are protected by national laws and international treaties.

UNESCO does not enforce regulations or manage the sites. That's up to the local and national authorities, who promise UNESCO to preserve them in accordance with agreed-upon conditions. Once a site is nominated by local and national committees, UNESCO evaluates it based on ten pre-established criteria (six of which focus on cultural and four on natural standards) and advertises it by including it on the list and through its logo.

Though some countries (e.g., Italy, China, Spain) and continents (e.g., Europe) are vastly overrepresented in contrast to the rest of the world, the World Heritage program is widely accepted, well recognized, and reputed to be a successful initiative. This, we recognized, was good news for us. There it was: a list, an official list of places where we could go in our search of wildness and its diverse meanings. No longer would we have to randomly cherry-pick our sites. No longer could we be accused of seeking wildness in places we had ourselves pre-emptively defined as such.

The list gave us more than enough places to choose from in our global search for wildness – whatever that might mean to the people who lived, worked, and played there. Finding the ultimate wildness at those sites wasn't the point. Finding protected areas where a conversation about wildness could start was our goal. This idea morphed into a revised grant proposal, which we had submitted just days before we booked our tickets to Tasmania.

Before leaving, we had also contacted a graduate student at the University of Tasmania, Marisa MacArthur, who had expertise on the island's environmental politics. We asked Marisa to connect us with Tasmanians who could teach us about wildness and wilderness. She introduced us to a dozen people. Martin Hawes was one of them. We met him in Hobart twelve days after the premature end of our overland bushwalk.

"At the moment, I probably have the best job of my life." Martin beamed with joy under the warm December sun. He was exploring plans for a one-hundred-kilometre track across the Tarkine area, in the northwest of the state, an area that had been the subject of a forty-year conservation campaign. For Martin, who had long enjoyed and advocated the virtues of off-track walking, this was ironic. He had been the monitoring officer at Tasmania Parks and Wildlife for seven years, where he surveyed tracks and assessed the work to be done on them. A well-known photographer, he'd also kept himself busy writing articles and books on wilderness and its qualities.

We told Martin we were surprised by the amount of duckboarding on the Overland Track. The boardwalk separated us from the land, we explained, and it felt like a freeway in the wild. He understood exactly what we meant.

"I came across this quote years ago," he said. "It's said that a certain Native American tribe had a particular word for the psychic shock of stepping out of a teepee. And it struck me as being quite profound, because a teepee is just a flimsy thing, a very thin barrier between the world and oneself, and yet they recognized that the sense of being inside and protected and separated and then stepping out of that was actually a psychic shock. Living in so-called civilization, we've lost a tremendous amount of sensitivity to the wild, its subtlety, its depth, and its power. And one of the consequences of that is that we don't realize how profound the difference of putting a track in can be."

Martin spoke deliberately, and we listened intently, nodding in agreement. There had been times during our short trek when the only sound we'd heard was that of our boots on the boardwalk, the clambering noise of rubber banging on metallic mesh.

But Martin told us the effect wasn't just sonic – it was also visual and conceptual. "To give you a very simple example, when you put a track in you divide the world into left and right. But with no track, the mountain is your guide, and one of the lessons of walking in wild country is the wholeness of life. It's not divided. And, unfortunately, tracks do divide."

Indeed, tracks divide. They make walking simpler, they speed things up, but they are also inevitable. The environment in Tasmania is incredibly fragile because of the nature of the soil, a large amount of yearly rainfall, the steepness of the landscape, and numerous other factors. Walking in such an environment causes severe erosion, so hardening trails is a necessity.

"It's important to keep some areas track-free," Martin said. But in high-visitation areas, boardwalks are unavoidable, and high-visitation areas become higher-visitation areas once you make it easy to walk in them.

Martin spoke and gave us a self-assured, convincing smile. He was in his fifties, and throughout his life he'd travelled enough into the back-country of the world that his words carried a heavy weight.

"First of all, it's not possible to experience wildness without going into it on its own terms," he said. "The word 'wilderness' has been debased. If you abuse it, it starts to become meaningless. After all, we could say we're in wilderness here and then have a cup of tea at the café, but the fact is that at the very wild end of the wilderness spectrum, you have to go into it on its own terms."

Martin's argument is well-accepted and recognized among wilderness enthusiasts around the world. Wilderness, the argument goes, is far out there – inconvenient, remote, uncomfortable – and therefore an immensely pleasurable antidote to the shackles of civilization. Accepting that argument, however, means raising the bar high, so high you start calling everyone who uses the world "wilderness" a boaster, or maybe a demagogue. Wilderness, in other words, is never quite wild enough. There is always somewhere else that's wilder.

But here is a thought. Let's assume that wilderness is far out there in remote spaces untrammelled by society, places such as deep in the Amazon, Antarctica, or the Arctic. By pushing wilderness to the edges, far away from where most people can get, do we do wilderness a favour or a disservice? We might be doing it a favour if we believe in its sanctity and scarcity, in its uncompromising character, in its clear distinction from everything that isn't wild. But by treating it in such a way, do we not also make it nearly impossible for most people to get a taste of it? Do we not exclude most individuals from accessing and appreciating its wildness? Or is that exclusion necessary to preserve the wild character of a place?

We told Martin that wildness in the Galápagos had been largely gentrified. Boat schedules and access regulations ensured that wilderness remained out there, far from wet and dry landings. And now, it seemed to us, something similar was taking place at Cradle Mountain. The real wilderness seemed to lay far off the boardwalk – somewhere in the bush, far away from where the hikers travelled. Wilderness seemed impossibly elusive, always ahead, never in full grasp. Because of that elusiveness, we could imagine it, fantasize about it, but never quite experience it authentically. Cradle Mountain, like the shoreline of the Galápagos, was nothing but a gateway drug: a little tease, a small taste of what might have lied beyond if we could have just been able, been allowed, to venture farther.

After turning around, crestfallen, we walked to the park headquarters at Cradle Mountain to explain why we had given up. By the early afternoon, the headquarters had quieted. Overland Track hikers had left for the first hut. Day trippers were either busy with lunch or taking the last photographs of the day before their bus journey back to town. We were the only ones with our backpacks on.

We approached the desk. Our daughter was sick, we pleaded, but she would feel better the next day, so could we delay our departure? Nothing could be done about it, we were told. Tomorrow was a different day. Other hikers had reserved that departure day a long time ago. There was no extra space at the huts.

We had a planning disaster on our hands. For the next five nights, we had made no plans other than camping at huts along the Overland Track. Now, a campground across the road from the park's headquarters was our only choice. Since we still had our meals-in-a-bag, tents, sleeping bags, and mats, we resigned ourselves to the notion that camping for almost a week would be better than returning to Launceston.

Autumn felt guilty and distraught that her passing illness had ruined our plans. But our parental responsibilities trumped our research obligations. We knew that she would soon feel well enough to do day hikes around Cradle Mountain.

The next morning, we woke up in our tent, laced our boots, packed a lunch full of nuts and dried fruits, and headed for the shuttle bus stop at the park's headquarters. The shuttles obligated visitors to drop off their car at a single lot by the quarters and take transit to the trailhead of their choice, thus reducing congestion inside the park. We also found them convenient because they allowed us to observe who was coming and where they were going. These visitors could be said to belong, roughly, to two groups.

The first group was comprised of people who stayed overnight. On their day hikes they carried cameras, water bottles, and packed lunches in small backpacks and wore trail shoes, not quite hiking boots, but good walking shoes, nonetheless.

Second, there were day visitors who returned to the city at the end of the day. Time pressures clearly appeared to curtail their ability to walk. Some carried water bottles, though most didn't. Only a few wore back-packs and most wore sneakers rather than trail shoes. For the most part, their ambulations were nonlinear – they walked for a bit in one direction, turned and walked for a bit in another, looking for a different photo-op, then turned again.

Members of the latter category included large groups of tourists from eastern Asia. To make their travel easier, the Hobart Airport had been recently expanded to allow China-bound larger-bodied jets to take off and land. However, Cradle Mountain was far enough from most airports that the only way in and out was by bus. Bus travel from the nearest cities meant an early wake-up, a late return to the hotel and, thus, a rather brief outing at Dove Lake. Their movements were tightly planned. Escorted by Cantonese- or Mandarin-speaking guides, groups had two hours at Dove Lake to snap a few photos within a 500-metre radius of their bus.

We spent the day walking around Dove Lake jotting notes in our journals, recording images, and adjusting to the temperature. By midday, strong winds lifted from the south, carrying dark clouds that soon obscured the top of Cradle Mountain. The first raindrops fell as we closed the loop on the lake hike and boarded the bus back to the campground.

Cradle Mountain, as seen from Dove Lake

The tent held up well during the overnight downpour, and we woke up late the next morning. The faint morning sun broke through the clouds as we mixed our instant coffee. The temperatures had cooled ten to fifteen degrees since the first scorching day. After a meagre breakfast of cereal bars, we set out for the trails. On the day's schedule: a short hike to Wombat Lake followed by a visit to the Waldheim Cabins. Hardly wild, we thought, but we were wrong.

We have always been independent travellers, and independent travel lends itself to two competing approaches: tight scheduling versus the happy-go-lucky, go-with-the-flow (even if it means sleeping a night on a bus station floor) style. Though we have no philosophical reservations with the latter, we are too ambitious to let chance dictate our path. Our family has always travelled on schedules – not tight plans, as in the North American sense of the word (today in Rome, tomorrow in Venice, Paris the next day, and then four European countries in five days before flying home) but tight from a logical and organizational standpoint. It's a logistical thing for us: if we only have three weeks in a country, then we're going to make sure that we research the place, list every destination we wish to see, and arrange everything in advance – hotels, trains, flights, permits, everything – to make sure we don't miss out on anything. We don't want to rush between destinations or waste a day looking for last-minute accommodation.

Having said this, we find that nearly every time we travel, chance magically throws a cosmic wrench in our plans. We call these black holes in our scheduled itineraries "travel lulls." A travel lull can last a few hours or even a few days. During a travel lull, our personas seem to morph into something different. We become more relaxed, less controlling, almost fatalistic. A travel lull is a time to explore what we never thought we would, a time to meet people we never thought we'd meet, a time to do things that simply aren't quite our style. Travel lulls are slow, at times even boring. But it is out of that temporal quagmire, and fuelled by boredom, that a travel lull turns into a time to wonder and wander. It is during a travel lull that the unpredictable happens.

And so it was on the slowest, least-scheduled day of our entire time at Cradle Mountain – itself an entirely unscheduled travel lull of its own – that magic happened. The boardwalk from Waldheim Cabins back to the trailhead crossed the same buttongrass field we'd traversed on our first day on the Overland Track. The view was familiar. A wooden path stretching before us. Asymmetrical Gondwana trees. Round hills rising above the valley. Stubby triangular mountains. Nearly square wombat scats dotting the duckboard. Rectangular signs indicating the direction and how far to the next car park (as if one could ever get lost walking on a duckboard). It was there and then, in the dullest of moments, that unforgettable wildness came to life.

"What's that thing ahead, right below the boardwalk?"

Autumn, several steps ahead, rushed forward and within moments reached a family standing nearby the thing we had spotted. She slowed. Stopped. Kneeled. Her right arm reached down. Two blond girls her age were doing the same thing. We sped up, but by the time we reached her, she'd already pulled up her arm and stood on her feet.

"I just wanted to see what its fur felt like," she said with a cheeky look. "It's kind of rough."

The "thing" was a wombat. A short-legged, quadrupedal marsupial of the Vombatidae family. The wombat – without a care in the world for the three girls who had gotten a feel of the fur on its back – ate grass. Our ten-year-old, who a year before had asked us if we could buy her a platypus for a pet, was now gaga over wombats.

Wombats have strong teeth and powerful claws, tools they use to dig deep, extensive burrow systems. Wombats are herbivores: they eat grasses, roots, bark, and herbs. They mostly hang out in the open at dawn, dusk, and night, but daytime sightings are not uncommon at places such as Cradle Mountain. We had read that wombat attacks on humans are extremely rare, yet their powerful teeth and claws can leave deep puncture wounds. When startled, wombats can also bowl over humans, causing dangerous falls. Yes, yes, and yes, but did we mention how adorably cute they are? About one metre in length and half that in height, they are chubby and have grey spiky hair. Their pudgy faces – small beady eyes and a button nose – make them look like a cross between a raccoon, a cat, and a bear cub. They might as well wear a sign that says "Go ahead, I won't bowl you over. Pick me up and cuddle me!" Yet you shouldn't. We shouldn't. Most of all, Autumn shouldn't have.

During a travel lull, the unexpected reigns supreme. Chance rules over plans. Even in a place guarded and controlled, a place like a board-walk, wildness can spring to life in the shape of a magical encounter with another species.

"I'm going to call him Spiky," Autumn said.

"Okay, but be sure not to touch wildlife again. It's not good for you or them." We turned our camera toward Spiky and snapped a shot.

Cradle Mountain didn't quite seem like a wilderness. At best, it's a "wilderness area," a broader zone comprising a wilderness core and a peripheral area through which the core can be approached. Regardless, the potential for wildness to come to life was still there, very real, very much present.

Wildness is an expression of our lack of control over our environment. It is chance, spontaneity, ephemerality. Wildness is life unrestrained, excited, unruly, indulgent, and full of wonder and amazement. Wildness is a travel lull in a more predictable journey.

After a week of camping, we left Cradle Mountain on Christmas Eve and travelled to Hobart to interview people Marisa had put us in touch with. As we spoke with them, we delineated a few rough conceptual differences between wilderness and wildness. Bert Spinks, a bushwalking

A daytime sighting of Spiky the wombat, named by Autumn after touching its fur

guide, taught us to view wilderness as a noun, wild as an adjective. Nouns are categories, he told us, whereas adjectives are more open, fluid, less easy to prescribe.

Wilderness, on the other hand, had been subjected to a great deal of operationalization in Tasmania, as Martin Hawes and his friend Grant Dixon explained to us. We met Grant Dixon in Hobart. He, Hawes, and Paul Smith had contributed to the definition of wilderness used by the state of Tasmania for mapping and planning. Grant – a Tasmania-born earth scientist, photographer, and wilderness recreationist – had been bushwalking since the age of fifteen. In his late fifties, his long list of adventures included mountain climbing in Antarctica, Africa, the Himalayas, the Andes, North America, and Europe.

"I've seen a lot of the world, a lot of wild places," he admitted in a self-assured but soft-spoken tone. It was his love of wildness that had persuaded him of the usefulness of advocating for and participating in a wilderness-mapping project as part of his work with the Tasmanian Parks and Wildlife Services.

"Many of my recreational colleagues who don't see things in quite the same sort of scientific way as my brain seems to work think it's unnecessary to classify things and come up with ways of measuring wilderness, because they think it's just about the experience. But if you're going to look at it from a land-management point of view, then the fundamental idea behind that is maintaining and enhancing wild character."

Though we sympathized with his colleagues' argument, we couldn't help but see the validity of his point. Systems for categorizing and measuring wilderness have their limitations, but they have their uses, too, especially in conservation management.

Grant told us the definition of wilderness had to be simple to facilitate a reliable measuring system. The definition depended on assessing two variables: remoteness and naturalness. Naturalness could be measured using a variety of basic indicators to assess how much change humans had brought to an environment. Remoteness was a more difficult criterion. "Remoteness is how you get there," Grant explained. But the calculations aren't simply based on distance. "In the more recent versions, we changed it to time because time is more relevant than distance."

Having walked at high speeds on the first few kilometres of the Overland Track, we agreed that time mattered more than distance. Ten kilometres on a boardwalk could take as little as a couple of hours. The same distance on a rough track could take a day.

Grant agreed. "Once you upgrade a walking track and make it easier to walk further in a given unit of time, the time-remoteness contour pushes out and, therefore, the wilderness quality of the wilderness area you're walking through declines. So, developing tracks is no different than developing resorts in the wilderness, except in terms of its scale."

Unlike resorts, however, it's difficult to do without tracks. The Western Tasmanian high country is so sensitive to tramping that it needs protection from as few as one hundred visitors per year. Building tracks, Grant admitted, is much easier than restricting access. Tracks are a "necessary evil. They are another blot on the landscape visually and, therefore, they have an impact on the naturalness of the landscape and therefore the wilderness character of the place."

Regulation, management, and control, in our experience, were other key forces behind the appearance of naturalness. "I don't think it takes away from naturalness, but regulation certainly takes away from overall freedom," Grant said. That had been a necessary compromise in the twentieth century. Preserving the exclusive feel of wilderness meant restricting access, and that entailed regulation, control, and enforcement. Nevertheless, regulation, too, reduced the naturalness of the experience.

We recounted our experiences at Cradle Mountain to Grant. We noted that mass tourism detracted from naturalness and remoteness. Even when perfectly sustainable, mass tourism results in crowding, noise, and annoyances of various kinds. He agreed. The trend of mass tourism to the edges of the wilderness was a relatively recent one in Tasmania. "Tasmania's marketing angle is wilderness-oriented, and people think they can come here for a couple of days and see the wilderness. It's impossible," he said. Mass tourism brought bus tours from China. New middle classes bringing money to the state was more desirable – from an environmental sustainability perspective – than dealing with the consequences of a resource-extraction economy, but it, too, had an impact.

"These folks don't get out on the tracks," Grant said. "They might walk around Lake Dove, but otherwise, they're staying somewhere in Devonport or Launceston and go up there for the day, and that's all possible because of the development at Cradle Mountain, because of the roads."

The idea of wilderness as the sum of (time)remoteness and naturalness is intriguing in its practicality, simplicity, and usefulness. Give us a place, tell us how far it is, how intact it is, and we'll give it a score. But how valid, how comprehensive and diverse, was that score?

Unfortunately, the one Australian we wanted to ask had passed away. By the time of her sudden death in 2008, Val Plumwood, an ecofeminist philosopher, was universally recognized for her contributions to wilderness thinking and writing. Unlike other philosophers who had a penchant for writing about nature from the confines of a city library, Plumwood had lived all but an urban existence.

Born as Val Morell, she spent the first years of her life with her parents in a shack made of hessian sacks dipped in cement, deep in the Terrey Hills near the Ku-ring-gai Chase National Park, north of Sydney. Her father was a hod carrier then poultry farmer. After completing her studies in 1965, she and her husband, the philosopher Richard Routley, became involved in movements to combat deforestation and promote biodiversity. Their work became a central point of reference for scholars and students interested in anthropocentrism.

In 1975, Morell and her husband decided to build a home near Plumwood Mountain on a 120-hectare clearing in a rainforest seventy-five kilometres from Canberra. After their divorce in 1981, she changed her last name to Plumwood but continued to live there, writing and lecturing at various institutions. She was found dead on March 1, 2008, presumably of a stroke.

Plumwood's writings on wilderness were revolutionary. The idea of wilderness, she found, is both androcentric and ethnocentric. She argued that the notion of a pure and inert virgin land, separate from civilized society and awaiting conquest and taming by courageous explorers was chauvinistic and disrespectful of Indigenous peoples' relations with their environments. It was a faulty notion created by urban men unreflexive about their settler mentality.

It was also an anthropocentric notion, she believed. Anthropocentrism is an ideology premised on the notion that humans are at the centre of the cosmos and occupy a special and privileged position in the universe. One of the manifestations of that special position is the separation between humans and nature, an idea that deeply permeates Western culture.

That idea lies at the foundation of what philosophers call reduction-ist thinking. Reductionism is a way of analyzing and explaining complex phenomena in terms of other phenomena believed to be of a larger, more powerful magnitude. Examples of biological reductionism include reducing human behaviour to the ways neurons fire in our brains and explaining natural processes as sociolinguistic constructions.

For Plumwood, reductionism is a mistake. It is a mistake to explain away culture in terms of natural processes, an argument favoured by many evolutionary biologists. But it is also a mistake to reduce nature to a social construction – an argument typical of many philosophers keen on demonstrating that wilderness is purely an arbitrary idea produced by historical circumstances. Nature and culture are not opposed, Plumwood argued, because they are bound to each other, forming a complete whole. The idea of wilderness, and wildness, should not, there-fore, denote a dualist separation between culture and nature, between people and wildlife, between society and environment, between civiliz-ation and biodiversity, between modern and premodern ways of life. To extend Plumwood's argument: viewing naturalness and remoteness as conditions of wilderness might help us distinguish between wild spaces and cities, but it reinforces the very ideas that separate us humans from the natural world, to which we are bound.

Our trip to Tasmania left us rather discouraged. For the second time in our travels, we had failed to get a taste of "true wilderness." Of course, as ethnographers, we knew that measuring wilderness by the criteria of remoteness and naturalness was simplistic. Yet our job was to learn from the people we met and to view the world from their perspective. From the perspective of people such as Grant and Martin, what we experienced at Cradle Mountain was clearly something other than wilderness.

We learned something else. Wilderness was one thing, wildness another. Wildness may very well be a quality of wilderness, a fundamen-tal aspect of its condition, but it is also a fleeting character that can appear nearly anywhere, any time. "Wild," as an adjective, seemed more fluid, more open-ended. "Wilderness," as a noun, seemed like a definite cat-egory that something either fit into or did not.

On the morning of December 31, 2015, while the world readied to celebrate the arrival of the new year, we packed our bags and made our way to the Hobart Airport. Though the word "wilderness" was nowhere in the name Te Waipounamu World Heritage Site, part of the South Island's Fiordland National Park, we knew New Zealand could teach us something new.

3

Wild Can Be Ephemeral

AOTEAROA-
NEW ZEALAND

IN DOWNTOWN QUEENSTOWN, New Zealand's outdoor leisure capital, snowboarding, rafting, hang gliding, bungee jumping, aerobatics, skydiving, kitesurfing, parasailing, climbing, and countless other adventure outfitters competed fiercely with cafés and pizza joints for tourist dollars. Set against the background of the Southern Alps and majestic Lake Wakatipu, the town teemed with cool lads and lassies cruising up and down Beach Street while busloads of older travellers meandered through golf resorts and wineries.

After landing and struggling for half an hour to find a parking spot downtown, we picked up our trekking passes from the Department of Conservation and headed for the road. About an hour's drive from Queenstown lay the pretty and much quieter town of Wanaka, tucked at the end of the eponymous lake. It was there, at their gorgeously stylish home overlooking a distant mountain chain and sweeping valley, that we spoke with Martin Hill and Philippa Jones. We had learned about Martin and Philippa through their environmental artwork. Their projects featured assemblages of found natural materials such as shells, sticks, and rocks that they arranged, balanced, or knotted into mind-bending shapes set against wild landscapes and photographed before the landscape reclaimed them through waves, tides, or other natural processes.

The middle-aged couple – he a UK expat and she Kiwi-born – had given extensive thought to the meaning of wildness and had keenly agreed to meet us for our first interview in New Zealand. "For me, wild is in my consciousness," Martin reflected as we sipped tea. "I take the wild wherever I go, and wild, to me, is the way nature works."

Wildness is inherent to any ecological system, he told us. Wildness isn't something that resides only within animals, or within places, it is a force that could be awakened, or sidelined, depending on how an eco-system functions. Wildness can come and go. Unlike ideas of virginal wilderness that hinge on the notion that once development occurs, wild-ness is gone forever, Martin and Philippa told us that wildness could be brought back to a landscape even after it had been scarred by industry. Rewilding, the name of this practice, was, indeed, well-established in Europe and in places where "original" wilderness zones had long been lost.

"However," Philippa said, "New Zealand is quite unusual in the sense that we have a lot of native flora and fauna, and once you wipe that out with weeds and pest species, you lose it. So, whereas Martin might look at them and think that a piece of ground is wild, it may have actually been destroyed, farmed, and eventually gone back to the first species that colonized it, but I wouldn't call it wild. Martin comes from a very tamed country."

Martin smiled. "Yes, that's why I came here!"

Quite possibly it's why we chose to go there too. Whether it's a prod-uct of successful marketing or something more authentic, New Zealand enjoys a powerful status among the world's nature lovers. We were opti-mistic we could finally find a sense of wildness there, and as it would turn out, Martin and Philippa's ideas about wildness as an ephemeral force would be foundational to our experience in the coming days.

Unlike artists who capture wildness as a snapshot in time, Philippa and Martin's artwork profoundly epitomized ephemerality. Their art, like wildness, wasn't meant to last forever. "The materials we use come from the land, and they go back to the land where they've come from, and they might be leaves, which go back and become soil, so then they become food for something else, so on and so forth," Martin said. "Nature doesn't know waste on a permanent basis because it reuses everything. So, our practice is about the subject. It's about making beauty out of what we see in front of us, not only beauty and imagery but the beauty of its design."

Wildness, they noted, came and went, came again, and went again. "The trees live and die," Martin said. "So do the birds, so do the animals, so does the grass. The stars are changing before your eyes. Everything out there is being affected by everything else and changing. It's ephemeral. Our work is about drawing attention to relationships between us and wildness, or the natural workings of things."

"So, what brought you here," Philippa asked. "Why did you decide to come to the South Island?"

It was Te Wāhipounamu, we told her. Not to be confused with Te Waipounamu (the Māori name for the South Island of New Zealand), Te Wāhipounamu is the World Heritage Site we hoped would give us our first taste of wilderness. The site stretches 280 miles along the southwestern coastline of the island and includes Doubtful Sound, Milford Sound, Aoraki/Mount Cook, and Tititea/Mount Aspiring. Inscribed in 1990 and covering twenty-six thousand square kilometres, Te Wāhipounamu is reputed to be the home of the world's best remnants of the original flora and fauna of Gondwana: an ancient megacontinent that encompassed Antarctica, South America, Africa, Madagascar, the Arabian Peninsula, the Indian subcontinent, Australia, and today's New Zealand.

With sapphire glacial lakes, snow-capped peaks, fast-rushing waterfalls, deep fjords, narrow valleys surrounded by thick vegetation and kept hidden by distant active glaciers, Te Wāhipounamu seems mystical and surreal, the ultimate wild place. Making things even more seductive for us was the presence of countless animal species not found anywhere else on earth, nearly all of them elusive birds that tantalized visitors not so much with their looks but with strange calls from the bush. Te Wāhipounamu's broader region is New Zealand's least densely populated area, and the surrounding towns are small and sparse. Much of the human presence is, for the most part, temporary.

"If we don't find wildness here," we joked with Martin and Philippa, "we may never find it anywhere."

Our original plan had been to tramp along the Milford Track, one of New Zealand's "Great Walks" and arguably one of the greatest in the world. Alas, the first two weeks of January are peak tourist season. The bookings system left us no choice but to shelve our idea. The area was also home to the Routeburn and Kepler Tracks, but they, too, had seen their maximum quotas for hikers fill up early. This was New Zealand after all. The Kiwis' reputation for being adventurous backcountry lovers was proving itself true. Unfazed by our poor luck and bad timing, we decided to hike the Hollyford Track, a newer and lesser-known fifty-six-kilometre track that promised to be just as wild and spectacular as its more renowned counterparts.

Autumn was chomping at the bit. She was eager to put her bad day on the Overland Track behind her and prove to us she was as tough as we thought she was. But we knew it wouldn't be easy. The Hollyford was shorter than the Overland Track, but the terrain was infinitely more challenging with not a single foot of duckboarding. The skimpy Department of Conservation brochure we'd downloaded off the internet back in Canada was also rather vague about a potential issue: three-wire bridges. Whatever they were, it seemed we'd have to traverse a few of them to cross fast-running rivers. To make sure Autumn wouldn't feel unnecessarily anxious about them, we didn't tell her about them. We'd worry about them as we faced them.

The Hollyford Track ran the course of the Hollyford Valley, an inlet nearly parallel to Milford Sound, one of the South Island's most popular destinations. Before tackling the hike, we thought we'd drive up to Milford Sound. We got there on January 2, 2017, during a busy lunch-time hour after a long and tortuous drive from Te Anau.

Back home, a screensaver portraying Milford Sound had flashed on and off our desktop for years. The photograph showed a view from the fjord made famous by countless photographers. No people – only waves, trees, and mountains. When we got to Milford Sound, we discovered tourist coaches, vans, and shuttles next to rental cars and SUVs. And there were boats, floatplanes, and helicopters too. Martin, Philippa, and at least five other New Zealanders we'd interviewed had warned us about it. Milford Sound was gorgeous, but its wild beauty was fleeting, ephemeral. To enjoy its wildness, we were warned, we'd have to show up well before or after everyone else did, either at sunset or sunrise.

The wildness of the place was temporal, but we realized, as we ate an overpriced egg salad sandwich, that it was also spatial. People were flying over the Sound, they were cruising on it, they were taking pictures around it, they were driving and stopping by it, but no one seemed to be truly in it. The wildness of Milford Sound not only came and went with time, it also depended on the effort it took to go into it, to enter its depths, something no one seemed to be doing. The place could be as magical and wild as it looked in that photo, but for 99 percent of its visitors, it seemed to be nothing more than a two-dimensional backdrop for a duck face selfie.

Where the road ended, a busy dock promised travellers an adventure down the fjord by way of a variety of sailing choices. Among the more popular options were two choices of day cruises. Cruise A – which we and a few dozen European, North American, Australian, and Kiwi travellers boarded – featured small sailboats with plenty of space on sun decks located at the bow and stern. These were labelled "nature cruises," presumably because a naturalist would provide commentary for part of the trip.

Cruise B – which seemed to exclusively attract Chinese visitors – featured larger motor vessels with ample seating room inside, where passengers could enjoy a buffet lunch and gaze at the outside from behind large windows. We promptly added "behind" to our list of prepositions to describe how one could get a sense of the wildness of Milford Sound. The next day, we went into the fjord.

Our five-day itinerary started at the base of the Darran Mountains in Fiordland National Park and ended at Martins Bay on the ocean shore. As in Tasmania, we had our mixed nuts, our salami (we really did pack it this time), our wraps, and our dehydrated foods. Plenty of water could be collected from creeks along the way. And even though small unserviced shelters were located along the way, we'd packed tents and sleeping mats and bags.

The only tangible differences from our Tasmanian outing were the weather – the temperature kept in the range of twenty degrees during the day – and Autumn's backpack. In Tasmania, her large rucksack had weighed her down from the first steps. This time, we limited her burden to a minuscule day pack that contained little beyond a couple of changes of clothes. So it was with a smile, not a pale and weak look, that she set off with us on January 3. Our only constraint on this trek was that a bush pilot was scheduled to pick us up at the Martins Bay airstrip on January 7, at 10 a.m.

As we took our first steps, we read in the Department of Conservation leaflet that the river we would coast for the first two days of our trek was the Hollyford/Whakatipu Kā Tuka. The green depths of its frigid waters rivalled that of the immense fern trees. Mountains still capped in snow cut through the cerulean sky in the distance. Inland scents redolent of the ocean wafted on a breeze. The compact soil, soft but not muddy, was utterly pleasant to tramp.

Whereas it had taken us nearly one and a half hours to cover about one kilometre on the Overland Track, we reached Hidden Falls Hut – nine kilometres away from where we'd parked our car at the end of Hollyford Road – by lunch. It sits in a field teeming with tall grasses and sand flies. Our first day was in the books.

We sliced the salami, filled a wrap each, and ended our lunch with dried fruit and a granola bar.

"Well, what do we do now?" asked Autumn. She lay on a bunk bed inside the hut and looked vaguely bored.

We cast a confused look at each other. Should we open a book? Nap? Conduct a census of the hundreds of sandflies that had snuck into the shelter? Or keep going?

We asked a grumpy-looking eastern European solo traveller whose bad mood reeked more sharply than our socks. "The next hut doesn't have as many sandflies. I was just there yesterday." A glance at the map revealed that Lake Alabaster Hut was ten and a half kilometres away. It felt as though he wanted to get rid of us.

"What should we do?" April asked.

Elevation wasn't a concern. The Hollyford coasted the river nearly all the way, and the highest point was Little Homer Saddle, a mere two hundred metres above sea level. The real concern, we reasoned, was the terrain. Our brochure told us the first twenty-two kilometres would be easy. The real trouble would start afterwards, at the beginning of the Demon Trail. As if the name wasn't enough to make the point, the leaflet spelled out in italics that "this section of the track is maintained to a much lower standard." It continued in a menacing tone: "Use the orange markers on the trees to guide you. It can be muddy, rocky, or wet underfoot. Tree falls may obscure the track. Be aware that after heavy rain the river can flood and you may be stranded in the hut until river levels are lower and it is safe to cross."

"Ok, let's go," April said. She packed the leaflet away. "We might end up needing the extra time on the Demon Trail."

We left Hidden Falls Hut, and the track entered a section of lowland ribbonwood and podocarp forest. Ferns and mosses closed in on us, making the trail narrower and narrower, then the first uphill ascent presented itself. The tall beech forest trail rose gradually, infinitely longer than any trail should have taken to rise a mere two hundred metres in altitude.

Autumn led the way. "Mom, you're way faster than us on levelled ground, but I'm faster than you uphill."

April didn't respond. She wasn't feeling well. We stopped. April looked pale and sweaty. She sipped water. She reasoned she must be having a sugar crisis.

"Give me your backpack, honey. I'll carry it all the way up to the summit."

She refused. We walked slowly, hoping her energy would pick up.

An hour later, we reached the summit of Little Homer Saddle. It was now mid-afternoon. Alabaster Hut, we guessed by looking at the map, had to be another five kilometres away. April was close to fainting. It wasn't a good sign when, minutes later, she agreed to surrender her backpack. Wondering if we would ever make it all the way to Martins Bay, we resumed walking.

Martins Bay had been a busy Māori settlement between 1650 and 1800. Known as "Kotuku" to the Ngāi Tahu people, the bay allowed for easy access to the food resources in nearby lakes and forests as well as the sea. *Pounamu,* or New Zealand jade, was also sourced there and used to make tools such as ornaments and weapons. In 1861, David McKellar and George Gunn explored the Hollyford Valley, and in 1863 Patrick Caples came by looking for gold, becoming the first European to reach Martins Bay. Later explorations yielded favourable reports on the status of other resources in the area, such as iron, copper, zinc, and, of course, timber. Caples recommended that a road be built. Neither the road nor resource exploitation ever happened, but the trail carved in those days eventually gave form to the track we walked.

A kilometre after the summit, we got two major boosts. A park warden announced that Alabaster Hut wasn't too far and there'd be no more elevation gain to worry about. "How old is your girl? Ten? That must be a record." He'd never seen a ten-year-old complete the track.

Then we encountered a strange group of mostly Europeans and North Americans, dressed in identical T-shirts. During the first six hours of walking, we'd run into only a handful of people, probably fewer than ten altogether. A group of about twenty was quite a sight.

"We're a guided group," a Kiwi guide explained as we and the other group refilled our bottles from the creek. "You'll see our private hut about half a kilometre before you reach Alabaster Hut," she said and smiled. "Feel free to stop by for some tea." She led a three-day "guided wilderness experience" that provided cozy refuges furnished with showers, mattresses, and soft pillows; food freshly prepared by the guides; and a speedboat ride on the River alongside the dreaded Demon Trail. "Alongside," we noted – another preposition for our growing list.

The guided group faded in the distance. "To hell with this," we said. "Let's finish this trek on our feet and show these spoiled lazy asses what real trekking is like." Our pace picked up. An hour later, we passed the fancy hut. On a log by the path, the friendly guide had laid out a plate of cookies and three glasses of orange pop for us. She waved from inside as we marched on.

Five hundred metres past the cookie plate, exhausted from walking twenty-two and a half kilometres, we reached the Department of Conservation hut. A few minutes later, we cooked our dehydrated dinner on our butane stove and set up our tent. We fell asleep to a manic symphony of sandflies dancing on our flimsy tent. One of our last conscious thoughts was of the first wire bridge of the trek, which awaited us three to four kilometres away.

Sandflies on the outside of our tent at Hidden Falls Hut

The next morning, we woke up late, after a solid ten-hour sleep. The dozen or so hikers we'd shared the Lake Alabaster Hut with must have been a third of their way to Demon Trail Hut by the time we walked our first steps on the trail. No big deal, we thought, we'll have the trail to ourselves.

The path went on in its merry and pleasant way for about two to three hours. Our legs were tired from the day before, but our spirits were high. Though we weren't breaking speed records, we were covering ground in earnest, and it was utterly remarkable that we'd essentially covered half the distance of the track by lunch the previous day. It was obvious, however, that things might get tough. Why else would the luxury hikers pay good money to dodge the trail by taking a boat?

Dodging the challenge, rather than enjoying it, seemed to run counter to our notion of a wilderness experience. The Western idea of wilderness is deeply interconnected with notions of fatigue, discomfort, inconvenience, and sacrifice. Historically, wilderness began to take root in the Western imagination when urban living became the norm. As cities expanded and urban dwellers became more dependent on the trappings of modern society, a small but growing number of writers such as Henry David Thoreau began penning words about the virtues of excursions to the countryside and the mountains. To spend time away from the city, in closer contact with nature, strengthened the body and reinvigorated the spirit, they wrote. To struggle with primal challenges such as collecting water and food and making shelter was a test of one's physical and moral fortitude, a fortitude that had been softened by the comforts and conveniences of the city. To spend time in the wilderness, they argued, was a way to go back to the basics, to appreciate the pleasures of deprivation in the name of struggling for achievement.

We explained to Autumn that to feel tired was to feel good, nearly quoting Thoreau. Along the same lines, we lectured that to be brave in the face of challenges and to conquer one's fear were ways to manifest ... um ... she wasn't listening anymore. She had turned the corner and sped off. Moments later, we caught up with her. She stood still, staring at the three-wire bridge. "Mom, Dad, what the heck is that?"

We stopped dead in her tracks and exchanged a long look for what seemed like forever.

"Phillip, what is that? You never told me about this!"

"I did. It's a three-wire bridge. Remember, we talked about it and then we agreed to not worry?"

"Well, we should have worried! What do we do?"

"According to YouTube, we grab the right cable with the right hand, the left cable with the left hand. We need to walk at an angle, kind of like a duck, which will put more body weight on the crossbars that intersect the lower cable. It's important not to look down at the rushing water because that can be frightening."

"Your daughter—"

"Yeah, the interesting thing is, she's at an advantage because of her lower centre of gravity, and we just need to reassure her that everything will be—"

"No, I mean, shut up. Look at your daughter, right now! She's already halfway across the damn thing."

There Autumn was – 15 feet above the creek, 45 feet away from parental safety, 145 kilometres away from a hospital, and 2 minutes ahead of a proper safety briefing – duck stepping her way to the other side of the gorge. We hadn't even had a chance to give her a proper tutorial or reflect on the existential meaning of what we were doing and why we were doing it, and she was already too far for us to intervene (only one person at a time on three-wire bridges, or, well, you die).

"Phillip, do something!"

Do what? Run underneath and catch her if she free falls? Call her back for a quick safety briefing? Shout advice at the risk of distracting her? Pray to gods we didn't believe in?

It was then, amid all this tribulation, that Autumn stopped and turned. She had a blissful look on her face. "Whee! This is awesome! It's like that thing at the playground!"

Autumn on a three-wire bridge later that day, when our nerves were calm enough to record her.

The idea of wildness differs from person to person. While we may, as a global society, agree that some areas are deserving of receiving the official moniker of "wilderness" and the environmental protection that goes along with it, individual notions of what wilderness and wildness mean are less clear. What a wilderness is to you is not the same as what it is to us. And what it means to us differs dramatically from what it means to a polar explorer or the average city dweller.

We could suggest that some of these people are right and some are wrong. So maybe the polar explorer is right and we are wrong in thinking we found wildness along the Hollyford Track. But wildness isn't a fact like a mathematical equation, the length of a river, or the geographical location of the capital of a country. Wildness differs even from a legal standpoint: it changes drastically not only from country to country and in international systems of environmental protection but also within countries or cultures. In this sense, wildness is something akin to a beautiful landscape. What is beautiful to you may be nothing special to us, but you are still entirely within your rights to think of it, and feel about it, however you wish.

And that is why that moment, when Autumn led the way across the three-wire bridge, was the wildest moment of our family life up to that point.

On the other side of the three-wire bridge, the trail went deeper into inhospitable ground. Smooth compact soil gave way to mud pools. Then the mud faded into a meshwork of gnarly roots, sharp rocks, and pebbles of every shape and size. More three-wire bridges, less frightening but still time-consuming, lay ahead. And more roots and more rocks. We could close our eyes and see roots and rocks in our daydreams.

By that point, the guided hikers must have been toasting the day's "efforts" with a glass of champagne. We, on the other hand, were nine kilometres into our day's walk and still six kilometres away from our destination. We were exhausted and cranky. Even Autumn had lost her enthusiasm. "I'm homesick," she said as we reached another dubious suspension bridge.

"We need to make some decisions," we announced. We looked at the brochure. "We left too late this morning. We can't make it to the Demon Trail Hut tonight."

"What? I don't want to sleep here," Autumn whimpered.

She had a point. Where would we sleep? Laying our tent out trailside would mean sleeping on gnarly roots and pointed rocks. We needed a plan B. We studied the map. A couple of kilometres away, on McKerrow Island, there was a small Department of Conservation shelter. It wasn't the hut we had set out for, but it had a roof and a floor. It would have to do. With a favourable tide, we could cross the flood channel and rejoin the trail the next day.

Wilderness is a place. But it's also a feeling. A large component of that feeling, for a lot of people, is solitude. You don't have to be completely alone; it's possible to feel alone when you are in a small group – or a family. For us, feeling alone meant feeling responsible for our own safety, being aware that there was no one to help us, to guide us, to make us feel more comfortable. It felt intensely wild.

We kept walking in silence. Our fatigue drowned out our thoughts. Wildness was in every breath we took in the heavy wind; it was in every wordless feeling we sensed. With nothing but a sandy shore to guide us, we lost sight of the trail. We wandered in search of footsteps, looked for openings in the bush, searched for any sign of the shelter. We studied the map uselessly. Alone, we felt the wildness of the place. When we finally found the shelter, it felt like home.

The trek the following day was short and easy. We made it to the next hut early and decided to rest and recharge for the whole afternoon in the company of cold waters and sandflies. The Demon Trail awaited. "The Demon Trail is an historical cattle track," announced the Department of Conservation leaflet. "This section is both rocky and undulating but there are long sections of formed, flat track in between." It went on menacingly: "It can be difficult underfoot in wet weather, with the track becoming slippery and with loose rocks. Some of the creek crossings can be dangerous, so extreme care is required."

The next morning, we woke up early and set out after a breakfast of instant coffee and cereal bars. The roots and rocks continued to protest our hike, pressing through our boots with every step and threatening to sprain our ankles every time we took our eyes off them. Every so often, we stopped to chat with other hikers. The conversations always unfolded in the same manner.

"Good afternoon."

"Good day."

"Where are you guys coming from?"

"Hokuri Hut. You?"

"Demon Trail Hut. How long to Hokuri?"

"Probably four to five hours. How long to Demon Trail Hut?"

"Probably four to five hours."

Silence.

Stare.

Grin.

With no other, choice, we soldiered on, and our salami stock and trail mix depleted quickly. The trail passed through a forest of fern and podocarp. The march forward dipped dramatically for every creek and raised again sharply for the next hill. With every step, the terrain worsened. Thorny roots dug deeper into the balls of our feet. Sharper rocks poked harder into our heels. Boulders increased in size, making every step uphill harder on our quad muscles and every stride downhill more injurious on our knees. We slipped. We fell. We slipped. We fell. More rocks, more roots.

Hours later, at last, we reached Hokuri Hut. Our screams of joy and tears of relief startled the occupant of the hut, a lone British chap, who ran toward us to see what on earth was happening.

"We're okay, mate. Just happy to be here."

"I can tell!" He offered to relieve us of a backpack for the final three steps. "You look exhausted. Hey, hold on a second, is that girl ... uh ... Autumn?"

How did he know? Autumn nodded. We looked at each other mystified.

"I heard about you! Everybody on the trail's been talking about some ten-year-old girl who's trying to finish the track. Nice to meet you, young lady. You're a rock star!" He shook her hand and Autumn smiled proudly.

The trek wasn't over, of course. Our English hut mate, hiking the route in reverse, estimated it would take us about three hours the next · day to reach the airstrip. We added an extra hour for safety and set our alarm for five o'clock. The first hour and a half would still be challenging – the last stretch on the Demon Trail followed by an off-track shortcut along the lakeshore. With no way to contact our pilot, we simply had to be at the airstrip by 10 a.m., or risk having to walk back.

We rose the next morning at 4:45, one of the most memorable awakenings of our lives. Autumn would later recollect:

My eyes opened slowly and adjusted to the morning light. I'd been awakened abruptly by a noise reverberating throughout the hut. It sounded artificial, like it could be coming from some sort of electronic device. Did my parents set an alarm? I didn't even know they had packed one!

I rolled over onto my side to face my mom, who was already awake. "What's that noise?"

"It's coming from outside. I think it may be some sort of bird."

Throughout our travels, I had never heard any wildlife make that kind of noise. The closest comparison to it would be a video game sound effect, but even then, it still sounded so foreign.

After packing our things and getting ready, we began our hike down the dreaded Demon's Trail, whose rocky terrain had left our legs sore from the previous day. It was the final day of our journey, and to say we were relieved to be finished would be an understatement. The trail led us down to a flowing river with a rocky shore.

"We have to walk across the river to get to the end of the trek," my dad said.

With the Demon's Trail behind us, we continued along the lakeshore. I felt the rocks poke at my shoes. My face tensed with every step. I looked at the surface of the water to distract myself and noticed how the rising sun peeked over the mountain and reflected its light against the water. Even though the cold morning air stung my skin, I still felt warm. My energy was drained, but I kept on walking. As I gazed at the horizon, only one thought crossed my mind: I couldn't wait to eat my trek-completion ice cream.

At Hokuri Creek, the river was so low that we decided to wade it near its mouth rather than spending an extra half hour heading uphill to use the three-wire bridge. We'd rather cross the Amazon with a chesterfield on our backs than cross another one of those.

We waded the river, and the waters reached up to our knees. Then we had to find the trail again. Dawn had given way to sunrise, so we could look for footsteps left by hikers the day before. The pebbly lakeshore had enough footprints to give us a sense of comfort, but being alone, without a clear path to follow, made us feel more than ever like we were in a true wilderness.

Alone, away from home, far from any sign of development, immersed in the cacophony of rushing waters and bird chants, we were aware that our destiny was entirely in our own hands, and this realization brought us closer to one another and to the place we were in. That's right: the place we were in. The place that encompassed us, enveloped us, ensconced us. There was no ship to be on, no road to coast alongside, no trail to walk around. No other prepositions made sense anymore. Wilderness felt like a place you are inextricably, dependently, holistically, in. It permeated you from the inside.

Once the lake disappeared to our left, we saw a small but bright orange marker. The trail – suddenly smooth and easy – took less than an hour from that point to the airstrip. We had made the day's trek in three and a half hours, without encountering another soul.

Ironically, punishment rather than an award awaited us. New Zealand sandflies, for some odd reason, don't bite you unless you stand still. After hiking fifty-six kilometres through hell, pacing the airstrip for an hour and a half to avoid being bitten by the bloodthirsty bastards seemed an odd way to celebrate the end of our hike.

New Zealand has three World Heritage Sites. Two are natural sites: Te Wāhipounamu, which encompasses much of the southwest coast of the South Island, and the New Zealand Sub-Antarctic Islands. Tongariro National Park, on the other hand, is classified as a mixed heritage site, natural and cultural. There are only thirty-nine mixed heritage sites around the world, and since Tongariro is also the world's fourth oldest national park, we felt compelled to visit.

Located in the middle of the North Island, some three and half hours away from Auckland, the park, at 705 square kilometres, is rather tiny, but it makes up for its small size with history and vitality. The park's main geological and cultural attractions are its active volcanoes – Mounts Ruapehu, Ngauruhoe, and Tongariro. The last eruption was in 2012. The volcanoes are alive geologically but also in a cultural sense, and it was precisely their significance to the Māori that led the World Heritage Convention to create a new category – mixed cultural and natural, or cultural landscape – to capture the value of the sites.

The main park headquarters are located near the end of a lonely road that stretches up Mount Ruapehu. The road ends at Whakapapa Village, one of New Zealand's oldest and largest alpine ski areas. Whakapapa, save for its ample parking lots, isn't a busy place. There are the predict-able chairlifts, a few basic mountain-style chalets, and the odd eatery but nothing overly large, luxurious, or gaudy. The views are expansive, and the other volcanoes in the distance are mighty but perhaps unspectacular. Accustomed to the thick vegetation of the surrounding areas, the vol-cano's bare conical shape looked too stern and uninspiring. Its cultural significance would undoubtedly be more interesting.

Tired of trekking, we took a rain check on a popular day-long hike around the volcano and made an appointment with Amy Satterfield, partnership ranger for the Department of Conservation's Tongariro office, to learn more about the volcano's cultural value. Amy was a young and energetic American expat who had come to New Zealand for graduate research in conservation leadership and had fallen in love with the land and its people. Like others, her first introduction to Mount Tongariro had been through the Tongariro Crossing, a one-day, twenty-kilometre excursion up and around Mount Ruapehu that draws thousands of hikers from around the world each year. The same hike we had dodged. The hike was so popular, however, that as a ranger she had started to consider it as a possible management problem. "When you have an increase in population and an increase in people coming, you have issues with rubbish and waste on the environment. The impact of heaps of people on the trail is serious erosion." Amy had been in New Zealand long enough to pick up Kiwi expressions such as "heaps" but still spoke with an American accent. "And then when you look at the cultural implications as well," she continued, "you realize that those are ancestors that you're walking on. The mountains are the grandfather of this place, and that's a real deity, that's a real person to the Indigenous people."

This was a phenomenally important lesson. To many Westerners, persons are people, individuals, beings with a body and a mind, not mountains. Yet corporations are persons, in the full sense of the law. To believers, Gods and their apostles are persons, persons powerful enough to determine our fate. So are cars, planes, and ships – ask pilots and captains. And so are dogs and cats – ask any pet lover. So what's so strange about a mountain, a volcano, or a river being a person? Thinking of a volcano as a person endowed with being and free will underscores its aliveness and, therefore, its wildness.

A poster on the wall behind Amy proclaimed Tongariro a UNESCO World Heritage Site. It showed that it had been inscribed in 1990. That first inscription, Amy explained, focused on its biological and geological significance only. "Then," she said, "in 1993, it was the first to get recognized under this new mixed heritage status, and that is because of that significance it has to the people of this place, that this is their genealogy, this is their *whakapapa* – the mountain is their ancestor. It is significant in the sense that this is where they come from. When you talk to your local Indigenous tribes and people, they say, 'This is my river. This is my mountain. This is my hill. This is my house. This is the tribe I'm part of.' And so you never introduce yourself – it's your genealogy of the actual natural environment that you come from."

A mixed natural and cultural heritage site made perfect sense. The separation of culture and nature that we'd observed in places such as the Galápagos had only served to obscure the presence of the human species.

Calling a World Heritage Site "natural" without taking account of its cultural life reified ideas of pristine and untouched wilderness – ideas that are quickly dismantled once you scratch the surfaces of natural and social history. Mixed sites such as Tongariro somehow manage to convey the wildness of a place without excluding people.

Natural heritage sites, in contrast, often hide human components either through neglect or oblivion. Take the four criteria for inclusion in the list of natural heritage sites (not all four have to be met, one might be sufficient). Such a site

VII: contains superlative natural phenomena or areas of exceptional natural beauty and aesthetic importance.

VIII: is an outstanding example representing major stages of Earth's history, including the record of life, significant on-going geological processes in the development of landforms, or significant geomorphic or physiographic features.

IX: is an outstanding example representing significant on-going ecological and biological processes in the evolution and development of terrestrial, fresh water, coastal and marine ecosystems, and communities of plants and animals.

X: contains the most important and significant natural habitats for in-situ conservation of biological diversity, including those containing threatened species of outstanding universal value from the point of view of science or conservation.

The World Heritage List does not claim to be a list of wilderness sites. Yet the way it separates nature from culture seems to reify the notion that only pristine, untouched nature is pure, authentic, and wild. Moreover, much of the background discourse posted by UNESCO on its website refers to natural heritage as untouched and undeveloped nature, which is distinct from cultural heritage. And yet these distinctions made no sense for peoples such as the Māori who perceive mountains and volcanoes as ancestors.

By the time our research wound down in New Zealand, we were aware that the World Heritage List could serve a practical purpose for our project. Other types of lists and classifications were available that could be useful. Most notably, the IUCN – the International Union for the Conservation of Nature – had a clear definition of wilderness areas as "protected areas that are usually large unmodified or slightly modified areas, retaining their natural character and influence, without permanent or significant human habitation, which are protected and managed so as to preserve their natural condition."

However, classifications and lists such as that one were too prescriptive. If we used them, we'd spend years going to places too similar to one another. Furthermore, definitions of wilderness such as the IUCN's are too rooted in a Western way of thinking about our place in the world. When we define an area as wilderness because of its lack of permanent human inhabitation, we end up creating one category for nature and another for humanity.

Centuries of dualism, an ideology based on the neat separation of categories, has infiltrated Western culture so deeply that, on the surface, it makes sense to say that a place is wilderness because humans don't live there. But what if they once did live there, like many Indigenous peoples? What if their history, culture, and their ancestors are still alive? What if these people are somehow invisible but still present, despite evictions and attempts to segregate them? By calling their home a wilderness – a place emptied of presence – we'd simply be turning a blind eye to the fact that it has always been their home.

Soon after our return from New Zealand, we received the news we'd been waiting for. We now had research funding to travel to about twenty UNESCO World Heritage Sites. Ten of those sites, all Natural Heritage Sites, were located in Canada. The rest were scattered around the world.

The ten Canadian sites were set; our grant stipulated that we do research in all of them. The international sites came with greater flexibility; it was up to us to choose where to go. We determined that variety and diversity should come first, but we stopped short of generating a list with strict variables and criteria. It would become obvious in time where we should go, we thought. We also needed to keep finances in mind, as we would have to dip into family savings and Aeroplan points to cover expenses the grants didn't.

By giving us our first genuine taste of wildness in the fjords of the South Island, New Zealand had taught us an unexpected lesson. Though it may be defined on the basis of constructs such as naturalness and remoteness, wilderness felt too much of a finite concept for us. Sure, we could have followed the suggestion offered by our friends in Tasmania, who understood wilderness as something that comes in degrees, but that didn't feel authentic to us. We didn't want to assign points to places based on their naturalness and remoteness and then rank them on a scale. We'd much rather remain open to the qualities of a place, to how it felt.

Deep in the bush of Te Wāhipounamu, we'd experienced the wildness of a place carnally, in virtue of being authentically enveloped in it. We felt that the place had a will of its own. It was alive. It was in control. What we felt was a relational intensity that seemed to permeate every tree, every rock, every drop of water, and every air molecule. Wildness was a sensation and a force, but it was also a relation with a place. Unlike a numerical score on an objective scale, it was vivid, immediate, ineffable.

Wildness seemed capricious too. Relations with a place change, after all. A place can be wild one moment and then change a moment later, as Martin and Philippa had taught us. Wildness can evaporate without notice. The arrival of coach tours bringing day trippers from Queenstown took the wildness out of Milford Sound every morning. The landing of our bush plane at the Martins Bay landing strip did the same to the Hollyford Valley. And up at Tongariro, Mount Ruapehu could bring the wildness back to the landscape any moment it wished to erupt.

Moreover, wildness was a perspective. A volcano might seem wild to a visitor, but to a Māori, it is an ancestor, it is family. Whether it is dormant or not, to them, it is alive. Wildness is just that: it's aliveness, vitality. Wildness is unpredictability and effervescence. Wildness is a lack of human control and an openness to being immersed in the world. Experiencing what wildness meant to people was what truly excited us. Not wilderness, but wildness. Not the noun, but the adjective. Not the category, or the legal definition, but the process, the atmosphere, and the feeling. Not the classification, but the relation.

4

Wild Can Change

SOUTH TYROL

THE VIEW FROM OUR RENTAL APARTMENT in the village centre of Seis was incongruous. Two storeys below us, the narrow cobblestone street was alive with locals and visitors running errands and window shopping, just as they would in any central European small town. Before us, beyond the church steeple, the tall rocky face of the Schlern Mountain towered over the landscape. It dwarfed our collective human presence. Its shifting shadow reminded us that we weren't really on the high street but actually high in the mountains. But the sheer size of the Schlern was also incongruous. The mountain, in its finitude and verticality, felt oddly, inexplicably small. It was so close you could touch it, so finite you could walk around it.

Small mountains might sound like quixotic creatures if you've never seen them. A massive mountain feels majestic, foreboding, indomitable. In contrast, a small mountain feels approachable, friendly. A large mountain might look frightening, whereas a small one might look cozy, pretty. Because it is easy to see it in its entirety, a small mountain, in its visual finitude, feels distinct, discrete, identifiable, and familiar. When you find yourself in a large mountain landscape, you feel the power of immensity, the tyranny of distance, the pull of the remote. But when you find yourself in a small mountain landscape you feel as though you are a figure within a perfectly planned and meticulously assembled diorama. You feel the precision of detail, the harmony afforded by a sense of order, the power of a perfect assemblage of things that belong together.

There is a place in the world where the mountains are so small you can cast a stone at them from your balcony, or walk up to them and feel them, as if they were church steeples erected on city streets or tall trees growing on forest grounds. It's a place where you can travel among them and feel like you're meeting them, getting to know the peaks one by one. As you walk past them and encircle them, you see their different sides, you learn to appreciate their different feels, their secrets, their histories, and the memories you cultivate by hiking among them. That place is called Tyrol.

The actual County of Tyrol is no more. It ended in 1919. Established in the mid-1100s, from 1363 on it was controlled by Austria, first by the Habsburg Empire, then formally by the Austrian Empire in 1804, and finally by the Austrian-Hungarian Empire in 1867. At the end of the First World War, the Austrian-Hungarian Empire was dissolved, and as part of the Treaty of St. Germain, the County of Tyrol was split into three parts. North and East Tyrol were merged and kept in Austrian hands. South Tyrol was reorganized as an Italian region named Trentino-Alto Adige.

In recognition of the historical and cultural continuity of Tyrol, in 1998 the European Union formed a new political unity: the Euroregion Tyrol–South Tyrol–Trentino. Still straddling Italy and Austria, the new Euroregion was formed to strengthen cooperation across borders, promote mobility, facilitate cultural and economic exchange, and raise awareness of the cultural and historical heritage of the region of Tyrol.

South Tyrol is a three-hour drive north of Venice and a four-hour drive south of Munich. It is home to Europe's most beautiful Alpine landscapes and might be the world's most spectacular mountainous region. Yet it was only in 2009 – seven years before our visit – that UNESCO declared the Dolomite Mountains a World Heritage Site.

If anyone had their minds set on preserving a pristine wilderness, it was too late. Gondolas and chairlifts, smoothly paved roads, extensive networks of trails and ski runs, and busy mountain valleys equipped with some of the most advanced tourist infrastructures in the world had long made the Dolomites a favourite destination for middle- and upper-middle-class European holidaymakers. The place wasn't pristine, but this wasn't necessarily a flaw.

South Tyrolean mountain peaks are surrounded by high-altitude pastures that slope into a web of valleys dotted by small towns rich in history and vibrant cultural traditions. The valleys are busy during the winter and summer tourist seasons, but the farther you get away from them, the more the pace slows down. Even in the height of summer, you might have trouble finding a parking spot in town, but it's easy to catch a chairlift or walk a kilometre or two and leave the noise (there but bearable) behind. Development has unfolded in a relatively organic manner mostly respectful of local culture and historical traditions.

We chose to travel there to understand what made this possible. Our plan for our first dolomitic hike was unambitious but still exciting. After reaching the Lagazuoi Pass by cable car and departing on foot from the Lagazuoi Hut, we'd (in the company of our trusted gatekeeper, Emanuel Valentin, and our interviewee, Gustav Willeit) head not for the lower Falzarego Pass but north. North meant downhill toward the Badia Valley, where Emanuel's vehicle would await us so we could circle back by car. It was a downhill hiking strategy meant to familiarize us with the oddness of the small mountains, acclimatize us to the rarefied mountain air, and introduce us to South Tyrolean society and culture.

Emanuel and Gustav had been friends for many years. Now in their early thirties, they'd spent their childhoods in the town of Bruneck, in South Tyrol's Puster Valley. Emanuel had recently completed his PhD at the University of Bozen – the province's capital city – with a focus on cultural heritage. He'd been recommended to us as a gatekeeper by a university colleague. In the context of our research, the gatekeeper role had acquired greater importance. Until our trip to South Tyrol, our gatekeepers had played a limited role, recommending possible interviewees and providing logistical advice in advance of our travel. But after reviewing our practices, we realized we could use more help connecting with interviewees, learning about local contexts, providing translations when necessary, and understanding the nuances of intercultural communication.

Emanuel enthusiastically agreed to help. With a scruffy beard that matched his curly brown hair, he struck a rare compromise between reliable, laid-back cool and affable, educated (he spoke eight languages including Italian, German, and the local Ladin) confidence. Emanuel started off our experience by introducing us to Gustav, a visual artist with a passion for stormy dolomitic landscapes. Gustav liked to hike, and we agreed it would be best to chat about the mountains while surrounded by them, rather than just sitting down in Val Badia.

Gustav wasted no time in articulating what was unique about the Dolomite mountains: they were unusually small. And that made them uniquely suited to a dramatic kind of photography. Among some of our favourite photos of Gustav's were pictures showing the peaks shrouded in heavy, dark clouds, an image that stood in sharp contrast to the sun-kissed postcards of the region. Even more unique, Gustav included cable cars or roads in the frame. Though he knew that infrastructure like that lessened the mountains' wild character, he understood it also had a democratizing effect. "In my opinion, if you look at it in a visual way, these structures take away something from wild nature. The view is spoiled by the look of the structures built by men, but on the other hand, they give the opportunity to people to go up the mountains and enjoy the beauty." His simple statement brilliantly captured the essence of our experience of the region.

Gustav spoke the words in Italian. Though it is now part of Italy, and the Italian language is widely spoken, South Tyrol's main language is German. Despite Mussolini's attempts to "Italianize" the region with forced immigration from the southern regions, South Tyrol remained proudly autonomous. To this day, the region is still deeply rooted in Germanic and Ladin linguistic and cultural traditions, even though those traditions have had, at times, to go into hiding to survive.

As we hiked and talked – sometimes in English and at times in Italian, Emanuel and Gustav occasionally chatted with each other in Ladin, a Rhaeto-Romance language that only some forty thousand people speak. Hikers around us spoke Italian and German with a variety of regional accents and dialects. The linguistic diversity was matched in intensity by the rapid succession of different mountain landscapes. In British Columbia, we might have been in the same landscape for hours, if not days, but in this small mountain landscape, the views changed every few steps.

Hairpin turn after hairpin turn, the steep trail wound down below the treeline and the scree fields until we passed through small patches of red firs and grassy meadows. Mountain peaks, which had encircled us only two hours before, now towered above us. They changed colour with the passing of clouds and mutations in the sunlight. Gustav paused to take pictures while we caught up. As a photographer, he was innately aware of the mountains' ephemerally sublime nature. His moody, foreboding pictures, snapped during tenebrous weather, connoted that wildness was something that came to life intermittently in the Dolomites.

UNESCO had inscribed the Dolomites in 2009 because of the geological value of the rock and the spectacular nature of the landscape. And although the map of the World Heritage Site was confined to the mountain peaks and adjacent grounds, the inscription made a clear reference to the aesthetic character of the surrounding landscape by characterizing it as "sublime." It made no mention of the word "wild." Like other neo-Latin languages, Italian doesn't have a literal translation for the English notion of wildness. The word *selvaggio* can be used to say "wild," but expressions such as *natura intatta* or *pristina* – untouched or pristine nature – are more common. As in Italian, the Ladin word *salvario* refers to the qualities of forests and their trees rather than the Anglo-Saxon notion of will.

To talk about wildness with Gustav, we occasionally had to switch to English. Wildness, Gustav observed, "still exists, but it's diminishing too fast." He told us there are only a few places where you won't see a human footprint. "Although I can see they are trying to stop this virus, people are destroying nature."

It was hard to disagree with him, though rather than destruction, it felt more like a decadent upgrade. For instance, after we passed through the mountain scree fields, we approached a stylish hut that featured a fully functioning mountain restaurant two thousand metres above sea level. We drank large mugs of beer and ate a hot plate of homemade gnocchi with creamy pesto. Hikers laid in the meadow outside the hut on comfortable chairs sipping drinks and enjoying the warm sun. On our first day in the Dolomites, we experienced the paradox of sublimity

A map of the Dolomites surrounding the Seiser Alm

and comfort. The mountains were simultaneously indomitable in appearance and convenient in nature.

"We should get going soon, it's going to start raining any time," Emanuel said.

We downed a small glass of local grappa. Within minutes, the downpour began. Thunder followed. By the time we reached Emanuel's car, we were drenched.

After a few days filled with hike-free interviews, we set out, as planned, on our eight-day trek. The trek would take the shape of a large figure eight. We'd start at Seis and the Schlern-Rosengarten Nature Park, move through the Seiser Alm down to the Gröden Valley, trek back up to the mountains (first to Puez-Odle Nature Park and then to the Sella Joch) and up through the Langkofel, then back down to the Seiser Alm, and finally back to Seis. We planned to spend nights in mountain huts, but we did not need to pack food. In South Tyrol, unlike other places we had visited, we could stop at huts and sports hotels anywhere along the route to eat succulent meals and sleep in comfortable beds.

And so, with backpacks containing only our camera gear and a few changes of clothes, we set off on the morning of July 15. We forked out some forty Euros for the twenty-minute cable car ride from Seis to the Seiser Alm.

"I like this way of hiking," Autumn said after the first cable car ride ended. She lay sprawled out on the leather seat of a chairlift.

This level of comfort would not last, we soon found out. Our actual hike began at the Hotel Panorama at an altitude of 2,009 metres. We walked downhill for about an hour, south through the Seiser Alm, and then up the Schlern. We knew the six-hundred-metre elevation gain to the Schlerhaus – the hut where we had reserved a room – wouldn't be child's play. Phillip had hiked the route as a child, and he remembered the trail as a relentless climb with a series of hairpin turns. Yet the view from the top and the promise of a summit ice cream for Autumn were all the motivation we needed to start walking cheerfully.

A few days before, we'd gotten to know a little bit about what life was like on the meadows of the Seiser Alm. Thanks to a fortuitous last-minute introduction, we'd received an invitation to visit a working farm owned and operated by the Waldboth family. The farm, only a few hectares in size, had been in operation for over seven hundred years in a spectacular meadow a few hundred metres from the Panorama Hotel and its chairlift. It wasn't the only farm in the area. Many of the meadows had been passed down intact generation after generation to first-born sons in a primogeniture-based system anthropologists call impartible inheritance.

The meadows were part of the "sublime" landscape promised in the World Heritage designation. But they'd shaped the region's sustenance-based economy since the Middle Ages, along with its family economies, seasonal rhythms, and ways of life. As a result, the World Heritage Site was a unique puzzle composed of public and private land pieces – the latter's ownership complicated by rights of passage and historical patterns of common use. Here, natural heritage was so deeply knotted with history, society, and culture, it couldn't be separated from cultural heritage. It became obvious to us that the beautiful and sublime nature of the region was not spoiled but enhanced by human activities such as farming.

Like other smallholders in the area, Richard and his father used their land to raise a small herd of cows. The cows yielded milk, which they sold to the market through a farmers' cooperative whose small tank trucks could be seen every morning chugging along the narrow gravel roads that criss-crossed the Seiser Alm. The fact that a "working landscape" could be so stunningly beautiful was utterly remarkable to us, we explained to Richard, but he remained unfazed. Tall, thin, soft-spoken, and shy, the forty-year-old was confused as to why a Canadian filmmaking "crew" had bothered reaching out to him, "a simple farmer."

In a not-so-distant past, it had still been possible to make a living from farming alone, Richard explained, but life had changed. His family had found it necessary to open a guesthouse in town, called Mutzhof, to supplement their income from farming. Because of increasing wages and reduced revenues, they could no longer afford to hire seasonal workers as they had in the past. Despite the changes, they lived well, he said, and still enjoyed their work.

While we spoke, Richard's father patiently cut grass with a scythe, concentrating on spots too hard to reach with an engine-driven mower. We were lucky to be there to witness the rhythmic art of scything. Meadows were cut only once a year, in July, and the practice had a deep ritual significance. Scything unfolded as poetry, as a combination of sonic and visual rhythms. Wide swings of the scythe were followed by the grating sound of grass being swept away and then the raspy metal twang of a blade being sharpened by hand. It was a poetry accentuated by the melodic dinging of bells worn by cows munching away at the grass. It was useful poetry, in that it generated hay that sustained cows and, in turn, people.

In past times, the hay was stored in small wooden huts scattered on farmland around the meadows. As the snow melted at progressively higher elevations with the arrival of summer, herders gradually moved up the mountain, spending weeks at small huts. With the arrival of better transportation in and out of the high-altitude meadows, some of those rhythms changed, as farmers could return to lower elevations at the end of the day. But even though they are not used as often as in the past, the small wooden huts where herders spent their summers remain an unmissable architectural heritage, visible everywhere on the mountain landscape.

Not much has changed for the cows, however. As they did in the past, throughout late spring and summer, they eat fresh grass while farmers cut the rest and store it for autumn and winter. In late September, with the arrival of the first snow, the cows still go home down in the valley. The advent of motorized transportation means farmers can bring freshly cut grass down the valley faster, but the herds' seasonal rhythms continue as they always have.

Farming has become increasingly difficult, however, Richard explained, particularly with new rules and regulations to protect and conserve natural heritage. He directed our attention to a couple of marmots frolicking in the distance. In the past, marmots used to dwell only in higher mountain fields and rarely ventured down to the lower-altitude meadows. Enjoying higher degrees of protection than in the past, marmots multiplied and their population expanded. They dig holes on lower farmland, which creates problems for farmers. "It's easy for a cow or horse to stick a foot in one of those holes and get hurt really bad," Richard lamented.

Though admittedly less cute than marmots, cows, too, were inseparable from the dolomitic mountain landscape the World

A farmer rakes freshly cut grass in Puez-Odle Nature Park

Heritage Committee had labelled "spectacular" and "quintessentially Alpine." The prettiest among them were the grey ones, a local Alpine cow species that Richard and his father were happy to raise to help with their preservation. Though not as productive as other kinds, grey Alpine cows were a key element of local history, he told us, and it was stunning to see how "just a farmer" like Richard could play such an essential role in heritage preservation simply in virtue of his day-to-day work. True heritage isn't something you preserve, after all, it's something you do. Neither the English and German word "wild" nor the Italian word *selvaggio* could capture this entanglement, but it was easy to feel.

After our interview, we invited Richard and his father to lunch at the Panorama Hotel. "Thank you, but no," he said, "my mom is already waiting for us." After a five-minute drive down a gravel track, "mom" welcomed us to her table. We shared knoedels, cheeses, and breads and stories about the places we call home with the extended family. The grey Alpine cows – the very same cows that had given us the milk, cheese, and butter we ate – laid on the grass outside. The small mountains in the background became even smaller as they revealed themselves to us.

A half kilometre past Richard's farm, the trail to the Schlern raised its back. The midday temperature rose into the mid-twenties, and we had a limited supply of water and snacks. Our legs started to give in. Fortunately, these were the Dolomites, not the bushes of New Zealand or Tasmania. An hour later, after stuffing her face with a coconut-flavoured chocolate bar and a slice of carrot cake freshly baked by the Schlerhaus kitchen staff, Autumn's smile was back. We had made our first summit and found ourselves on top of the mountain depicted on the Loacker logo.

As awe-inspiring as they may be when they're moody pale grey during the day, the Dolomites show their uniquely beautiful face at sunrise and sunset. After dinner at the hut, as the sun descended behind the Schlern, the mountains shed their pale shroud for a warm orange veil, which gradually shifted to pink and then rose. A herd of cows munching short, thin grass provided a soundscape with the deep-toned bells that hung from their necks. "It's like being on the set of *The Sound of Music*,"

April noted. Though modest in its interior-design ambition, the Schlerhaus's exterior fit the scene well – stark, bare, and imposing in its linear and angular verticality. We fell asleep on hard but comfortable beds under a fluffy white duvet.

In the morning, Autumn was in top form. A good fifty to a hundred metres ahead of us, she led the way along the rocky and grassy ridge connecting the Schlern with the Rosengarten mountains. The evening before, however, we had adjusted our plans. Instead of descending to the Grasleitenhütte and then climbing to the Gasleitenpasshutte, we rerouted our path straight to the Tierser Alpl Hut – a more level trail at the foot of the imposing Rosengarten. Elsewhere in the world, this detour would have been impossible. This flexibility in trail and hut selection was a unique function of the social and geographical imagination that over the years had shaped the Dolomites into what they are now.

Unlike places familiar to us such as the forests of British Columbia, where a single route connecting remote campsites is often the only option, the dolomitic landscape is a meshwork of methodically numbered pathways – brightly signalled in white and red painted on limestone rock in the shape of the Austrian flag. The trails branch out from one another like a system of interurban highways. A 1:25,000 topographical map with a legend more detailed than Google Earth put us in an enviably controlling position over our route. Trails 1-4, 4 today, Trails 4, 8, 7, 8a, and 8 the next day. This felt profoundly Germanic and incredibly reassuring for our progress forward.

Making things even easier for planning purposes was the fact that the Dolomites, somewhat surreally, looked smaller each day we spent among them and walked in their midst. As we came to know the names of every peak, the mountains began to feel like friendly faces. On seeing them, we'd approach and feel them with our hands, as if to greet them. There was no need to climb on top of these mountains, we thought. Why "conquer" them when we were already inside them.

But the mountains could be dangerous. Their smallness creates narrow and precipitous ridges between them. These ridges are surrounded by remarkably steep scree fields, which can give way underfoot, causing sudden rockfalls. It's easy to slip and fall. Autumn, setting the pace with a gleeful smile on her face, was nonchalant about the danger. She also seemed to be unaffected by the approbation of Italian mountaineers as she trudged along the vertiginous passages.

It was only one o'clock when we made it to the Tierser Alpl, a brand-new hostel-style hotel whose metallic red roof gave it a clean and minimalistic feel in stark contrast to the richness of its international menu. Feeling somewhat guilty about calling it a day by lunch, we spent the afternoon and evening stalking marmots with our telephoto lens and failing, dismally, to visually convey with our cameras the smoothness and coldness of the dolomitic rock.

This was no "wild" place by common North American standards; no nature here could be reasonably called pristine or untouched, but the landscape felt no less sublime. As Gustav had noted, the trails and huts gave us the opportunity to experience these sublime landscapes, and that forced us to question whether wildness can be enabled, if not enhanced, by sustainable, intelligent planning.

On July 17, we woke up early and set out once again for the Seiser Alm, which we reached in one hour's time after descending from the Rosengarten. The Seiser Alm is what geographers would call an alp (lower case "a"), a grassy pasture on a mountainside. There are many alps in the Alps, but the Seiser Alm (Alpe di Siusi, in Italian) is one of a kind. Fifty-two square kilometres and on average 1,850 metres above sea level, the Seiser Alm is one of the world's largest meadows.

Making it even more remarkable, it is surrounded by a handful of mountain groups that reach above 3,000 metres, each marked by distinctive shapes. There is the diagonal and perfectly flat surface of the Plattkofel (Flat Rock), the hand-like shape of the Sassolungo (Long Rock), the neighbouring towers known as the Five Fingers, the saddle-shaped Sella (the Saddle), the postcard-perfect Schlern, and the jagged and slightly tilted Puez-Odle group.

Early tourism on the Seiser Alm dates back to the 1930s. The first gondola reaching the alp's northern edge from the town of St. Ulrich was opened in 1934. Four years later, the first chairlift was also inaugurated, opening up the first ski field in the area. Today, there are about twenty uphill transportation facilities on the alp alone: a mix of chairlifts, gondolas, and smaller cable cars, most of which operate in winter and summer. Partly subsidized by the province and the region to keep tickets affordable (sort of), uphill transportation infrastructures might encourage laziness and detract from the natural character of the highland, but they are a much better alternative to the car.

Back in the 1980s, you could drive up to the Seiser Alm from the town of Seis and have a picnic not too far from your vehicle. As a result, the narrow, paved pathways were congested, and many of the meadows on a busy August day could feel like a city park. Following World Heritage directives and capitalizing on the inauguration of the massive Seiser Alm Aerial Cableway, car traffic to the Seiser Alm has undergone a series of restrictions. It has been shut down to all but farmers and a few hotel guests permitted to drive to check in and out.

A few days before our hike, mixed-media artist Hubert Kostner had told us at his studio in Kastleruth that the cableway was part and parcel of a new philosophy of environmental conservation and tourism management that had taken root since the beginning of the new millennium. Dead set against mass tourism, Hubert told us, the region focused on quality tourism. Quality tourism meant restricted road access to high elevations, for example, and data-driven environmental management.

But quality tourism also had pernicious effects, according to Hubert. "Quality" had become synonymous with exclusivity and high prices. Three-, four-, and five-star hotels competed with one another to provide new frills. Crowding and environmental impact were thus being fought with funds raised by offering the latest artisanal food fashions, relaxation massages, saunas, and silk-covered comforters.

Born and raised in the Dolomites and in his early forties, Hubert's art, inspired by his admiration for the landscape and by a critical attitude toward the consequences of tourism, adorned public buildings and spaces around the region. "My work can be traced back to old postcards," he said. "What characterizes these places is our 'scenography.'" By "scenography," Hubert meant the sublime and scenic value of the idyllic landscape: "Our landscape is so beautiful, so surreal, it's like a scenography."

The work of farmers such as Richard was an essential component of that scenography, and so, too, were the beautifully kept huts. The sublime nature of the place was, in fact, not "nature" at all but a more complex assemblage that some geographers have started to call natureculture, a neologism that reflects the inseparableness of the two concepts.

Hubert showed us around his studio as we talked. Much of his work was focused on exposing the notion of natureculture. Over time, he told us, he'd started collecting postcards and pieces of linden wood, which he'd carve with scenic landscapes and polish with lacquer. "Its essence is symbolic," he reflected, "because on one side you have nature, and on the other side you have a cultural intervention, which now has become touristic. And the touristic intervention is like a lacquer that covers the original substance."

Hubert's beautifully lit, cement-walled studio looked out to the mountains and the meadows. A chairlift not too far in the distance connected the town of Kastleruth with Marizenhutte, at the western edges of the Seiser Alm. The chairlift was not a blot on the landscape but an essential component of it. "To me, the image of a cable, with chairs hanging from it and going down, it's just gorgeous." Growing up in the Dolomites meant an easy association between chairlifts and a way of being outdoors. "It's part of my inner child," he said with a smile.

But from an environmental standpoint, there had to be a limit, he observed. Chairlifts and gondolas in and of themselves may have had a limited footprint, but mechanized uphill transportation brought restaurants, hotels, roads, cars, and endless problems. "Once you reach a certain point, you have to stop."

Hubert's warning rang in our ears as we neared the Sporthotel Floralpina at the end of our third day's hike. Offering an indoor and outdoor swimming pool, a 520-square-metre spa with indoor and outdoor jacuzzis, a Kneipp basin (we weren't sure what that was), a biosauna, a steam room, a Finnish sauna, and a relaxation room to all guests, the Floralpina's rooms featured a minibar, satellite TV, a telephone, balconies, more toiletries and bathroom appliances than we could fit in our backpacks, and an outdoor café and fine-dining restaurant.

"This is too much, guys, what kind of 'mountain hut' experience is this supposed to be?" April said as we approached the entrance.

"It's for research," Autumn said with a devious smile and led the way to the check-in.

The next day, things got even easier: two chairlifts and three gondola rides with only a few kilometres of walking in between. A subterranean conveyor belt of the type you might find at a Tube station transported our bodies from gondola number two to gondola number three. As silly as it looked, the conveyor belt nearly annihilated the need to use a private vehicle to get from one side of town to the other. Previously choked by traffic jams, the town of St. Ulrich was quieter and cleaner than it had been in the 1980s.

Though it would be easy to condemn the whole experience as utterly gentrified, we realized just how drop-dead gorgeous nature could be when managed effectively, expansively, expensively, and thoroughly. Nothing was left to accident, just like a diorama or a miniature world in which everything had been thought out and fit perfectly. Rather than a gentrified neighbourhood, the place was akin to a scenography, in Hubert's words. The result was mesmerizing, so impossibly beautiful and inviting that anyone but a wilderness-tested purist would fall in love with it at first sight.

In fact, landscapes such as the Dolomites aren't so much gentrified or manufactured – to refer to filmmaker Edward Burtynsky's visually arresting documentary on factory spaces and industrial wastelands, *Manufactured Landscapes* – but rather manicured. To manicure is to take meticulous care of something to make it look more attractive. To manicure is to polish, to trim, to shape, to beautify. The Dolomites were on the UNESCO list for a good reason, but rather than natural heritage, a more proper classification for them might have been placing them next to any other work of art or architecture on the long list of Italy's cultural heritage sites. And that would take nothing away from their sublime nature, and quite possibly their wildness – if we understand wildness to be something other than the separation between nature and culture.

Little of this natural-cultural dichotomy made sense to Giovanni Mischi. Giovanni, a Ladin historian, had recently published a book on the role played by the larch tree in the ecology and history of the Dolomites. He lived in a *vila* (the spelling is correct) in the Gader Valley in the small town of Longiarü – at the northeastern edges of the Puez-Odle Nature Park. In South Tyrol, a vila is a hillside compound of several buildings (anywhere from three or four to a dozen) called *masi*. Neighbours within a vila can be relatives or friends, but regardless of their relation, they share some common facilities and help one another out with work and everyday life as needed.

"Masi" is the plural noun, "maso" the singular. "A maso is the combination of house and barn," Giovanni explained in Italian. On one side of a maso, you'd find the people, on the other side the cows. Culture and nature living together, in the same place, taking care of each other. It was a good arrangement for both, and having an expression of antidualism right in his living environment meant Giovanni had little sympathy for the separation of cultural and natural heritage. His maso, called Ciasa de Mair, or the mayor's house, was a fully renovated home: modern, spacious, comfortable, and impeccably polished and orderly. The cows' quarters were almost as hospitable.

Despite their heritage value, many vilas and masi had disappeared over the past fifty years, either to make space for residences or because they were remodelled as mountain restaurants called *malghe*. "What has happened over the last fifty to sixty years is impressive," Giovanni said. "Every town in the Badia Valley used to depend on local agricultural revenue. Nowadays, agriculture is still somewhat important in the local economy. However, it is perhaps the smallest link in the chain. Economic development has depended on tourism. These days, nearly everyone lives off tourism, even agriculture indirectly, and all of this has consequences for our natural environment."

In his fifties, Giovanni spoke using wise and measured words that carried the authority of a teacher. "Look at the ways our meadows are cut and our natural landscapes are cared for. Around here, the meadows are cut because there are still people attached to their land." We had, indeed, been looking. There was hardly a meadow that didn't look dreamy. Giovanni explained that they looked like that because of the farmers' emotional attachment and because they received economic incentives and subsidies from the municipal authorities. Even at their vila, the meadows were cut by Giovanni and his wife "for the love of it." "We do it for the sake of the environment," he reflected. "We just do it to take care of the landscape."

The geographical and historical significance of that fact had not escaped his attention. "The masi appeared here six, seven, eight hundred years ago. Before then nature was intact." Following that phase, there was tillage, deforestation. Deforestation led to the growth of meadows. "These meadows are not natural," Giovanni argued, "not even the high mountain meadows. High mountain meadows are, in part, the result of artificial work."

Lightning struck in the distance. "No matter how beautiful this landscape is, we should not think of a natural landscape or intact nature." Thunder roared for a few seconds. He collected his thoughts and drove the earth-shattering conclusion home: "We should think of this as a cultural landscape."

On the fourth day, our trek ended within the boundaries of the Puez-Odle Nature Park, right underneath Mont de Stevia and the Odle group. Checking in for the night at the Regensburger Hut, we ordered a dinner of eggs, bacon, and rösti and then retired to our separate rooms. The Regensburger was an old-fashioned mountain hut: no pools or saunas, just shared bathrooms and dormitory-style spaces. It was a welcome change. Autumn took to her drawing journal (no TVs available either). We ordered a pair of ice-cold radlers then wrote field notes and consulted our trusted map as the sun created pink magic on the pale rock.

Scattered around us in all directions, we realized, were a handful of the *malghe* we had read about. Malghe were small huts that offered local agricultural products. They weren't restaurants or cafés or teahouses or pubs; they were all that and more. They'd been converted from their former life of hard agricultural work, having served either as *masi* or as summertime lees for herders. Typically serving food from mid-morning to late afternoon, malghe featured a few savoury Italian and German dishes made with ingredients farmed or harvested nearby, as well as beers, wine, and a selection of goods baked onsite. Their presence enabled hikers to rest their legs for an hour or two while enjoying, say, a cold Bavarian beer, pumpernickel bread with Alpine cheeses, knödels with melted butter and parmesan cheese, and a slice of strudel filled with local apples.

Next to the malghe, at times, were beautiful hotels that perfectly fit the landscape. For reasons that remain a deep mystery to us, mountain hotels in North America either look utterly out of place or, when they're designed to fit in the environment, irreparably cheesy and forced. In the Dolomites, hotels seemed to belong in the landscape. Fritz Bromberger owned one of them: the Ütia de Börz hotel situated on top of the Würzjoch, a 2,006-metre mountain pass between the town of Brixen and the upper Gader Valley at the northern edges of the Puez-Odle World Heritage Site, just a couple of kilometres away from the Regenburger Hut.

Located right in front of the imposing Sass de Putia (an iconic triangular slab of grey rock reaching 2,875 metres) and atop a meadow surrounded by scattered patches of forest, the hut-style hotel featured a quintessentially Alpine dining lounge and cozy bedrooms appointed with Swiss pine furniture. "Guests' expectations have increased," Fritz recounted as he joined us for a day hike: an eighteen-kilometre loop around the Sass de Putia. Lean, stocky, and with lungs accustomed to the thin air, the sixty-five-year-old could simultaneously talk and sprint up and down the steep trails while we gasped for oxygen.

Minutes into the first hill climb of the day, he noted, "Even at 2,000 metres of altitude, people don't want to have cold water or candlelight, they want comforts." Years ago, the people who went high up the mountains were expert walkers, people who knew what it meant to go up a mountain, who had an idea what to expect, Fritz observed. "Now, the group is broader, and many people don't care about the significance of mountains. They want the same comforts they have at home. And the question is, is it sustainable? The costs for building and maintenance at such heights are enormous."

Fritz had developed a unique mechanism to cope with the stresses of running a growing business: he hiked. Or more accurately, he galloped. Every day, he would set aside some time to hike at high speed around the many trails branching around the Sass de Putia, occasionally even accompanying guests all the way to the summit in the middle of the night. "On a clear day, at sunrise, you can see glimpses of Venice," he said.

Tourism in the region had changed dramatically over the years, Fritz reflected, as we reached the halfway point of our hike. People used to take a whole month off for holiday. They would drive up to the Dolomites, park their car, and hike new trails day after day. During the winter, most employers would give their workers a week off so they could enjoy what middle-class families called "the white week," an entire week spent on the slopes skiing and relaxing. "Now, it's all changed," Fritz commented with a tinge of melancholia. "Nowadays, people have this hit-and-run mentality. They show up for a few days, maybe a weekend, and then they're off to the next destination: Venice, Tuscany, Rome, or maybe somewhere in Austria or Bavaria."

Like most dolomitic hikes, the Sass de Putia loop traversed a wild variety of grounds. Hard, fractured limestone soil, faded to creamy white and ash blonde. Loose scree, which occasionally gave way under heavy boots. Forest dirt, tangled with red pine roots, moist with previous nights' rainfalls and ripened by random smatterings of cow patties. Open fields with short grasses growing in soft topsoil sequinned by myriad blue, red, and yellow wildflowers.

Every ground had its distinct smell. Alkaline dolomitic rock. Pungently crisp coniferous trees. A medley of smells drifting from gentians, geraniums, euphorbias, arnicas, and edelweiss flowers in open meadows. The full-flavoured, gamy odour of fresh cow manure – quite possibly the most soothing stench in the natural world. And the sizzling, savoury spice of German wieners or Italian-style thin pizza baked in an outdoor stone oven.

After a quick snack stop at the Schlüterhutt, we resumed walking on well-kept grassy soil adorned with wildflowers. "Farmers are well subsidized, from the province, from the EU," Fritz explained as we passed a farming couple raking their grass after a recent cut. "And that benefits tourism, too, because they take care of the place very well. Without the farmers cleaning up, the place would be a disaster. All the grass would dry up. From mid-August on, everything would be brown and ugly. Tourism benefits because nature is cared for and cleaned, and that brings lots of tourism, because tourists then find *una natura eccezionale* – an outstanding nature."

Clearly, this wasn't pristine nature; it was very much touched by the hands of farmers, but it was no less exceptional because of that touch, no less natural. Farmers' work, indeed, contributed directly to the biodiversity of the soil and the region. Without farmers' activities, the low-nutrient soil – called *prati magri* in Italian, or thin lawns – would have been home to significantly fewer species.

"Thanks for the *passeggiata*," Fritz said as he began his final sprint on the last stretch of the trail. Aussies did bushwalks, Kiwis tramped, Brits rambled, Americans hiked, and Fritz took breakneck high-altitude *passeggiate*, or strolls, we noted in our journal later, after one long nap.

"The Dolomites have always had a huge impact on those who admired them for the first time, and it is not a secret that they are acclaimed as the most beautiful mountains on earth," declares the official page of the Dolomites World Heritage Site.

This wasn't always the case. Before the eighteenth century, mountains were often thought to be grotesque, ugly abominations of nature. Alpinism itself is a recent invention. Before people from the city turned up with ropes and boots, ready to climb and enjoy the highest peaks, residents of mountain regions would never dare go up. "And why would you?" they might have reasoned. "It's dangerous. It's exhausting. It's pointless." Alpinism took off in large part because of the same attitude that encouraged the cultivation of an artistic education and imagination. Mountains were monuments, according to this ideology; their raw natural purity corresponded to the essential creativity of the artist's mind.

Like high culture and the fine arts, however, the mountain's sublime beauty wasn't, at first, meant for everyone. For a very long time, skill, physical prowess, sacrifice, fatigue, and danger were understood as crucial tests for anyone keen on appreciating their character. Amazement, transcendence, grandeur, mystical asceticism, and all that poetry could be experienced only after an arduous day of walking. To appreciate them took cultivation, refinement, and education, just like art.

The notion that the natural sublime is something you have to strive for, something you have to work to appreciate, something you have to earn, is rapidly disappearing from our world. Places such as the Dolomites are still as beautiful as they have always been, but the conditions for the appreciation of that natural beauty have changed. Comfort and convenience are now part of the experience of nature, and for many people, without that kind of comfort and convenience, the experience of beautiful nature is simply unimaginable, much too hampered by fatigue, risk, and inaccessibility.

A few hours' walk away from the Regensburger Hut lay the SellaJoch Resort. It was day six of our hike. Only a few years ago, our final destination had been called the Sellajoch Hut. Rusty, gritty, and unkempt, it had been a functional hostel with a long history as a basecamp for high-altitude climbers. Now, after a massive renovation, it featured a swimming pool, a sauna, a steam room, a wine cellar, and a fine-dining lounge. "All our rooms," the hotel's website boasted, "are furnished with pine wood. This fine wood has a relaxing effect and, thanks to its scent, it improves the quality of sleep, transforming every stay into a rejuvenating experience." Rooms also featured private saunas and large-screen entertainment centres equipped with a PlayStation.

The next day, we left the Sellajoch Resort and caught a cable car to the Langkofel Scharte. From there, we descended through the vertiginous scree fields separating the Langkofel from the Plattkofel. The loose scree and a few patches of snow made our advance slow at times, but we eventually made it back below the treeline, to the meadows of the Seiser Alm, en route to the Zallinger Hut.

This is Autumn's recollection of the moment:

> My forehead dripped with sweat, and my stomach growled from
> hunger. It was the longest day of our trek through the
> Dolomites. Perhaps it wasn't the longest in terms of duration,
> but the constant change in terrain and the wavering weather
> conditions made this day feel like a week. We had ventured
> through mountain paths, rolling hills, and small towns all for
> the purpose of finally making it to the next hut. It felt as though

my legs could collapse at any second. In spite of this, I kept my eyes focused on the trail ahead and continued walking. Trailing behind were my parents, who had managed to keep a balanced pace throughout the day. A couple of extra sugar packets in my hot chocolate that morning allowed me to remain fifty metres ahead of them at all times. Because of this, I was the first to notice the hut at the end of the path. My face lit up with delight.

"Guys, the hut is at the end of the trail!"

"Really?" my mom said.

I heard their footsteps getting closer, and soon enough, they were right next to me. We pursued the hut as a group, all with gleaming eyes. We hadn't arrived yet, but I could feel the warmth of the heated room and the comfort of a bed. Just as I thought this, a drop of water struck my skin. Then another. Before I could even put a hood over my head, rain began to fall from the sky faster than I'd ever seen before. My parents threw their hoods on and ran toward the hut. But as the rain increased in speed, I stopped in my tracks. I looked up at the sky and felt every raindrop sink into my skin. People always talk about how they dislike rain, but there's something about the sound of raindrops hitting the ground that puts my mind at ease. I was soaked head to toe, and my whole body ached from fatigue. Despite all that, there was nothing I'd rather be doing in that moment than feeling the rain strike my skin.

On the morning of the eighth day, tired from the long downhill walk of the day before, we dragged our sore knees and toes to the Panorama Hotel, where everything had begun. We walked proudly into the lounge and announced to the confused desk clerk that we had been walking for eight days straight.

"So, you don't need a parking permit then?" the desk clerk asked.

Our trek had been a walk in the park in comparison to our experience along the Hollyford Trek in New Zealand. Yet it had been more work than the average hotel guest had likely accomplished in between spa treatments, reading the newspaper, and wine tastings.

"You know, guys" Autumn said, as we entered our bedroom, "this hike was fun and everything, but I don't feel any accomplishment. In New Zealand, I kind of hated it, but in the end, I felt like I achieved something. This one was so beautiful, but it wasn't really challenging." The Romantics had a point about earning their appreciation of sublime nature through hard work.

At lunchtime, Emanuel joined us at the Panorama Restaurant. His work had kept him busy all week, and like many locals, he was happy to be up in the mountains for the weekend.

This alp, Emanuel observed as we waited for our meals, had once been dominated by agriculture. "Now, agriculture has increasingly been replaced by the monoculture of tourism." For example, he noted, traditional dresses worn regularly a few decades ago were now worn only during selected ceremonies and rituals, such as going to Mass on Sunday. "Nowadays, you have the presentation of these traditional dresses to tourists in settings disconnected from traditional rituals, and so it has become a kind of public performance of your culture, and so sometimes there is a question about the authenticity of this performance."

"Have the locals lost their souls to tourism?" April asked.

"Maybe, somehow, it's a normal development. Culture is always changing and adapting to new situations. The Dolomites fifty or sixty years ago were inhabited by peasants who produced what they needed for a living. Now they, and the hoteliers, and the restaurateurs, and the shop owners have found another way to survive. You might say it's not authentic, but what exactly is authentic culture anyway?"

Change, Emanuel reflected, was part of culture and nature. Not only had the Dolomites region experienced drastic economic change following the early arrival of tourism and its subsequent evolution toward mass consumerism, but it had also experienced another source of change more recently. After environmentalism developed deeper roots in the 1980s and early 1990s, commercial and residential developments and road building slowed down. Then UNESCO arrived, bringing even more prestige and even more regulations.

"You now have a lot more people coming to this area," Emanuel said, "and the issue of protecting the area now has become an international issue. No longer is it up to only national or regional lobbies. I've heard people say that at first everyone wants to be a World Heritage, but once they are in, they want out because they recognize the burden from all the restrictions and obligations. So, yes, it brings prestige but you also risk becoming expropriated."

That was the condition of the new sublime, unfortunately. A stunningly beautiful place that no longer attracted just a few people from the surrounding regions, people with the time, the patience, and the passion to cultivate its appreciation. The new sublime attracted people from around the world who were there one day, in Venice the next; people who needed to get to the summit fast, post a selfie on Facebook quickly, and move on; people who, unprepared and unwilling to invest time, could maximize comfort, convenience, and luxury in two or three days of plush decadence.

"So is this a wild place, Emanuel?"

"Yes, it is a wild place. But for me, the issue of control comes up. Wild places are places where we lose control a bit, we lose control over nature." But this was hardly a place out of control. From the amount and type of cow manure that could be spread out on the fields, to the landscape liens that regulated the architectural design of masi and homes, to what foods could be served in a malga, to the sections of a meadow that a path could cross, absolutely everything was under control. This was a scenography, a diorama, a carefully manicured place that was anything but out of human control.

"But you see, this isn't a place like the Amazon," Emanuel was quick to clarify. "This isn't a wild place where there are no paths to walk and untouched nature everywhere around you. You've seen for yourselves how if a hiking path here brings you to the top, to the very top of a mountain, it gives you a feeling of wildness, a feeling of being out of control and being exposed to the forces of nature," like the fog and the sudden thunderstorms that Gustav's photographs captured. That was the feeling of the wild thunders and the lighting bouncing against bare rock walls, echoing through hollow valleys of cold, pale stone, the feeling of the rain drenching our skin as we walked freely. And that feeling, thankfully, was still free of charge.

There are powerful conservative tendencies in environmentalism. At times, these are well justified, because the "progress" espoused by extractivist politicians with their interest in developing the planet's resources is not real progress at all but mere rhetoric meant to hide their self-interest. But at other times, a much more thinly veiled conservatism pervades ecological sciences in often unreflexive ways. This is a kind of fetishism of stability and an antipathy toward change. The notion of ecosystem equilibrium, for example, so central in ecology, is rooted in conservative values – in the idea that change is naturally destabilizing. Given that so many nature lovers are otherwise politically progressive people, this conservatism can be quite paradoxical.

There is a conservative vein in anthropological sciences, too, and Emanuel was quick to point it out. This comes in many different forms, but most often it can be seen in the way cultural authenticity is valued above many other things. Tourism, for example, is often seen as a corruption of earlier pastoral ways of life. By this token, one should be critical of how old mountain huts are turned into luxury sports hotels, of how malghe are taken out of their traditional agricultural context and repurposed for tourism, of how grass cutting with machines is replacing scything by hand, of how vilas are welcoming fewer cows and more international travellers, and so on.

These two conservative sets of values often coalesce in the appreciation of wildness and wild nature. Wilderness, wild nature, wild places are thought by many people to be ecosystems based in equilibrium, places that shouldn't be subjected to the change brought about by social and economic pressures generated by humans and their shifting cultural values.

We understand why wild places are sacred and why they matter, but we are also skeptical about the conservativism implicit in their appreciation. When we equate wild nature with stasis, or wilderness with a place frozen in time, we shortchange wildness and its power. Wildness is change, wildness is growth, wildness is the will to evolve, unbounded, unrestrained by the status quo.

We are not the first to say this, of course. Within the science of ecology, the view of nature as a balance has long endured challenges from those who espouse the value and the reality of the fluxes of nature. Some ecologists have even gone so far as to suggest that disturbance, not equilibrium, is the normal state under which ecosystems live and thrive. In the context of wilderness studies, authors such as J. Baird Callicott and Michael Nelson have argued that wilderness is something that has always been subjected to the disturbances introduced by ubiquitous humans. Disturbance isn't new; it isn't a sign that the world has fallen from grace. Stable wilderness equilibria are extremely rare outside of Antarctica, perhaps even nonexistent.

Nevertheless, environmentalist movements, wilderness conservation movements, and the broad notion of wilderness within Western cultures have not been updating themselves as regularly as have the ecological sciences. Views of nature as something constantly experiencing change and flux have not been uniformly taken up within conservation philosophy and politics. And yet they should be. When we realize that there are no original states of nature, we begin to understand that conservation policy should be rethought, and its values reviewed. As J. Baird Callicott writes in *The Great Wilderness Debate*, "Preservationists therefore must consciously develop and defend criteria for determining which historic states of nature should be selected as worthy of preservation." Which states of nature should be selected and why, of course, is the key.

Places such as the Dolomites are knots of natural and cultural dynamics entangled together. Rather than frozen in time, they are always in the midst of growing and flux, of becoming something else. The reality is that such growth, such change, isn't always bad (except in those cases where it destroys ecosystems) or always good. At times, growth and change are positive, as they free people from unjust cultural and social restrictions. Growth and change are also good when they increase and promote cultural diversity and biodiversity. But, at times, growth is untenable, and change is tacky and disrespectful of time-tested relations. And, unfortunately, change, at times, can be outright destructive and should be prevented, no matter the cost. Regardless, change happens, and preservationists must make conscious choices over what should be conserved and why.

South Tyrol had changed dramatically over the last few decades. Some of that change was good; it made living conditions better for residents, and it increased both cultural and biodiversity. Some of that change also had an unintended consequence: it made the place impossibly exclusive for many.

Wild natures can be changed; they can be enhanced by people and the disturbances and the policies they introduce into an ecosystem. The appreciation and enjoyment of wild nature and wild places can be fostered and improved when people act intelligently and respectfully toward their land and the cultural heritage embedded in that land. South Tyrol, with its beauty and rich land-based cultural traditions, had taught us that. And above all, it taught us that people can and do belong in beautiful natural landscapes and that their presence can enhance their wild beauty, as long as we are willing to believe that wild doesn't always have to remain untouched.

5

Wild Can Be Reimagined

BELIZE

WE WERE BOTH PRETEENS when Madonna recorded "La Isla Bonita" in 1986. *True Blue* was an annoyingly catchy album, and hardly a day seemed to go by without Madonna's lyrics getting stuck in everyone's heads. Yet neither of us in 1986 gave any thought to whether the famed "tropical breeze" and "the nature wild and free" that Madonna sang about in "La Isla Bonita" might be found in an actual place. The place was real, however. It was Ambergris Caye, Belize. San Pedro – where Madonna longed to be (as the warm winds carried her on the sea) – was the island's main town. It is there that we rented an Airbnb for Easter week, 2017.

And now the song is stuck in our heads again.

Madonna's claim that Ambergris Caye was wild wasn't the reason we chose to travel there, however. The reason was that time seemed to be running out. In 2009, UNESCO placed the Belize Barrier Reef Reserve on its list of World Heritage Sites in danger, and eight years later, in 2017, things only seemed to get worse. According to the World Heritage warning, "Management challenges and threats that impact on the integrity of the property" included "overharvesting of marine resources, coastal development, tourism, industrial development and proposed oil and gas exploration and exploitation."

The Belize Barrier Reef is the Northern Hemisphere's largest and the world's second-largest barrier reef after Australia's famous counterpart. It is a roughly three-hundred-kilometre-long section of the nine-hundred-kilometre-long Mesoamerican Barrier Reef System, which runs parallel to much of the Caribbean side of Central America. In the north of Belize, the reef is as close as three hundred metres to the land, whereas in the south it lies farther ashore, as distant as forty kilometres. Stretching the entire coast of the country, the reef includes idyllic off-shore atolls, hundreds of picture-perfect low-lying sand cays, and a vast network of mangrove forests, river estuaries, and coastal lagoons that are home to marine turtles, manatees, and marine crocodiles, among countless other species.

The reef was inscribed on the World Heritage List in 1996 and sub-divided into seven protected areas: Bacalar Chico National Park and Marine Reserve, Blue Hole Natural Monument, Half Moon Caye Natural Monument, South Water Caye Marine Reserve, Glover's Reef Marine Reserve, Laughing Bird Caye National Park, and Sapodilla Cayes Marine Reserve.

We arrived in San Pedro, Ambergris Caye, on Easter weekend via a high-speed foot passenger ferry from Belize City packed with inter-national tourists, a handful of locals, and a few domestic visitors. For the other internationals, San Pedro was a chill party town, a better alternative to the nearby Mexican coast. For us, San Pedro was a convenient base camp, an ideal place to connect with organizations, speak with key people, and launch expeditions to the reef.

Most tourists will appreciate San Pedro as much as Madonna did, but given our preferences for peace, quiet, and relative solitude – the small town wasn't our favourite place in the world. On the plus side, San Pedro had managed to keep cars off its narrow streets. On the minus side, the cars had been replaced by golf carts driven by unsober tourists in search of the nearest beachside bar. In all, the place was busy and at times tacky, but it was also convenient and not unbearable. Luckily, its planned strategic value had come through: our appointment requests were granted by welcoming locals who cared deeply about the barrier reef and seemed eager to let the world know about their plight.

Alyssa Carnegie, communications director at Oceana Belize, offered to speak to us about the latest developments in the ongoing environ-mental crisis. Oceana is one of the world's largest NGOs dedicated to protecting the planet's oceans. For most of the last decade, its focus had been fighting offshore oil exploration. The World Heritage designation of the barrier reef, Alyssa told us, was something Belizeans were proud of. "But we're not so proud of the fact that it's been listed in danger."

Pride would turn out to be a recurring theme throughout our conversations in Belize. Unlike other parts of the world, where natural heritage areas were almost forgotten in the back corners of the country, Belizeans were deeply proud of the reef. Interview after interview, from fishing folk to environmental activists, from business owners to tour operators, the reef stood as a national symbol that united Belizeans. It wasn't just a geological feature; it was a national monument, and many people were doing their part to protect it.

"The issues that are confronting us are very real developmental issues," Alyssa told us. "As a developing country, there's a lot that we'd like to see in terms of investment, development, jobs, but there's so much that we're currently making from the reef that we would be jeopardizing if we were to go that route." Alyssa explained that economic research clearly showed the number of services that people received from marine resources. People would give up a lot if they sacrificed the reef for economic development.

Alyssa told us that they had seen good progress in some areas, but political pressure still needed to be applied to stop offshore oil exploration. But restoring ecological systems long affected by development, tourism, and fishing would be a whole other ball game. The most positive fact, however, was that so many Belizeans had united in a front against oil exploration.

"Their stance has been a resounding 'no' to offshore oil exploration," Alyssa told us. In 2011, Oceana held a people's referendum. About thirty thousand people – almost 10 percent of the population – participated. "But we need policy, legislation, something that would ensure protection for future generations," she said. "Belizeans care about it. They need this, they want this, and they're willing to fight for it."

One of the reasons many Belizeans seemed ready to fight was a widespread sense of resentment toward the government's lack of transparency. In Belize, the oil-extraction business was like a fly-by-night operation. One morning, Alyssa told us, just a few months before our arrival in Belize, coastal residents woke up and noticed suspicious-looking ships collecting data and doing seismic tests of a mysterious nature. No one knew exactly what they were doing or who they were.

Despite a long history rooted in Mayan civilization, Belize is a young nation. It earned independence only in 1981, when it dropped the name "British Honduras" and adopted the name "Belize" (though it wasn't until 1994 that the last British troops, apart from a small contingent left behind for training purposes, left). Unlike several other Central American nations, Belize enjoyed political stability and somewhat regular economic growth. In speaking to Belizeans, it's easy to get the feeling they have little patience for the Banana Republic ways of some of their neighbours. Transparency of governance is of the utmost importance.

Over 190,000 Belizeans, by Oceana's calculations, depend on the barrier reef for their income, through either tourism or fishing. Twenty-five percent of Belize's GDP is derived from tourism (in Canada, by comparison, the rate is 6.5 percent). An oil spill would cripple the country for decades and the reef forever. "And that's something I don't even want to imagine, to be honest," Alyssa admitted. "The loss would be huge, and it would be devastating. Belize is known for this amazing coastline, and that's why people are here. So is fishing, same thing."

And then there is the issue of coastline protection. "We live in the hurricane belt, and we in recent years have been hit by several storms," Alyssa added. "Though there have been significant losses, they could have been far worse if we didn't have the reef, if we were exposed. The loss would be tremendous, and it would be incredibly detrimental to our country. I think it would change the face, the shape, the nature, our culture, our identity beyond what we know."

In 1971, famed French explorer, conservationist, and filmmaker Jacques Cousteau led his ship, the *Calypso,* to chart the depths of a unique sinkhole roughly seventy kilometres off the mainland of Belize. The sinkhole had a uniquely circular shape, nearly a perfect circle, 318 metres in diameter and 124 metres deep, which had been formed during a succession of episodes throughout the quaternary glaciation, 153,000 to 15,000 years ago. By filming his adventurous dives, Cousteau made the sinkhole famous around the world (though few people know that his crew actually dug out a giant opening through the southern wall to allow boats to access the centre!). In 1988, the famed sinkhole received its name – the Great Blue Hole – from British diver and author Ned Middleton.

Today, the Great Blue Hole is a massive magnet for travellers. Day tours leave nearly every day year-round from both San Pedro and Belize City. Many of the visitors are divers wishing to relive images Cousteau imprinted on the world's psyche, but there are also snorkellers, swimmers, and even those who prefer to see it from above.

Few Belizeans get the chance to visit the Great Blue Hole. The typical cost for a day tour is around US$300 per person, which is considerable in a country where the median monthly income is less than a grand. This is probably why grandmas, aunties, uncles, and children didn't hesitate to jump on the speedboat we managed to charter through the executive director of the Belize Audubon Society, Amanda Burgos-Acosta. Lyra, our Belizean gatekeeper, and her boyfriend, Peter, volunteered to come along too. The presence of extended family was something we welcomed deeply. Rather than a cookie-cutter tourist or scientific expedition, a long weekend with the Burgos-Acosta family and a few members of the Belize Audubon Society sounded like a genuine way to experience the cultural significance of the famed sinkhole.

With the boat packed and on her way, we learned that the Belize Audubon Society was dedicated not only to raising environmental awareness but also to comanaging (among other sites) two of the protected areas inscribed within the borders of the World Heritage Barrier Reef Reserve: the Great Blue Hole Natural Monument and Half Moon Caye. This was part of a unique comanagement agreement between the Belizean federal government and a host of NGOs. Unable to tend to all its protected areas (because of limited monetary resources and its overall small size), the government gave authority to NGOs such as the Belize Audubon Society to look after its most precious environmental gems. This arrangement, incidentally, made our work easier too: rather than dealing with a central bureaucracy and being fed the party line, we could establish relations with a variety of people who cared about the place and weren't afraid to tell it like it is.

Roughly two hours after leaving the family dock in Belize City, our speed boat came to a halt. The afternoon sun was still high in the sky, and no signs of land were in sight. The winds were calm, and the azure waters surrounding us darkened. Before we could even guess why we'd stopped, a seaplane appeared a few hundred feet above us and encircled us. You could almost hear the cameras snapping pictures from above. That was the clue we were at the Great Blue Hole. From our vantage point, it was virtually imperceptible.

"Jump up here with the camera," the captain encouraged. "You'll get a good view." We followed his lead to get a better visual perspective on the sinkhole. Everyone else slipped on fins and snorkels and jumped into the water. By that time, the day-trip diving vessels had left, and the Great Blue Hole was ours to enjoy alone. The key to appreciating the experience, we were told after the camera was stored away, was staying away from the centre and keeping to the edges. We dove into the warm water and followed schools of midnight parrotfish, blue and queen angelfish, queen triggerfish, banded butterflyfish, and damselfish.

Wildness has a different feel under the water. It's quiet. The only sounds are your breathing and the water displaced by your arms and fins. Fish seem unconcerned with your presence. Some see you and pretend to ignore you; others make way for you, perhaps out of respect for your size. Others, every bit as big as you, like the great barracuda or nurse sharks, remind you that you are a guest and that you should be careful. But in all, there is a wildness underwater even more pervasive than on the surface of the planet. It's the kind of wildness that feels peaceful because it's everywhere around you, because it enfolds you. It's a place that feels wild because you know that you don't quite belong there; you're not in control. It's also a place where you can't linger too long.

After an hour of snorkelling, we collectively decided to head to the cabin. In a manner of minutes, we docked at Half Moon Caye. The atoll measures a mere forty-one acres. Shaped like a banana slug, it's covered in coarse, light-coloured sand that bears the faint traces of hundreds of hermit crabs side walking. On its northern side, a grove of palm trees provides shade to an abandoned pair of shacks and a decrepit communication tower – something that gives the atoll an indubitable aura of haunting abandonment. At its centre is the dock, a lone pier for the occasional boat of wayward Blue Hole divers in search of diversion and terra firma for their bagged lunches. And on its southern side lies a thick littoral forest of primarily orange-flowered siricote trees, the boobies' favourite hangout.

At the edge of the forest, set metres back from a swimming beach, was our cabin. More a lodge than a cabin, the spartan compound had enough rooms to host a handful of guards from the Fisheries Department, a few long-staying members of the Audubon Society, and our large party.

We could have done fieldwork there for years. But we couldn't. So as soon as we managed to find an electrical outlet to plug our camera into, we sat down for an interview with Amanda. The cay was the first marine protected area in Central America, and since 1924, it has been a bird sanctuary dedicated to the red-footed booby. As part of criterion vii, UNESCO had inscribed the barrier reef on its World Heritage List because of "the spectacular picturesque natural setting of brilliant white sand cayes and verdant green mangrove cayes [and] surrounding azure waters," and we wanted to know if Amanda held a similar sentiment. We sat in the shade of a swaying palm tree to talk.

"Halfmoon Caye," she said, "has a strong hold on your heart because it feels like you're coming to the end of the world. It has that feeling of isolation. You can find solace. You can really just reconnect and recharge yourself."

During the people's referendum a few years before, Amanda had worked at one of the polling stations, and a man there told her how badly he wanted his kids to be able to go out and see the Great Blue Hole. He wasn't the only one, Amanda said. "I've met fishermen who come here and say to me, 'I've made my life off of this. I want my kids to be able to make their life off of this.' I really think that it's important."

Most Belizean kids would never see the Blue Hole or the reef in person, Amanda explained. To enable some kids and families to enjoy the place and learn about the importance of environmental conversation, the Audubon Society offered youth programs, summer camps, and a yearly field trip to members of the general public at a nominal cost that ranged from fifty to seventy American dollars. The program was meant not as a fundraiser but as a consciousness-raiser.

For Amanda's children, too, the place was an especially unique one. Her nine-year-old boy and twelve-year-old girl had the good fortune of routinely accompanying her in the field and had learned to make the best of it. She glanced at her boy, who was introducing Autumn to his favourite spots on the beach. "I think it creates that kind of ethos of really believing in what is right for the earth and thinking in a much bigger context than just themselves." Children, she continued, "can really be focused on only themselves and leave their phone or tablet at home. And I think being here really forces them to get out of that bubble. Some of their fond memories are probably out here waking up. You really do wake up with the sunrise, and you go to sleep when it gets dark because you're just so tired and knocked out."

"What does 'wild' mean to you?" we asked.

"I think 'wild,' to me, means untouched. It means pure. It means the idea that it's not tainted by that societal kind of branding, or impact. It's being able to maintain its integrity and its essence of what it is. That's wild."

"Is this place wild?"

"It is. It has human interaction. But when you go and you stand on that platform" – she pointed at an observation deck situated above the tree canopy – "and you're surrounded by the boobies and the frigates and the smell of the guano, that is wild."

We told her we agreed.

"And when you're snorkelling, and you're in your own world watching the fish, it is wild. It still has that essence to it. Even though there are people and some degree of infrastructure, we've tried really hard to maintain the integrity of that. I think if you leave here with a sense of calm and peace, it's because you've experienced the wild."

"Do people belong in wild places?"

"They do. I think they have a role in maintaining the wild and the wild spaces. But I do think that you have to experience it, because if you don't experience it, you don't appreciate it. And I think that's fundamentally important. Our tagline is 'Balancing people and conservation,' and there's many ways to do that. But I think one of them is allowing people to taste the wild."

First-hand experience is the key to appreciation because it builds a relational bond, it allows a connection with a wild place to take root.

But until the opportunity for experience manifests itself, a place has to be imagined, to be fantasized about, to be mythologized even. As we packed and started making our way back to Belize City, Lyra and Peter thanked us profusely for inviting them to join us. They, too, had only seen the Great Blue Hole in books and televised images. It had lived only in their imagination for years. "You don't have to pay me for the work I did," Lyra told us. "Being able to come here is more than enough."

Belize's road system is a bit like its coconuts: they're there, but most of them have fallen down. Only two major roads bisect the spine of the country, and one of them is impassable for most vehicles. The other one is open, but it's overrun by manically aggressive local drivers who seem to live hectic lives. It's a bit of a paradox, given that no one in Belize, when not in their cars, ever seems to be in a hurry.

From Belize City to Placencia, the road passes only one large town – Belmopan, the country's administrative centre – and a handful of sleepy farming communities surrounded by verdant hills. After the turnoff to the Placencia Peninsula, the traffic slows down, and the landscape changes. Gone are the coffee plantations and errant chickens, the green fields and roadside stands. As the newly paved road insinuates farther south, wedged between open sea waters and a meandering canal, vulgar subdivisions funded by foreign capital and teeming with villas, mansions, and the odd golf resort eventually give way to discreet palm-shaded hotels and sandy beaches.

While Placencia isn't immune to the imperial notion that cheap real estate is a sufficient justification to build a pricey vacation home in a foreign country – no matter the consequences for the locals – the town has maintained enough charisma to be enjoyable even to the most cynical traveller. Sure, it's busy and expensive (by local standards); sure, there are one too many restaurants on the beach; and sure, the place is odious on the odd day a cruise ship stops by, but it's still infinitely mellower than San Pedro, and its impeccably colourful and full of character.

As soon as we arrived, we met up with Lyra and her boyfriend, Peter. Lyra had just finished her PhD in cultural anthropology at Indiana University, and she'd been recommended to us as a local gatekeeper by her former adviser, an ethnographer colleague of ours. Wise enough to not take up an academic career, Lyra and Peter had recently started a cultural tourism business, guiding visitors to experience Belizean culture beyond the sun and sand. One of their tours focused on chocolate making and farming cocoa beans. It neatly wove together a chocolate tasting, lessons on sustainable economy, and well-placed references to the anthropology of food.

Blonde, fair-skinned, and tall, Lyra's strong voice and presence gave her the air of someone smart, practical, and pragmatic. And true to character, the arrangements she made for us weren't "appointments" in the sense that we'd come to expect after visiting South Tyrol and Tasmania. We learned that Villamar Godfrey, known as Mr. Villa, was "happy to chat with you guys." Lyra smiled. "Just head down to the fishing pier."

"Okay, when?"

"Whenever he's there."

"When is he there?"

"He goes there most days. Just ask around if people have seen him."

"What does he look like?"

"Everyone knows him. Just ask whoever is around to point him out."

The fishing pier was the end of the road. Beyond that, and over the waters, lay Punta Gorda, and then Guatemala and Honduras. Like any pier at the end of the road, the Placencia dock was the domain of fishing folks and the odd migratory worker or two, some more legal or official than others. It was also a great place to hang out if you were a retiree or an ethnographer.

"Excuse me, have you seen Mr. Villa?" we asked a fisherman cleaning a barracuda.

"He's over there, walking this way."

Try that tactic in London or Vancouver and see if it works.

Barefoot and relaxed in his stride, Mr. Villa wore a white ball cap, long loose pants, and a green shirt. He shook our hands gently and invited us to sit down at a shaded picnic table midway down the pier. Lyra's notes on Mr. Villa had prepared us well, and with his soft speech, thick accent, and humble demeanour, it was easy to feel like we were in the presence of a local legend, an Elder in the true sense of the word.

Mr. Villa had grown up in a much different Placencia and Belize. He had retired from lighthouse keeping and fishing, he told us, but he still loved the sea. Born in Punta Gorda, he moved with his father to Belize City, where he went to school. But his father had a boat for him to work on, too, so he worked, mostly catching barracuda. Then, a few years later, he moved to Placencia where he eventually founded the fishing cooperative.

"We'd catch lobster, conch, fillet fish, cold fish, all kinds of fish. Good. Very nice." He had lived in Placencia for fifty-four years, he said.

"Why did you decide to start the cooperative?"

"Well, there were a lot of young fellows here. They'd catch fish, and then they couldn't sell them. So we said, 'Let's form a cooperative.' We used to ship this stuff to the United States. So any amount you'd bring in, we'd sell it, then you'd get your money. It was good." He paused to remember. "Now, it's not working that much, because everybody went into tourism. One of the young guys said, 'No I don't want to dive that much.' They want tourism. Take out tourists, show them the cayes and different spots. That's where they make their money now."

"Is that a problem, that nobody wants to fish anymore?"

"No, no, no. One or two still do it, but young guys say they are not in it for that. They want to take out tourists, make their money and then come back."

It was odd, we noted, that there were no tourists around the wharf. A couple of grade-school boys fished with a makeshift rod. We found it amusing that one would hold the rod while the other dove into the water to cool off but scared the fishes away. Three other middle-aged locals worked quietly, tending to the booths that housed their unnamed businesses. Caribbean music floated from a nearby dinghy.

It was as if our meeting with Mr. Villa had opened a time warp into the halcyon days of Placencia's past, a time when days were quieter and lives slower. But perhaps it was simply an atmosphere Mr. Villa created with his words, spoken idly, economically, and deliberately. Some people are easy to transcribe and adapt to the written page – they read just as well as they sound. Other people, like Mr. Villa, have a cadence and a tone that transcription cannot help but render nearly empty of meaning and character. Above all, it was the pauses between Mr. Villa's short sentences that punctuated the performance of his persona. The pauses pulled you in, asked you to listen, asked you to take your time.

We weren't the only ones who felt that way in his presence. In the early 1970s, a young correspondent from *National Geographic* made his way to Placencia from the United States. He met Mr. Villa and fell in love with his charisma. In January 1972, a photograph of Mr. Villa free diving for conch landed in the hands of magazine subscribers around the world.

"I don't like tanks. I never did try. They wanted to teach me, but I said no. I'll go out for a while then come back up." A simple philosophy. "Without a tank. Forty feet down. Freediving. Seven, eight hours a day," he said. A twinkle formed in his eyes as he remembered those days. He looked away from us and the camera, toward the sea. "I wasn't afraid of it. I loved it."

"How long could you stay underwater? One, two minutes?"

"No. Longer than that." He paused. He spoke proudly, without attempting to boast. "I used to be perfect with that. I loved it. I'd see sharks. I'd see barracudas. But I wasn't afraid of them."

We asked Mr. Villa if he had a copy of the famous issue of *National Geographic*. He did. He offered to walk back home to fetch it and came back after a few minutes. Our camera captured his fingers thumbing through the worn pages, tracing the words written about him, his eyes glaring at the photos as if it was the first time he'd seen them, his voice shaking with joy and pride.

At the end of the municipal pier where we met Mr. Villa, a small billboard featuring a bright photograph of coral, told passersby about the activities of an NGO called Fragments of Hope. The next day, we sat down on the beach to talk with Lisa Carne, a California-born marine biologist who had been living in Belize for over twenty years. She'd been at the helm of Fragments of Hope since 2013.

There are three taxa of coral in the Caribbean, she told us, commonly known as elkhorn, staghorn, and fused staghorn. Corals, Lisa explained, are animals; as such, they can not only sexually reproduce but also asexually reproduce, just like some plants. Fragments of Hope had been working on growing and planting corals on the Caribbean Sea for a few years, with great success. "We can take a cutting of a certain plant and its roots, and it starts all over again, and this is primarily how we're fragmenting the corals and restoring them. However, genetically speaking it's important to have multiple individuals of each species so that they can sexually reproduce. Only when you have sex, do your genetics recombine and do you have adaptation."

Following Hurricane Iris, nearby Laughing Bird Caye had become the ideal place to begin coral-restoration efforts. Fragments of Hope staff began transplanting naturally broken pieces of coral from one site to another in underwater nurseries. Scuba divers operating in shallow waters worked their way around growing beds and large containers, picking up pieces and planting them on the seafloor. Thanks to funding from the WWF and Inter-American Development Bank, Fragments of Hope managed to scale up their efforts, at one point working on nineteen different nurseries all over southern Belize. "To date," Lisa remarked with a hint of an acquired Caribbean accent, "we have out-planted over seventy thousand corals at Laughing Bird Caye alone, as well as several other sites."

Rewilding corals might very well be one of the most spectacular rewilding practices. It takes drive and ingenuity. And it saves lives. Among all its many functions, coral reefs offer shoreline protection, a kind of safety guard against waves drifting in.

"Why restore the reef, beside shoreline protection?" April asked.

"For years, we have been documenting the decline of reef health even prior to the hurricane impact. And that is primarily due to climate change effects. And these are coral bleaching and disease events. The first bleaching event was documented in Belize in 1995. The big event famous all over the world was in 1998 when people first began speaking of this."

Bleaching, she explained using simple words, was caused by the decaying health of the algae living inside the coral. They are responsible for the lively colours of the coral, and when conditions become adverse, as has happened with climate change, the algae leave, and the coral turns bright white, just like a skeleton.

"The other main things that reefs do for us is provide so much protein," Lisa continued, "so much food, because they provide home for so many organisms. And finally, they have a key aesthetic purpose. Reefs provide us with natural, wild beauty."

Just as grey Alpine cows in South Tyrol munched grass to provide milk, yogourt, butter, and cheese, coral reefs in Belize fed the nation. The reef was not just a pretty place to have fun in but the very protein behind the constant regeneration of the collective body. The death of coral and subsequently of fish would spell the demise of the country.

A few weeks after our visit, Lyra emailed us to tell us that Mr. Villa had just passed away. He was eighty-three years old. We realized that we had a video in our hands of Mr. Villa describing his life story in intimate detail. We quickly cut a few clips together so they could be played at his memorial service. As we edited the video, our eyes locked in with Mr. Villa's, and we realized how much his eyes explained his charm. The camera captured the light in his diminutive brown eyes better than the written word ever could, a light that had undoubtedly kept his family and community brighter throughout his life.

The private marina north of Dangriga that served as our meeting point with the crew from the Wildlife Conservation Society was glacially quiet. A lone family of yachters from the United States confirmed that this was the place our map claimed it was. No one but a bored storekeeper was around. We tentatively offloaded the rucksacks onto the dock and made sure the remaining cargo and our rental car would be safeguarded. "No problem, everything's gonna be all right," said the elderly park warden. He spoke in heavily accented Creole English, sounding almost like Bob Marley's lyrics in "Three Little Birds."

An hour went by. Nothing happened. Then a quasi-military-looking vehicle appeared. Four serious-looking guards jumped out and made their way toward the dock, where we had been lolling around, eating ice cream and drinking coke. We exchanged a shy hello. They glanced at us skeptically. Were they our ride? Did they know who we were and why we were there? And why were they there? They rolled a heavy barrel full of fuel down the dock, presumably to refill a distant generator. They loaded the heavy barrel onto a skiff, which had just arrived, and spilled a bit as they heaved it onboard. No words were exchanged.

Moments later, another man arrived, alone. Smartly dressed, business-like in appearance and demeanour, Kenneth Gale walked toward us and introduced himself. "The coast guard is hitching a ride with our vessel today," he told us matter-of-factly, "and they'll be staying on the island with you and the rest of the WCS crew." Apparently, the boat the guards had been loading was our ride. The rest of the crew, we learned, would be Captain Buck, two Wildlife Conservation Society staff, and Ms. Alva, our cook. Since Kenneth would be heading back to the mainland after checking on a couple of things, the three of us would be sharing Glover's Reef with a grand total of eight people.

Autumn lifted her head from her book. "So, what's going on, exactly?"

"We're jumping on that skiff, and we'll be heading to a fifteen-acre atoll in the middle of nowhere. Once there, we'll have to share the sleeping camps with the coast guard. Captain Buck will drive us."

She said okay and returned her attention to her book. Two and a half years into our project, our weird, half-baked plans had clearly become a standard affair.

Glover's Reef Atoll was an assemblage of five main small islands, one of which was the site of a pair of idyllic but simple resorts (less like the Club Med and more like expat ma and expat pa) and two of which were privately owned. Our island, Mid Island, was the main outpost. It was publicly owned and comanaged by the Fisheries Department and the Wildlife Conservation Society and had been designated as the main landing site for the park and World Heritage. Once a day, one or two vessels would stop by so tourists could take pictures of the World Heritage plaque, go for a fifteen-minute walk around the island and, if Captain Buck was around, try to buy a souvenir T-shirt from him. Being the main island in the atoll also meant that people could come to our headquarters for help, shelter, or rapid transportation to safety.

After an uneventful ride, we docked on Mid Island and were given the tour by Kenneth. He told us about the basics and advised us that electricity (generated by solar panels) was as limited as water. He reminded us to stay safe and wished us the best with our work. "I almost forgot," he added as he departed, "the internet is available in the evening."

Captain Buck navigating the boat while standing up

The days went by languidly, and our cameras were our main source of work and entertainment. Fancy cameras may be a source of unwanted attention in some parts of the world, but on a small island, where hardly anyone is terribly busy, they can turn out to be a magnet of opportunities. Captain Buck was the first to come forward. "Would you like to go over to the next island and interview the resort owners? ... Would you like to go snorkelling to get a few good shots of a few cool fish species? ... Do you want me to show you where the nicest coral is?"

As time went on, Captain Buck acquired depth and – if possible – even more character. The man appeared monumental at first sight. Six foot three inches tall and with a deep voice that made him seem at least five inches taller, he rang in at some 250 pounds. He had short dark hair and the white in his beard contrasted with his black skin. The lenses in his cool plastic shades had a way of hiding his eyes and reflecting the world around him in much higher definition.

Buck liked to drive his boat while standing. He steered the wheel with his left foot, and that only contributed to his sang-froid kind of charisma. For example, one lazy afternoon, Autumn and Phillip set their eyes on a coconut that had fallen from a tree and decided, in the way all gringos do, to free it from its green casing without a rod planted in the ground, a machete, or any other modern tool. Buck observed from his hammock with a knowing smile, little by little casting doubt on the futility of the endeavour without saying a single word. Hours later, the coconut was peeled, thanks to the use of a sharp conch shell. "Faster than most," he said with a dry smile.

Ms. Alva, the cook, was equally fascinated and filled with curiosity about us. "It's nice to see that researchers could work together as a family," she said. She asked us what kind of researchers we were. Social, we said.

"Social? What is that? Oh, you're not actual scientists?"

"Well, sort of, but no."

"Ah, that explains why you are so friendly."

She asked if we'd like to film her in the kitchen while she made Johnny Cakes and told us about Garifuna culture. Ms. Alva, like Buck, drew her coolness from the fact that she was in no hurry. She spoke at a pace of her choosing. She moved in the same fashion. And she cooked what she pleased, when she pleased (though quite punctually, it should be said). Like Buck, with every passing day, Ms. Alva grew fonder and fonder of Autumn, whose never-ending appreciation of the food she cooked and the perfectly ripe bananas she laid out punctually on the snack table seemed to make her day.

Ms. Alva giving us a Johnny Cake tutorial

Between Buck, Ms. Alva, and the reclusive but friendly coast guard, we were quickly elevated to the status of preferred guests of the year. Requests and offers were cast our way with unending regularity. Would we have any interest in jumping aboard the coast guard vessel to film the enforcement of fishing regulations? Yes? Maybe an interview with the coast guard first?

Coast guard Chicas, who went by his last name, told us he had been working two-week shifts at Glover's Reef for the last four years. As cool as the other side of the pillow and in his thirties, the biologist was the acting manager on site. And as it turned out, there was quite a bit to manage: enforcement, research and monitoring, and revenue collection.

"On a typical day you go out on patrol," he explained, "and you inspect to make sure that the fishermen that are around the area are abiding by the rules – the fisheries regulations. You make sure that what-ever product they have is in season and the sizes are within limits." The atoll, he explained, was divided into different zones. The general zone was where all the fishing activity occurred. In the conservation zone, only nonextractive activities such as snorkelling, diving, and catch-and-release were allowed. Then there was a seasonal closure area designated as a spawning migration bank for the Nassau grouper.

"So do fishers free line or spearfish around here?"

"Well, it depends. We have different communities that fish in this area. We have people that come from the north. Typically, we will find six to twelve individuals in a sailboat. The sailboat will be like the moth-ership. Then they'll have their canoes. These are the guys that mainly free dive for conchs and lobster, and they also spearfish. Then we have the other community, from Hopkins and Dangriga. They will be more focused on finfish, which will be handlining. They will be here just for the opening of the seasons, for the conchs and lobsters." Neither gillnets nor traps were allowed in the area, Chicas clarified.

"Anyways, would you like to join us on a patrol so you can see for yourself?"

Given the small size of the vessel, only one of us could join them on their patrol, Chicas said apologetically. Because he held the biggest cam-era, Phillip was the chosen one.

"Can I film the fishermen?"

"Sure, that will be no problem, but they mainly speak Spanish, so we'll check with them first on your behalf, and if they're okay, you can shoot and ask them whatever you want. We will leave tomorrow early."

The morning patrol began after our Johnny Cakes breakfast, with Chicas behind the binoculars and Harris behind the wheel of the skiff. With their hyper-cool sunglasses and thinly disguised firepower, Chicas and Harris looked like the most bad-ass characters of the most unlikely COPS episode ever.

After a twenty-minute cruise on shallow waters so clear you could pick and choose the fish you wanted to aim at, Chicas and Harris spot-ted a lone, empty canoe. A nearby buoy indicated someone was free diving nearby. Minutes later, an elderly man, someone who looked too old to still be doing this job and too tanned to still be out in the sun, emerged. Chicas and Harris chatted him up in Creole. He agreed to be filmed. He genuinely seemed to not care or even be surprised a cameraman was with them. "All in order," they said after a couple of minutes of friendly banter.

Freediving, Chicas explained, is fishing with a snorkelling mask and fins, just like Mr. Villa did it back in his day. "These guys will just go as deep as their lungs can take them. They can pick up whatever they can pick or strike. We do not allow spearfishing with tanks."

The boat resumed cruising at medium speed. Five minutes later, another vessel appeared, this one a sailboat full of fishers. Some dangled off the mast; others wrapped around this or that piece of the boat. They looked like birds – at one with the boat and sea. Something about their attitude was fishy, though. Chicas and Harris demanded to see their papers. They exchanged a few words. They spoke heavily accented Spanish. One of them seemed to be complaining about the camera. "They're saying that cameramen are becoming more common than fish around here," Chicas translated with a grin.

Conservation-zoning policies for fishing were implemented around Glover's Reef in the early 1990s. As was the case at Laughing Bird Caye, the heart of the atoll functioned like a sanctuary, a birthing place where fish could reproduce undisturbed and eventually venture outside. Nevertheless, overfishing had been listed as a concern by the World Heritage program, and the Fisheries Department had been charged with solving the problem.

"A lot of people want to come to fish at Glover's Reef because they know that production is high," Chicas said, "but it's really challenging to keep the numbers as low as possible. We have some studies and research. It's been shown that we can sustain 140 fishermen fishing in the area. Last year, the individuals that had licences were 135 or something around there. So, if you say 135 to 140 can be the max, it's pretty close, right? So it's pretty challenging, because people just keep submitting applications. They want to go into Glovers Reef."

Illegal fishing did occur, though, and Chicas and Harris were tasked with making sure everyone fishing had the right papers.

"So, do you see a lot of illegal fishing?"

"We mainly have problems with night fishing, but it's very difficult to navigate during the night."

"Do you patrol at night?"

"Only when we see night lights. So we'll go and verify what's happening. Last month, we caught two individuals that were night fishing. And two months before, we did another bust with two water skiffs from Hopkins."

As the morning sun rose higher in the sky, Chicas and Harris patrolled more of the zone, stopping to check about ten vessels and crew in all. No shots were fired, no tempers flared. The more fish the men caught, the happier they were to show them off to the camera and answer a few questions. They all complained that fish catches used to be more abundant, prices better.

Our days at Mid Island were an idyll, just as one would hope on such an atoll. But in fewer than seven days, we managed to interview two-thirds of the resident population of our atoll and the one immediately north of us. Most of our time was spent filming iguanas, hermit crabs, and marine birds. "You can never have enough b-roll," filmmakers say, and by the fourth day on the island, we had not only seen every corner of the place but also filmed it and photographed it.

The island was encircled by a trail, which began and ended by our compound. Farther away, two buildings served as residences for staff tasked with longer stays. We discovered thick sand dotted with fallen coconuts between the buildings. It all felt a bit like a toy village, something that could have come out of a LEGO box. Any time a tinge of boredom surfaced, or perhaps a fleeting feeling of cabin fever, or simply overheating from the Caribbean sun, Captain Buck would show up. "Ready to go if you are," he'd say, fins and snorkelling mask in hand. It was time to put on the GoPro and capture underwater b-roll.

One afternoon, Ms. Alva volunteered to show us how to make Johnny Cakes. We turned the camera on for an impromptu cooking show that soon turned into a conversation on wildness. "The reef is a protector," she told us, it keeps people safe from storms, and it keeps everyone fed.

"It's important to us," she observed as her hands kneaded dough. "It protects all of us. All of Belize."

"What does 'wild' mean to you, Ms. Alva?"

"To me, it's the animals that are out there which need protection."

The fact that people associate wildness with wildlife in need of protection wasn't original, but the way she phrased the rest of her sentence was thought-provoking.

"You are not supposed to destroy the fish, the conch, the turtle, nothing," she continued. "You are to be their protector. That's why we're out here. The reef protects us. So we must protect it."

By envisaging wildness as reciprocal protection between the human and animal worlds, Ms. Alva was telling us that wildness is, above all, a relation, a bond.

"We are here to protect them, not to destroy them," she added. "Because if we destroy them in the future, nothing will be here. It will all be gone."

Wild places aren't always wilderness zones. You don't need to backpack days into a jungle, away from traces of civilization, to find wildness. You don't necessarily need to dispossess yourself of access to a kitchen, a dock, or a mattress to feel that you've arrived in a wild place. Wildness can be associated with a feeling of adventure but also with something that isn't scary or dangerous, something as tranquil as life underwater and as placid as the rhythms of life above the surface, something as comforting as reciprocal protection.

In June 2018, UNESCO removed the Belize Barrier Reef from its list of endangered World Heritage Sites. The removal followed the Belizean government's announcement of an indefinite moratorium on oil exploration. The good news was welcomed by all the people and organizations we spoke with in Belize. Oceana, the WWF, and the Audubon Society, together with many other groups and individuals, had managed to convince their national government that the barrier reef was too important to be sacrificed to oil extraction. The reef was and is essential to the nation and Belizean national identity.

A nation is nothing but an imagined community, political scientist Benedict Anderson famously argued in 1983. It is imagined, he wrote, "because the members of even the smallest nation will never know most of their fellow-members, meet them, or even hear of them, yet in the minds of each lives the image of their communion." National imagination, therefore, coalesces around mythical images, foundational stories, visions of the collective generated by mass media and national institutions and accepted by all those who imagine themselves as part of that group.

Wild nature, wilderness areas, and largely undeveloped land and water are essential components of those foundational images of the nation. It is precisely because these places have never been subjected to extensive development that they are often associated with a timeless essence of the nation, an incipient nature that forms the very basis of the commons. Very few citizens of Belize are affluent enough to travel to the Blue Hole or many other areas of the barrier reef. Yet the place resides in their imagination as an essential element of their national identity, economy, and shared land and water. But this phenomenon doesn't just happen in Belize.

In Canada – to name our country, among the many examples we could come up with – the North is essential to the collective imagination of the country as a unified whole. The North, loosely defined as the land and water above the sixtieth parallel, is also a place few Canadians have experienced or travelled to, outside of territorial capitals or work camps. But it is precisely that lack of direct experience that fuels the imagination of the Great White North. It is the lack of knowledge, of familiarity, of roots and immediate relations that fuels the mythical power of the North and countless other places we – Canadians or otherwise – imagine as wilderness spaces.

Halfway through our research, it became obvious to us that the wild was often associated not only with the imagination of the nation but also with the imagination of nature. This is why the wild, for many people, is often distant, remote – a place and a nature as far away from their home as possible, a place they've never been to, a wildlife they've never encountered, and likely will never experience first-hand. And so, when a place like that becomes threatened – whether it's the Belize Barrier Reef, the Arctic National Wildlife Refuge, or the Amazon jungle – what is threatened is not simply an environment but a core image in our imagination of the nation or humanity as a whole.

Imagination can be energetic and mobilizing and, ultimately, a powerful motivator for environmental defence. It has been an extremely beneficial force in Belize. But imagination can also be dangerous, as it can quickly slide into ignorance. Countless places around the world have been imagined as empty wilderness or *terra nullius* – despite rightful Indigenous inhabitation – and colonized not only in the name of wild but also in the name of the nation and its imperial expansion.

6

Wild Can Be a Foreign Concept

JAPAN

THE *OGASAWARA MARU* LEFT PUNCTUALLY from Tokyo's Takeshiba Port at 11 a.m. on the dot, just as you would expect from any Japanese means of conveyance. Modern, functional, neither luxurious nor gritty, the ferry boat made that journey about once a week, sailing the one thousand kilometres separating Tokyo and Chichijima, the largest island in the Ogasawara Archipelago.

Living on a small island and having conducted research on ferry transportation in small island communities, we are no strangers to boats and the mundane rituals that take place onboard them during the routine of commuting. As usual, we'd stocked up on things to read, snacks, motion-sickness pills, and extra blankets, and we'd passed without hesitation on the option to book a private cabin – an unnecessary extravagance.

Yet there was something about the *Ogasawara Maru* that felt undeniably different from our typical ferry experiences. For starters, there were no trucks or cars onboard. That meant that all the goods the islands needed had to be loaded in neatly stacked containers. Second, the sleeping quarters (save the few private cabins) were more democratic than any ferry we might have boarded in Canada. Large open-space rooms had floors covered in tatami mats loosely marked into individual sleeping compartments with basic arrangements of spartan furnishings bolted to the walls. It looked like an elementary school classroom had been partially converted into a martial arts training hall, which had in turn been converted into common sleeping quarters.

Moreover, the ship was grand. Not luxurious, by any means, or even particularly elegant, but simply a bit too large to be docked into an island the size of a small town. Its size was simply incongruous, a bit like driving into a Costco parking lot in a Boeing 747. And yet, just hours into the journey, life on the *Ogasawara Maru* started feeling resoundingly familiar, even downright modest and pretense-free, we thought, as we sat down in the canteen for a bowl of ramen.

Though he had only been to the Ogasawara once before, Yosuke Washiya, our trusted gatekeeper, translator, and mediator, seemed at home too. We'd met up with him the night before at Narita Airport. His train from Kyoto had arrived just a few hours before. In his early thirties, Yosuke was in the final stages of completing his PhD at the University of Toronto. As he awaited his doctoral defence, he'd found a position at a private university in Kyoto.

Autumn – who had a deep fascination with Japanese popular culture – had been patiently waiting to meet Yosuke so she could submit a battery of questions about anime, high school culture, food, and growing up in Japan. She wasted no time subjecting him to an interrogation. He seemed amused, even a full hour into it.

We needed Yosuke's help with more practical things. Given our limited understanding of the Japanese language and social relations (an understatement), we'd had asked him to help us plan our fieldwork in the Ogasawara well in advance of our arrival. He took it upon himself to do a reconnaissance trip to set things up. Only a few of our conversations with the islanders could be in English, so Yosuke agreed to be with us for our entire journey. As we ate our lunch on tables firmly bolted to the floor (fortunately, with the ship still sailing smoothly), we went over our planning notes.

The Ogasawara Islands were inscribed on the World Heritage List because they have an abundance of unique endemic species. Thanks to evolution processes unfolding largely in isolation from the rest of the world, and because of the absence of human residents well into the 1800s, the thirty islands had become the habitat for unique species and rightfully earned the nickname the "Galápagos of the Orient." Unlike the Galápagos, however, the Ogasawara are virtually unknown to the world.

To find them on a map, draw a line straight south of the main island of Japan or straight east from Guam. Look a bit right of Taiwan and the Philippines. Then zoom in on the water. And zoom in some more.

"Even most Japanese would have a hard time placing the islands on a map," Yosuke told us over a cup of green tea.

Although our cafeteria table was still unfazed by the growing swells, we thought it time to ingest double our recommended dose of motion-sickness medication. The medicine worked as planned. We woke up groggy the following morning, with six hours left in the journey. The sea was calm enough to allow us to walk on the deck to get a sense of how much the world around us had changed. We had left Tokyo on a cold winter day when the temperature was barely above freezing level; in as little as eighteen hours, the *Ogasawara Maru* had transported us to a subtropical place with temperatures in the low twenties and warm humid winds. Even the colours seemed to have changed dramatically. The closer we got to the Bonin Islands (the Ogasawara have long been known in the West by that name), the deeper the blue of the Pacific Ocean became. The water looked like a dark iris, known as "Bonin blue," the more so as the sun burned through the morning clouds.

With an hour left in the journey, islands appeared on the horizon. The first apparitions were nameless: massive rectangular slabs of rock erupting from the water like gargantuan container ships. Then, as the *Ogasawara Maru* began to slow, the island of Chichijima appeared in the distance, angular in shape, much like a stone fortress. Though only twenty-eight square kilometres – exactly half the size of our home island in British Columbia – the island seemed much bigger from the water. As we approached, more of her vertiginous walls took form before our eyes. From a distance, this looked like no tropical paradise. Chichijima – the largest island of the archipelago – felt forbidding, awe-inspiring, and dramatic in her presence, unperturbed by the white waves violently crashing against her craggy shores.

If you know a word or two of Japanese, you'll likely find the name "Chichijima" interesting. "Chichijima" literally means "Father Island." It and Hahajima (Mother Island) are the only inhabited islands in the archipelago. There are other islands, too, all uninhabited: Mukojima

(Bridegroom Island), Yomejima (Bride Island), Anijima (Elder Brother Island), Magojima (Grandchild Island), Otōtojima (Younger Brother Island), Anejima (Elder Sister Island), Imōtojima (Younger Sister Island), Meijima (Niece Island), and most uniquely, Nakōdojima or Nakadachijima (Matchmaker Island). Among the remaining islands of the archipelago – less imaginatively known as East Island, West Island, and so on – we spotted our absolute favourite on the map: Mukōjima (Island over There). We told Autumn all this with a great degree of excitement. She barely opened her eyes. "Are we there yet?"

We docked on Chichijima on time, wedging starboard side against a terminal unduly abuzz with life, busyness, and excitement. Live music welcomed us on the pier. We stood with our luggage at the edges of the terminal and watched the hubbub for a few minutes, marvelling at the bedlam – containers finding their way onshore, islanders reacquainting themselves with their families, and tourists seeking escort to their shuttle vans. We were the only visitors from outside of Asia.

A few days later, we met a young man whose heritage wasn't so uniformly Japanese. Ludy – short for Ludovico – had moved to Chichijima from Tokyo five years before. The son of an Italian man from Tuscany and a Japanese woman, Ludy had studied at an International school for his entire youth, and his English, spoken with a placeless American accent, was flawless. We sat down for a cup of coffee made from beans grown onsite.

"You wake up on the boat, you look outside, and right in the middle of the ocean suddenly there is a rocky island standing there," Ludy told us as he sipped his Americano. "It just pops out. It feels wild."

Besides teaching English and working as the island's unofficial translator, Ludy ran Ogasawara's newest arts and culture magazine. He knew the islands intimately. "This island is rougher. It's pretty different from the typical vacation destination type of island." He spoke with the insightfulness of someone familiar with a place yet still objective about it. "The population is low, the settlements are all confined to one small corner of the island, and the place is mostly comprised of undeveloped forest, cliffs, and secluded bays. It feels pretty wild."

Even though the archipelago is one thousand kilometres away from Tokyo, a world away from the metropolis, it is still part of Tokyo's municipality. Besides the limited development and rough feel, a clear aura of mystery surrounds Chichijima. That aura works like a magnet for many people, including Ludy. He first heard about the place through a manga called *Tennis,* he told us. But *Tennis* wasn't the only popular culture product to depict the Ogasawara as a remote and mysterious creature bordering on fantasy. In Pokémon, the Ogasawara are known as the Orange Islands, a place where rare Pokémon, capable of unique evolutions, exist aplenty. Godzilla itself is said to have been born in the Ogasawara Islands.

"This island is very mysterious," Ludy said and smiled. "Some people know it exists, but people do not know much about it." Most Japanese have only heard of the Ogasawara through weather forecasts when the islands make the news because of hurricanes. The place promised enough adventure for Ludy and his wife: "I just said to my wife, 'Why don't we go?' And soon after, we came."

Unlike other remote islands around the world that suffer from the twofold threat of depopulation and population ageing, Chichijima's vibe is young and chill, but in a pretenseless and relaxed way, Ludy observed. "People are more laid-back and very open. People are very welcoming of those from the outside, and they are not too nosy about other people." Eighty percent of the island's population came from the main island of Japan, so it made no sense to treat newcomers as outsiders.

"Who comes to these islands to visit, and how long do they stay?" we asked.

"Mostly Japanese people. They stay a week, or however long it is from one boat arrival to the next departure. Daily life on the island has very distinct rhythms. Most weekdays are busy, and weekends are relaxing. When the ship is in port, it is always busy. But it's quite different every week, depending on the ship's precise schedule."

The schedule varied depending on the time of the year, but the *Ogasawara Maru* typically departed roughly once a week, which meant it was in port for about five days then out to sea for three days (one day northbound, about a day in Tokyo, and one day southbound). During those three days it was out to sea, Ludy clarified, the two thousand full-time Chichijima residents largely kept their island to themselves. They relaxed and enjoyed their temporary freedom from the obligations of the tourist industry.

Ludy, we would later find out, wasn't exaggerating. When the ship left port a few days later without us, many shops and restaurants closed, and hotels stopped serving dinner. Not catching that boat after a one-week stay felt a bit like going over to a friend's house for dinner and then hanging out for three days.

Following Yosuke's recommendation, we settled at Papa's Island Resort and Diving Studio at the far northern edge of town, steps away from Ohmura Beach. The word "resort" was misplaced. The place was a modest, clean, functional minihotel with the vibe of an upgraded youth hostel. Its dining room served tasty meals on days the ship was in port. The friendly staff was unaccustomed to Euro-American tourists and went out of their way to make us feel welcome and comfortable. We returned the gesture by learning enough new words each day to compliment the chef, whose vision of what foods were acceptable for breakfast expanded our minds and stomachs unmeasurably.

Many visitors to the Ogasawara dive or surf. Others seek wildlife encounters, especially with whales. Chichijima, as a result, had a handful of outfitters who specialized in cetacean action. Though whales are a rather ordinary sighting on our island back home, we gladly accepted the invitation of Takezawa-san, Kitake Nature Academy's head guide, to go for a whale-watching ride. After a punishing forty-minute journey southwest of Hutami Port (whales may or may not have been spotted between the three-metre swells), the skiff's course was set for the calmer waters of Minamishima, one of the uninhabited islands of the Ogasawara Archipelago.

The rocky landscape, the sparse vegetation, the endemic wildlife, the imposing bays, the tidy queues of small groups of camera-wielding tourists, the tight regulations over how many people could be on land at any point in time. Minamishima could have been plucked from the Galápagos and flung across the Pacific Ocean. It felt a lot like déjà vu.

In his late forties, Takezawa-san had a good business enterprise on Chichijima – a youth-oriented burger joint, a lodge, and a thriving ecofriendly diving and outfitting operation. Minamishima's environment, he told us as we started walking around the small island, was strictly regulated to make sure the rare snails that inhabited the island thrived.

"The special thing on this island is the unique landscape. The coral reef appeared due to declining sea levels, and the famous cave was collapsed by the rain. Eventually, these natural circumstances created the unique landscape," Takezawa-san explained and Yosuke translated. The famous cave stood in the distance. A rock arch created a blue lagoon sheltered from the outer shore. The seas had taken on a stunning turquoise colour.

The land snails, known as *Mai-mai*, went by the genus name *Mandarina*, and while cute in the unique way snails can be, they were unassuming and uninteresting. Then again, our reaction arguably said more about our standards for charismatic species than about the colourfulness of their character. Regardless, the Ogasawara Islands had been inscribed on the UNESCO World Heritage List not only because of the friendly mollusks but also because of 195 endangered bird species, the rare Bonin flying fox (not actually a fox), and 441 native plant taxa endemic to the islands. Like the Galápagos, the Ogasawara Archipelago was a living, breathing, festival of endemism.

Endemism, in biology, is the state of a species being native to a single defined geographic location. But endemism is also an ideology of sorts, a value system that revolves around the importance of indigeneity and its implicit wildness. Endemism is important in biology, but it often slides into fetishism. At its best, endemism valorizes the local and the unique. At its worst, it slips into a xenophobic species-ism that can become downright paranoid: what's local and native is good, what's foreign is evil. This notion was reinforced, but also challenged, throughout our stay in the archipelago.

On Minamishima, only one hundred people per day, three days a week, were allowed to dock, with a maximum of fifteen at a time, Takezawa-san told us. All groups had to be accompanied by a certified guide, and no one could stay longer than two hours. "People cannot come here from November to January, except for New Year's holiday.

New year's holiday is very popular for tourists, so we decided to open only this special week for tourists." We were fortunate, as New Year's Day was only one day away.

These regulations had been in place for thirteen years. Two official-looking monitors, each armed with a clipboard and a stopwatch, sat on camping chairs perched above a small cliff to keep count of who came and went. We pointed our telephoto lens at them from fifty metres away and, as if on cue, the two smiled and waved giddily at the camera. We wanted to ask them why they had a stopwatch, but it didn't seem like a polite thing to do.

"Many tourists arrived after the UNESCO inscription," Takezawa-san said. "They would line up from early morning to make sure they could get access. They knew the limitation was one hundred people in a day, so over one hundred people came and tried to get onto the islands." Since then, a better schedule and more efficient regulations had been put in place. The World Heritage inscription had, in fact, been a welcome event. "After the UNESCO inscription, the Japanese government decided to take responsibility for the protection of this island," he told us. And because tourists could only come to Minamishima via small boats, it was easy to manage access and ensure protection.

"This is the wildest place in the Ogasawara Islands," Takezawa-san noted, "and one of the wildest natural places in Japan. We need to protect the island from invasive species. No place has true pristine nature in the world because even deep in the forests in Africa, the air from the outside is contaminated. But 'pristine' and 'wild' are different. Here, nature takes care of itself. This island is a pure natural island."

The ideology of endemism was clearly at work in Takezawa-san's argument. But, here, nature did not truly take care of itself so simply. Humans were very much in control of invasive species and limiting who could live there, who could stay, and who could visit, when, how long, and why. Humans, who are not endemic to the Ogasawara, and are, in fact, recent newcomers, were instrumental in making and keeping the place feel as wild as possible. Endemism, paradoxically, survives thanks to the protection afforded by the most dangerous invasive species around.

The contradiction in Takezawa-san's argument was obvious, but wildness in Japan wasn't a paradox in the same way it might have been in the West. Whereas people elsewhere seemed certain about the meaning of wildness, at least in abstract terms, in Japan the word "wild" caused confusion. Throughout our time on the islands, our usual questions about the meaning of "wildness," "wild," and "wilderness" were met with bedazzled stares, apologies for lack of understanding, and laborious sidebar conversations with Yosuke, who painstakingly tried to translate these mysterious words from English into Japanese.

April (behind the camera) and Yosuke (right) conducting an interview with Mayu Inada and Shuzo Kishi

The problem wasn't so much literal translation. Yosuke had fully prepared himself for the challenges of translating our questions, and he had even worked with us to adapt our questions for interviewees who spoke no English. The problem was the lack of a shared agreement over the "true" meaning of the word "wild."

The core idea behind our project, the idea of wild, had been conceived by us in English, and it carried connotations and consequences along with it. To translate a word for the sake of a conversation, as Yosuke did so patiently every time, allowed us to carry out a dialogue. But translation, no matter how accurate, could never carry the whole "baggage" the English concept of wild carries with it.

"Wild," in fact, has no easy translation into Japanese. The closest words refer to being natural and pristine. Translations such as *yasei* or *mikon* lack the same cultural baggage as "wild." Yet, rather than an obstacle, this felt like an opportunity to understand something new and present the limitations of concepts – such as wilderness – that environmental politics and ecology often export unreflexively across the globe. We reflected on these challenges with Takezawa-san, but our conversation came to end when our group had to pull up the anchor.

With the island of Minamishima behind us, our small boat cruised past Enen Bay, heading straight for Tatsumizaki, the southeasternmost point of Chichijima. The midday sun shone above us and the water turned into the deepest Bonin blue we had seen yet. The captain stopped the engine, and a moment of unscheduled confusion followed, filled with fast-paced, excited utterances in Japanese. Goggles, snorkels, and fins were handed out. We English speakers remained in the dark about what was going on.

"The captain just spotted dolphins underneath us," Yosuke said as soon as he could get a word in. "Do you want to swim with them?"

Swimming with dolphins is an activity frequently included in people's bucket lists. Entire dream vacations are built around it. Successful therapy programs are built around it. But look a little deeper, and you will find a catch. "Swimming with dolphins," if you read the fine notes, typically consists of getting a few minutes of pool time with captive dolphins trained to act cute and cuddly. Swimming with those lovely critters also means swimming with a trained guide. It's a bit like a wet petting zoo, if you think about it.

But swimming with wild dolphins in rough, open waters? Sure, they looked cute and cuddly, but these guys had a tough edge to them. One also needed to be a decent swimmer, we were warned. The water was choppy, the boat captain told us, and the dolphins "untrained" – as if this needed to be spelled out. We had to move quickly in and out of the boat to be respectful of their space.

"So do you want to go in?" Yosuke asked.

"I'll go," Phillip said.

He later wrote in his field journal:

December 30, 2017

I counted six dolphins, all of them bottlenose. Five adults and a baby. We dove into the water three times. The first time we were in the water for less than a minute before our guide called us back. I did not understand why. The second time, once again, we were told to dive and then recalled back on board right away. Yosuke explained that strict regulations were in place to protect the dolphins. Outfitters were only permitted three dives. For each attempt swimmers could only be in the water for a certain number of minutes. Another outfitter boat was nearby so we couldn't be in the water when they were in. If the dolphins moved toward them, we had to get out of the water in order to not waste our limited time and to limit the number of swimmers in the water at the same time.

The third attempt would be our last one. Nervous moments went by before we could jump. Then the dolphins' fins poked through the water right beside our boat. I immediately jumped in and started swimming alongside them. For several seconds I was in our group who was the one nearest to them. The dolphins glided underwater effortlessly while I strove to keep up the pace.

They seemed unconcerned about us. As I swam alongside them my mind drifted toward what their thoughts might have been. Did they care that I was here? Were they curious about me? Was I bothering them? Was I safe? Were they safe? Were they making eye contact with me or was it just my imagination? What would I write about this? Would this be a wild moment? Or just another time slot in the eco-friendly wildness adventure business? Another moment of wildness on the clock? Or was it unethical, and wild only in the worst of anthropocentric ways?

"How was it?" April and Autumn wanted to know as soon as I got back on board. It was pretty wild. But, I told them, I couldn't stop thinking about whether it was wild for them. What were they thinking about me?

As the boat ride resumed, I started thinking about summer months back home when wasps become hungry. When they do, especially during the month of August, they suddenly take notice of humans. That's when wasps suddenly become interested in us. They want to get closer. They want to smell us, to taste our food, to drink our drinks, to get our protein. Maybe they're just curious about us. Maybe they want what we have. But to us, to us humans, the wasps' interest is just a dreadful nuisance. We can never seem to get away from them. I wondered if the dolphins felt about us humans the same way we humans feel about wasps.

Chichijima is shaped like a caricature of a little dragon. Its hands and feet protrude east and west. Its long neck stretches out of its body and curves left, and its head is bent downward, as if it were staring at its feet. The top of the dragon's neck is the neighbourhood of Okumura. The dragon's mouth is "downtown" Chichijima, where all shops and most lodgings and restaurants can be found. Save for a few pockets of homes and accommodations, the rest of the dragon's body is forested.

Downtown Chichijima stretches about a kilometre between the Japanese self-defence force base and the island's only gas station on one end and the harbour on the other. Between them, you'll find businesses, a soccer pitch, tennis courts, the island's two grocery stores, a town hall, a coral beach, a small park, and the island's only traffic light.

The place felt calm, serene, and pretty without any pretense of being fashionable or enchanting. There was something rather enchanting, however – a mysterious jingle. The melody played every day at five o'clock throughout the streets. The jingle seemed to be an anthem of sorts, not the Japanese anthem, but somehow equally meaningful. The song would last for about two minutes, broadcast from invisible loudspeakers. Playing at a loud but discreet level, the anthem did not seem to require standing up or arresting oneself mid-step. But where was it coming from? What did it mean? What were we supposed to do when it played? Was it a performance of remembrance? Of pride? Of unity?

We found another interesting feature downtown – the Japanese flag. It hadn't always been there. It was only in 1543 that the islands were first visited by humankind, when Spanish explorer Bernardo de la Torre saw and named them the "Forfana Islands." But the islands remained free of human residents. The Japanese first explored them in two successive expeditions in 1670 and 1675. They were renamed "Bunin Jima" – literally "uninhabited islands." In the West, a misunderstanding of the word "Bunin" meant that the islands became known as Bonin. But still, no one lived there, and no one owned them for many years. No flag flew over the Ogasawara, so to speak.

The first temporary residents of the Bonin arrived in the early 1800s. The first ship to arrive was the HMS *Blossom*. In typical British fashion for the time, Captain F.W. Beechey quickly claimed them as a British possession. But it was a later arrival that would change the Bonin forever. In 1830, American Nathaniel Savory and twenty-nine other people from Hawaii, the continental United States, and Europe founded a permanent settlement on the islands.

Savory brought along a Bible. When Commodore Matthew Perry visited the island in 1853, he noticed that Savory owned the sacred book and thought that such possession made him more qualified to oversee the island than anyone else. Perry appointed him governor. The islands became an American possession.

The archipelago changed hands again in 1862, when they were claimed by Japan. In 1867, they were named Ogasawara in memory of Ogasawara Sadato, a *ronin* (lordless samurai) who had claimed, in 1727, that the islands had been discovered in 1593 by his ancestor Ogasawara Sadayori. Little did it matter that the claim was proven to be false in 1735. The name Ogasawara stuck, and all islanders – Japanese- or non-Japanese born – were granted Japanese citizenship in 1882.

In the early 1940s, the Battle for the Pacific began. Chichijima quickly became a key target because of its strategic significance. Allied forces and the Japanese military fought for years throughout the island, indiscriminately dropping bombs (from American planes) and even committing acts of cannibalism (by the Japanese army major Sueo Matoba).

When the Second World War ended in 1945, Americans retook possession of the "Bonin Islands." They evicted all residents of Japanese ethnicity and established a Navy base on Chichijima. They also allowed the return of the non-Japanese prewar inhabitants, who had been expelled by the Japanese army.

To hear the story from someone who lived it first-hand, Yosuke set up an appointment for us in Okumura with a lady by the name of Kyoko Kimura, who lived not too far from the island's only traffic light.

Kyoko greeted us with the warmest smile, as if she had known us for years. We returned the greeting with fanfare. By now, we were starting to become well-versed in the ritual of introductions and small gift exchanges demanded by Japanese propriety. Following Yosuke's greeting, we worked up enough linguistic confidence to formally "beg" Kyoko's "forgiveness" for gifting her with "such trivial tokens of appreciation." Yosuke smiled at our formality and old-fashioned language expressions, undoubtedly excessive on laid-back Chichijima. Kyoko seemed amused, too, but partly impressed – we hoped.

The excessive politeness seemed apropos because Kyoko was ninety-six years old. Her life story was fascinating. She was born on Chichijima as Edith Washington, a direct descendant of one of the early American settlers. She grew up on the island, but as chance had it, she happened to be in Osaka in 1941 when the war broke out.

"I was nineteen years old," Kyoko said, "and that's when I received a letter that ordered me to change my name. My brother was on the main island of Japan to get his driver's licence, and he had to do the same. He changed his last name as 'Kimura.' Eventually, I changed it to the same as my brother – 'Kimura.'"

"Kyoko" was an adopted name too. Edith Washington was way too Western, according to the Japanese imperial ideology that reigned during the war years. When the war ended and the Americans retained control of the Ogasawara, Kyoko decided to keep her new name. Still living on the main island of Japan, she applied to the American occupying forces for permission to return to her native island. Since the Washingtons were her ancestors, the Americans permitted her to return.

Kyoko Kimura, born Edith Washington, was ninety-six when we spoke to her and had been born on Chichijima

Tortoise weighing approximately four hundred kilograms, Galápagos

The boardwalk near Cradle Mountain, Tasmania

View of the Seiser Alm (*below*) from the Schlern Mountain, with the Puez-Odle group in the centre and the Langkofel group on the right, South Tyrol

Cable cars leading to the Langkofel, South Tyrol

Mr. Villa, Belize

Chicas checking in with a group of fishermen, Belize

The view from the cliff above Heart Rock, Japan

Harada-san showing a picture of Heart Rock, Japan

Viedma Lake and the steppe, as seen en route to El Chalten, Patagonia

Iceberg on Lago Argentino, Patagonia

People posing for Instagram on Reynisfjara, Iceland

View from Reynisfjara, Iceland

Soldiers on the lookout for wayward elephants, Thailand

Elephants at Kuiburi National Park, Thailand

View of Trout River, Gros Morne National Park, Canada

Phillip capturing a view of the Rocky Mountains outside Banff, Canada

Speaking with us in her living room, she directed our attention to a couple of photo albums laying on the dining table. "This photo was taken in September 1946," she told us through Yosuke. "When I came back to the island in October, I wanted to get this photo, so I asked a fisherman to bring it to me. When I came, only 135 people were back on the island." The war had just ended, and Kyoko and a few other descendants of European and American ancestors had been allowed by the US Navy back in. Kyoko's status was unique, we were about to learn. "Over 20 years after WWII ended, people living on this island still could not contact their relatives on the main island since this area belonged to the U.S. at the time."

"Why couldn't people make contact with the main island?"

"It was quite difficult to make contact with them because we didn't have any tools to connect with the main island. However, some women came from the main island and got married here. So, sometimes, they allowed them to go back to see their family. If there was any reason to go to the main island of Japan, they would let us go. But if somebody had an emergency or got sick, we went to Guam via airplane instead of Japan. So we could not communicate with the mainland."

Because she had lost many of her friends, Kyoko felt quite lonely, she told us. "There is a picture here from when the Japanese Emperor visited this island," Kyoko skipped ahead in the chronology of the events, "and I spoke with him many times. Did you see a tennis court when you drove here? It's next to the gateball court. While we played gateball, he came to see us and individually talked with us. I talked a lot, especially about my ancestors."

"She spoke to the emperor?" April asked Yosuke.

"Yes," Yosuke confirmed, striving to hide his surprise.

Kyoko flicked more pages. "And here's me and Shinzo Abe," she muttered.

"Shinzo Abe? The current prime min—"

"Yes," Yosuke confirmed. "Oh, here's me and Mr. Bush Senior."

Yosuke smiled and nodded before we could even say anything. George Bush's plane had crashed in the Ogasawara when he was a war pilot. While president, he made a point of visiting Chichijima as part of a tour of Japan. We were beginning to feel like we were in *Forrest Gump*.

"Were you happy when you came back here?" April asked.

"Of course, I was so happy because it's my hometown, but I felt lonely over time because I did not have many friends here. However, one of my classmates came here, so I was okay."

She pointed to an old photo. "This was my house, but I could not enter these areas because the US Navy told me that there was an unexploded bomb. Therefore, for a long time after coming back to the island, I wasn't sure my house was still intact. One day, my friend found my place. We talked to a commander about my house, and he allowed me to come back to my place."

We were starting to wonder why a movie about her hadn't been made yet.

"This picture here is me in a factory in Nerima, where I was forced to work during wartime. We made cartridges. This other picture was taken when I was performing with my cousin in a university auditorium."

Yosuke explained that Kyoko was a very famous singer. Kyoko told us she still loved to sing. She began singing the first few notes of one of her songs. Then she resumed her story. "This photo is from a party here. The US Navy served a lot of food during the US Independence Day. We celebrated together with all the Navy's children."

Kyoko did not speak English, but many people in her family did. "My sons went to a school that followed the US education system, so they spoke English at school. After graduating, one of my sons applied to the US military and became a soldier. He is the only US citizen in our family."

About seven thousand residents were forced to leave the Ogasawara Islands during wartime. Kyoko was one of the first to return. Twenty-two years later, in 1968, she was still struggling to keep in touch with relatives and friends stranded on the main island when her life changed once again. The Ogasawara saw the departure of the Americans and the islands' return to Japan.

"When I heard the news about the return of this island to Japan, I was so surprised. At first, people here did not believe that. After one week, we realized that it was true. I was so happy at that time. Immediately,

I sent a message to my friends who lived in Tokyo, but it wasn't easy because I was too emotional. I wrote and sent them a song, 'Henkann-uta,' a returning song. When my friends received my letter, they were touched and cried. I was supposed to send my voice to my friends, but I could not find the words, so I sang my message to them."

Today, people in Ogasawara still celebrate their Independence Day, their independence from America, that is. But many still carry English first names and last names, at times only thinly Japanized (the descendants of Nathaniel Savory, for example, go by "Sebori"), and many still speak fluent English with a distinct American accent.

Like many other old-time residents of the archipelago, Kyoko had lived multiple lives, it seemed. Her shifting identities paralleled the changing identities of the islands. Like nowhere else in the world we had ever been, the islands and many of their residents had undergone profound cycles of regeneration that affected the state of nature, the language spoken, their political status, and their minds, hearts, and very being.

But there was something else about her story and the island's human story. Endemism teaches us that the native is good and the foreign is bad. But who exactly was native or foreign here, as far as humans are concerned? Were they all foreign? Or had their presence by now been naturalized? And, if so, who was native to the islands? The Japanese, who allegedly spotted the islands first? The Spaniards or the Brits, who made the first expeditions? The Americans, who were first in charge? The Japanese, who took over? The answers were unclear, and it would be futile to try to find out. The reality was that an invasive species, humans, had made their home there, and whether they belonged would ultimately be judged by their actions.

Of all Chichijima's mighty cliffs, none was more famous than Heart Rock. Towering about two hundred metres above the water, the giant rocky cliff had a distinctive rounded triangular shape and a pronounced reddish tint that set it apart from the grey perpendicular walls flanking it on both sides. The heart-shaped stain was believed to have been caused by laterite soil getting washed away by rains. Chihiroiwa – as it is known in Japanese – could only be seen from the water, but the overland hike to the top of the cliff was reputed to be one of the wildest ways to experience the Ogasawara. Yosuke had arranged for a guided trek by working hard to convince our would-be guide, Harada-san, of our best intentions as researchers.

Unguided explorations within the forests of Chichijima were illegal, and anyone who wished to enter needed a guide. Harada-san was a diminutive but energetic former fisherman full of drive and opinions. Yosuke had met him by accident on the *Ogasawara Maru* and struggled mightily to convince him to meet with us. Researchers, especially natural scientists, had gotten a bad reputation in the Ogasawara for treating the islands like a data bank. But when Yosuke explained to Harada-san that we intended to listen to residents and learn about their place through their perspectives, he quickly changed his mind.

The hike to the cliff began with a steep trail that coasted along a feeble creek. The thick vegetation surrounding the narrow path provided shade from the throbbing late-morning sun. Harada-san had been involved for years in the citizen group responsible for maintaining and upgrading the trail. He was proud of how the group had managed to get their work done despite limited governmental support and even prouder that local materials had been employed to keep the trail's appearance natural and unobtrusive.

Invasive species were a key concern for Harada-san and the rest of the Ogasawara. If endemism were a religion, invasive species would be the devil. But Harada-san was about to teach us something much more profound. The lesson was complex, and we would learn it in due course throughout the day.

When the first settlers arrived in the Bonin Islands, Harada-san told us as we entered a thick forest, they made a home for themselves by bringing small farm animals such as chickens, pigs, and goats from their lands. When their ships docked, other foreign animals alighted, including mice and rats. Over countless millennia, the island's native species had grown in isolation from such outsiders, and their arrival had a vicious impact on the ecosystem.

Harada-san stopped in his tracks. "Goats," he shouted. He pointed toward a sun-exposed hill face rising above the forest canopy. Three goats hung on to the rock at an impossible angle, looking down at us. We watched for a few minutes. "Many native species don't exist anymore because of these goats," Harada-san told us. "We need to consider carefully how to get rid of these goats, because if we reduce the number of goats, the invasive species which are eaten by goats will increase and expand. We are considering this issue right now." We surmised that firing precision rounds from helicopters as they had done in the Galápagos wouldn't work here.

We resumed our hike. Yosuke conversed nonstop with Harada-san. He offered spot translations and context for both Harada-san's statements and our questions. It was the first time in this project and in our entire careers that we had to rely so much on the cultural interpretation necessary to do our work, and we thought it must have been infinitely harder to carry it out uphill on a hot day. Regardless, Yosuke was still remarkably sweat-free two hours into our hike, and Harada-san seemed happier and more laid-back as time went on, so we figured Yosuke was doing the work right.

As the trail reached the top of the hill, it flattened a bit and entered an even thicker forest, darker and thickly vegetated by plants that our Western eyes had no name for. Harada-san provided the language as we walked slowly by. English translations were less abundant. The trees that provided us with cool shade were Tako-zuru. The beautiful white flowers over there were Muni-Hime Tsubaki. The pungent smells came from Ogasawara-gumi. The crying sounds were made by a scaly thrush called Toratsugumi, and the coarse textures were those of a fern called Ootaniwatari. The most amazing of all species was a relatively short palm-like tree that produced an odd pineapple-lookalike cone called screw pine in English, or *Pandanus* in Latin. Though the species is common in subtropical areas around Asia, the Ogasawara has an endemic variation called *Pandanus boninensis warb.* With tiring hands, we captured them on film.

"This curious-looking tree is called 'Maru-hachi,' from its resemblance to the kanji character for the number eight, *hachi*, and the circle surrounding it, *maru*," Harada pointed out for the benefit of the camera. "And that one over there is a Nissan."

"Sorry, what? A Nissan?"

"Yes, over there, that pile of rust sticking out through the bush. You can tell by the engine."

Nothing in the Ogasawara came without a unique story, and the pile of rust before us was no different. The path we were walking on was at times barely wide enough for our shoulders, but during the Second World War, the vegetation had been beaten back to allow off-road vehicles to climb the hills and transport supplies to reach the many bunkers dotting the landscape. Parts of wrecked vehicles could still be found alongside the trail, their skeletons an eerie symbol of the wildness of fighting men fighting with one another and against the jungle.

"You can see a big conical hole over there where a bomb fell over wartime." Harada-san directed our attention a few feet below one of the burned-out vehicles. The Japanese and US military had a huge battle on the island of Iwo-Jima, not too far from the Ogasawara. "After finishing their bombing in the Tokyo area," Harada-san said, "some bombs remained inside the planes, so they dropped them here before landing. It was too risky to land while still carrying bombs. Four thousand people were killed on this island in that way." On an island that small, the dead bodies must have been everywhere on the landscape.

After about two and a half hours, the trail reached the top of the last small hill and exited the forest. The vista through the ferns – Minamijima in the distance and open ocean farther afield – rivalled the most beautiful landscapes we had ever laid our eyes on. From the vantage point of the hill, we could see a vast expanse of trees and shrubs, which we now had at least some names for. A cool, misty breeze carried the smell of the salt water. Minutes later, we stood atop Heart Rock. People in small boats down below captured the cliffs, and us, with their cameras. We could think of no other time when we had felt so far away in the world and yet so close with our planet.

We sat down and gazed at the horizon for a few minutes. By that point in the afternoon, Harada-san had become comfortable enough with us to share his life story. When he was a student, he told us, he heard the news of the Ogasawara being returned to Japan. Curious, he went to the library and looked up the islands.

"I was living in Tokyo at the time. I wished I could live by the ocean, somewhere where I could see the sun setting all the way down to the horizon line over the ocean. So I decided to visit the Ogasawara Islands, but only for a short term. I brought only some clothes with me. It was in May. I fell in love with this island and decided to live here forever. I think that the island called me to come and live here." He had lived on the island for forty-three years. "When I was twenty-two, I did not worry about moving here, and my parents were very accepting. They wished for nothing but my happiness. I was lucky they understood me."

After downing a few bottles of Pocari Sweat, we made our way back. Inside the forest, another interesting sight caught our eyes – a small cage. It had a story, too, quite possibly the most revealing of our entire journey to Japan. These small cages, large enough for a pet, were everywhere in the bush, Harada-san explained. When the first settlers realized the mice and rats they'd brought with them were creating enormous headaches for farmers and their agricultural products, they decided to fight the rodents with another imported species: domestic cats. Over time, and especially during the ravages of the war, many cats went feral and started preying on the island's birds. Evolutionarily ill-equipped to deal with feline predators, endemic bird species were decimated as a result.

"Having no idea what cats were," Harada-san explained while mimicking a bird's confused behaviour, "they just stood there and got eaten." Over the next few years, six of the island's species went extinct because of the cats. Traps had been laid out to catch the cats, but the task wasn't easy. "Thanks to this project," Harada-san pointed out, the number of Akagashira Karasubato (the rare Japanese red-headed wood pigeon) has finally started to increase a bit."

This is, so far, a classic lesson on the value of endemism. Native species are happy living in harmony until invasive species arrive. But Harada-san had a more nuanced view. "I think that it doesn't matter if it's a native species or an invasive species, because nature is nature. No matter what, nature is beautiful. We should just consider whether something is really harmful to a native species or not. Not all invasive species have a negative effect." One of the most negative invasive species on the island was us, humans, he told us, but at the same time, humans were now needed to rewild the place.

The trap that Harada-san had spotted for us in the bushes wouldn't be empty for long, as it turned out. Days later, a black cat was trapped there. Yosuke arranged for us to learn what would happen to the poor kitty.

A short walk away from the ferry terminal and the fishing harbour, right alongside the main road, stood a small, cottage-sized building with a roof shaped like cat ears. On its windowless exterior, wooden panels showed pictures and drawings of cats accompanied by extensive kanji. Kazuo Horikoshi, a US-trained zoologist and the director of a local NGO, the Institute of Boninology, dared us to guess what the writing said.

We had no clue.

"That part right there talks about the veterinary hospitals that have volunteered to take care of the cats," he explained. "We love the nature and culture of this island. We are committed to this activity. Someday, we would like to be something like the Darwin station in the Galápagos," he told us as we made our way inside.

About half of the organization's budget, he explained, was devoted to the cat program. In collaboration with organizations such as the Ministry of Environment and the metropolitan government of Tokyo, staff members of the Institute of Boninology worked to manage the number of domestic cats in the village and to trap those that had gone feral within the conservation area. Since 2010, they had caught about six thousand cats on Chichijima and Hahajima. But it's what they did to them that raised eyebrows around the conservation world.

The building with the cat ears was a "halfway house" where the cats were treated for physical ailments, fed, and spayed. After a short period of acclimatization to the domestic world, they got a free ferry ride to Tokyo.

"You send them to Tokyo?" we asked.

Kazuo explained. "In Tokyo, the cats are adopted by families who will care for them. These cats are our world's wild things. They are not pests."

"This must cost a lot of money," we observed. Autumn played with a fuzzy captive.

"Yes, it does. UNESCO, our international colleagues, laughed at us when we presented our plan because they thought it was easier to poison or shoot them, but it is not our way. Our people on this island love cats and disagree with killing animals, so if we kill these cats, they will not cooperate with us. We understand our project requires a lot of money and labour, but we prefer working with our people. If the island people see strange cats, they let us know; we have a great relationship. We are very proud of this project."

Island people weren't the only cat lovers. Japanese people in general love cats as much as North Americans love dogs, if not more. Japanese cities even have cat cafés where patrons can visit with kitties and play with them for a little while.

Catching the cats, Kazuo observed, was difficult but not nearly as challenging as working with the many individuals, organizations, and funders involved in the program. Both sides of the project required patience and perseverance. Kittens, he explained, were easier to catch because they were not yet as smart as adult cats. Females were the hardest to trap.

"Scientists have found that kids who grow without pets are less knowledgeable about animals. Keeping a cat as a pet is part of humanity itself. In Japan, because of our religion, we believe that animals have a soul too. We shouldn't kill any alien species."

Kazuo called the cats "wild," but by strict standards, they weren't. As an introduced and invasive species, they were not wild, but feral. But like all wild-related things in Japan, cats, too, escaped clear binary divisions and easy definitions. Whether they were wild or not, invasive or not, foreign or not, the animals simply had a soul, and they deserved respect. When we call animals wild, or feral, or domesticated, we forget to ask ourselves whether they have a soul like we do, whether they deserve the same respect as we all do.

"We don't want to teach the value that native is good and alien is bad," Kazuo observed, echoing Harada-san's words from a few days before. "We should focus on the protection of wildlife and not on killing. We need to regenerate nature ourselves."

Environmental protection, over the years, has become a global movement. It is a movement fuelled by a central body of knowledge fed by advances in ecological sciences. Ecological scientific writing is primarily dominated by the English language. Consequently, ideas rooted in discrete cultural contexts – for example, ideas about wilderness or wildness – take on universal value, as if they were the same all over the world. But the concept of wildness isn't the same all over the world. We realized this in South Tyrol, but the confusion and the silences of our Japanese interviewees spoke even louder.

Ecology, to work best, needs to be accompanied by ethnology. Without it, humans will remain a cumbersome invasive species. Advances in fields of study such as ethnobotany, environmental anthropology, and the environmental humanities are now starting to integrate local knowledge into scientific knowledge. But this, in a way, is an old way of doing science. Traditional ecological knowledge as shared, accumulated, and practised by Indigenous peoples around the world has always been based on Indigenous ways of knowing that blend story, spirituality, and science. Such knowledge helps us debunk facile notions of a wildness that cannot be regenerated over time as new relations between people, wildlife, and their lands develop.

Such knowledge also helps us poke holes in the ideology of endemism, often by teaching us that species do not sit still. They move, and they make new homes; by doing so, they enter into relations. It's the shape of those relations – how species treat one another – that matters.

Our time in the Ogasawara was coming to an end, but there was still a mystery to be solved. The five o'clock jingle heard on the streets of Chichijima was – we learned – the Ogasawara anthem. It played at five o'clock to call children back home. Playtime on the streets and the beach was over. It was supper time.

It was time to go home for us too. On the morning of January 10, 2018, we boarded the *Ogasawara Maru*, bound for Tokyo. What happened next – a strangely fun modern-day ritual – defies the imagination. Yosuke had alerted us about it a week before, when the previous sailing was about to leave. "Every time the boat leaves," he told us on January 2, without sharing too many details, "the locals give it a very unique send-off, and if you want, we can be part of it." Curious, and intrigued by his cagey attitude, we agreed.

On January 3, we joined a large group of locals on the pier to wave off the ship. There was no one on the boat that we knew, but it didn't matter. There was live music on the pier. There were people congregating, visiting, and having fun. We hung out next to Yosuke and a couple of young workers from Papa's who had come to say *itterashai* to the departing guests.

As the *Ogasawara Maru* blasted her horn and began pulling away from the dock, we were told it was time. Moments later, a van arrived. We were whisked away – the three of us, Yosuke, and a handful of the workers from Papa's. Tires screeching, we sped up to the nearby marina and jumped on a small vessel.

"Hold on tight," Yosuke told us as our vessel sped toward the *Ogasawara Maru*. Here's Autumn's recollection of the event:

> As heavy waves carried us through the water, the island seemed to be growing smaller and smaller, the *Ogasawara Maru* bigger and bigger. I gripped onto my seat to avoid falling into the rough waters of the bay encircling Chichijima. We still had no idea what was going on.
>
> Finally, Yosuke explained. With every departure of the *Ogasawara Maru,* he told us, many residents of Chichijima say their goodbyes by waving to passengers from their own boats.
>
> The large swells of the bay were amplified by the wake from the *Ogasawara Maru.* As we gave chase, our small boat swayed back and forth madly, causing my overly cautious father to grasp onto his camera like it was a lifesaver. The passengers' faint yells from the big ship drifted through the wind and reached our boat clearly as we got closer and closer to her hull.
>
> "Itterashai!" we shouted. "Please go and come back."
>
> "Ittekimasu!" they called back. This was the Japanese phrase for "I'll go and come back" or, more casually, "See you later." This went on for a while, as two dozen other small vessels and their passengers shouted "Itterashai!" with us.

Suddenly, our boat leaned sharply to the left. Barely catching my balance, I looked up to find that several of our boat's passengers had jumped off the boat and into the rolling waves. Passengers from other vessels, all wearing lifejackets and smiles, had done the same. While bobbing up and down in the large swells, they still managed to wave and shout out "Itterashai!" as loud as they could.

My voice was nearly strained from yelling at the top of my lungs. My mom hollered with laughter while my sea sickness-prone dad gave us a nervous smile, still tending to his heavy equipment with diligence. My feelings of excitement had completely overcome my other feelings – confusion, fear, and motion sickness.

Even though I'd never come in contact with the people on the ship, this moment and our words had drawn us together with the island.

"Ittekimasu!" I shouted one week later from the *Ogasawara Maru*, as the ritual repeated itself one more time, with us the recipients this time.

"Ittekimasu!"

7

Wild Can Be Alive

PATAGONIA

A FEW HUNDRED METRES NORTH of the village of El Chalten, Ruta 23 became a rough gravel track that wound its way upstream along the Las Vueltas. Sharp turn after sharp turn, the potholes became larger and the road narrowed as it rose in altitude until it reached the Río Cañadon de los Toros. The mountains surrounding us grew greener at their base as the aridity of the steppe gave way to forest. From that point on, the Andes leaned so far into the cramped valley they made passage from Argentina to Chile impossible for cars. The remaining kilometres to the border had to be made on foot, on highlands that in a not-so-distant past had seen their fair share of military skirmishes between the two uneasy Southern American neighbours.

Rodrigo, a soft-spoken ecologist in his mid-thirties, drove, and Benji, our Argentinian gatekeeper, sat in the backseat. We saw mountains to our left and the river and its tributaries, occasionally flanked by fields teeming with huemuls (deer), guanacos (a camelid closely related to the llama), and horses to our right. Above us, and by now fully inside our heads, the Patagonian winds swept large billowy clouds against the cold rock walls of monolithic peaks. We had been driving for nearly an hour, sightings of one-lane bridges and roadside waterfalls vastly outnumbering passing vehicles or any other evidence of human presence, when Rodrigo slowed and mumbled something in Spanish to Benji.

"Que pasa?" Benji asked. What's wrong?

Rodrigo looked down at the brake and gas pedals, which didn't respond to his feet, and pulled the limp vehicle over. He turned the key over to fire the engine. An empty click then a mysterious series of beeps. He looked confused and a bead of sweat now forming on his forehead, Rodrigo flicked the key one more time. Another click followed.

"It's the battery," Benji said in English.

The vertiginous mountains had hijacked the last faint cellphone signal at least thirty kilometres behind us. Ahead, nothing but the mountain pass into Chile. Rodrigo, who spoke no English, looked at Phillip. "Lo siento." "Sorry," he whispered.

We exited the vehicle. Rodrigo and Benji leafed through the dusty car operation manual but found nothing to troubleshoot the situation. We were too far to walk anywhere, too remote to call for help, in a place too deserted to do anything but wait for a passing vehicle.

While Benji and Rodrigo worked on the car, growing more frustrated with every failed solution, we walked into the forest that flanked the road on both sides and marvelled at the quiet that enveloped us.

"Are you guys okay?" Benji asked.

"Sure. Why not?" April said. "It's nice here."

"The forest is so lush compared to the desert just a few kilometres away," Phillip commented from behind his camera. Autumn took pictures of a cobweb.

The Argentinians looked perplexed at our calm disposition. "Canadians," Benji observed in Spanish to Rodrigo, "must be from another planet."

Truth is, the world around us, the forest we had been scheduled to drive by at fifty kilometres an hour, had suddenly come to life, to our lives. It had become present in our lifeworld. No longer something to drive by, it had revealed itself to us as something to feel, something alive and wild.

Wildness is ephemeral. It's there one moment, fades away the next. Uncontrollable, it comes to life when it wills, and it vanishes when it wants. It can be dimmed, shut out in the world outside a car window, suffocated by the noise of rubber tires grinding through layers of gravel, and then it comes to life as engine noise is muted by the untimely demise of a battery and as the sound of the wind lashing against treetops reveals itself as a kind of natural music.

"Are you sure you're okay?" Benji asked again, interrupting the metaphysical reflections brewing in our minds.

"Nothing to worry about," April said. "A car will come by."

Minutes later, a car came by. It carried, of all people, a man who specialized in car alarms. He told us the alarm had malfunctioned, causing the system to shut off. There was nothing we could do to fix it there. We would have to hitch a ride with a passing car. And so we did. Nearly three hours later, we rolled back into El Chalten, happy about how our day had gone.

Wildness is ephemeral but also fickle, capricious in its instability. Patagonia, more than any other place, taught us this. It taught us that seeking wildness is a bit like trying to dance to a constantly changing tune – you try to catch up, step after step, to an unpredictable rhythm.

The most unpredictable thing in Patagonia? The winds. The winds of Patagonia aren't just strong, they are wild forces that dwell in the sky: alive, vibrant, and utterly unbearable whenever they choose to come to life. The winds wreaked havoc on our plans daily, forcing us to change and adapt our schedules.

We aren't the first to complain about them. Memoirs of early European settlers to the region are full of references to furious winds sweeping the steppe, winds so relentless they drove newcomers mad. Some of those stories seemed like an exaggeration when we read about them back home, but the day we arrived in El Chalten, they became easy to believe.

We'd landed in Patagonia in the last week of December 2018. After a three-hour journey from the El Calafate Airport, we reached El Chalten. We checked in and then stepped outside to stretch our legs. Minutes later, barely a few steps upwind, we realized that breathing – let alone walking – in the violent headwinds was impractical. The relentless winds felt like a wall. They insinuated themselves inside our bodies, suffocated our breath, and extinguished our will to walk.

This frustrated Autumn, whose antipathy for the sky's blustery forces had been intense since her first days of life. We remembered her gasping for air one day on the ferry back home when she was just months old, confused and enraged at the tempestuous force of the sky.

"I can't take this anymore," she yelled above the wind. "Let's go get a waffle."

We agreed to sit down in the busy "Waffleria," located just steps away from our cabin. We chatted with one of the owners, who was, incidentally, our landlady for the next ten days. Romina and her husband, Demian, had moved to El Chalten from Córdoba in 1988. They fell in love with the place, despite the winds.

"If you don't like the wind here, you must go!" she told us in English. She'd switched from Spanish to emphasize the importance of the subject. She switched back to Spanish to find the right words. "El viento es un demonio." The wind is a demon.

"Over here, you can't find a butterfly," she continued, "because the poor thing would fly away." We all laughed. "The winds here are extreme. We have gotten to the point of having winds that have shifted houses from one place to another," she told us with a smile. "To live in Chalten, you have to like the wind. Or at least you can't be affected by the wind. You go out, and you walk with wind. You can't comb your hair because of the wind. There are very few days that are without wind, and on those days, we send praise to the Pachamama." She laughed. "Our children have learned to live with the wind. They can only play soccer inside the gym. Otherwise, the ball just flies away."

Although they were an outstanding force of nature, the winds had played no role in the official inscription of Los Glaciares National Park in the UNESCO World Heritage List. One of Argentina's five Natural Heritage Sites, Los Glaciares is recognized as "an area of exceptional natural beauty, with rugged, towering mountains and numerous glacial lakes," where "three glaciers meet to dump their effluvia into the milky grey glacial water, launching massive igloo icebergs into the lake with thunderous splashes."

Los Glaciares is virtually uninhabited, though the towns of El Calafate and El Chalten lay at the doorsteps of the towering mountains and glacial lakes. El Chalten, to be precise, is the gateway to the most famous mountains in the region, while El Calafate lies among myriad glacial lakes. Without exaggeration, Los Glaciares National Park is "embedded into the enchanted and remote mountain landscape of the

Patagonian Andes," as the World Heritage List explains, "dominated by rugged granite peaks exceeding 3000 metres" on one side and glaciers on the other.

Unlike other destinations in Patagonia and nearby Tierra del Fuego, Los Glaciares hasn't yet achieved too much international fame. And yet, upon arriving in El Chalten, virtually anyone would recognize the mountains surrounding it. The logo of the internationally renowned clothing brand Patagonia depicts Mount Fitz Roy and its adjacent peaks as seen from the town.

"El Chalten" – everyone says – is a Tehuelche word meaning "Smoking Mountain," a reference to the often cloud-capped peak named Mount Chalten (also known as Mount Fitz Roy), which towers above the small village of sixteen hundred residents. But this is a myth. As Canadian anthropologist Javier Domingo's ethnolinguistic work shows, "El Chalten" is not a Tehuelche word. That notion was cooked up by the Argentinian government to legitimize their historical claim over the region as part of their long-term territorial dispute with Chile.

Another mountain in the area – Cerro Torre – is equally famed and just as controversial. Cerro Torre is a needle-shaped peak 3,128 metres in altitude and roughly within shouting distance of Mount Fitz Roy. Many climbers argue that it is the most challenging in the world. The story of its conquest is remarkable. In 1958, an Italian climbing expedition led by Bruno Detassis arrived in Patagonia with the intention of being the first to climb it. Others had tried. A few years before, for example, a French expedition led by Lionel Terray and aided by Argentinian president Juan Perón had succeeded in being the first to reach the summit of Mount Fitz Roy but gave up on Cerro Torre, deeming it impossible to climb. When Detassis saw Cerro Torre for himself, he, too, was struck by the foreboding peak, particularly the mushroom of rime ice that covered the very top. Though he had come all that way, he forbade his team from even attempting it.

But Italian climbers didn't give up so easily. The next year, two other Italian mountaineers, Cesare Maestri and his teammate, Toni Egger, reached the top of Cerro Torre. Well, maybe. As it happened, upon their descent, as Maestri recounted, Egger was swept away by an avalanche and lost his life. Egger, Maestri claimed, was the only one with a camera. His demise meant there was no proof to back their claim. Hardly anyone believed him.

Fed up with the endless scrutiny and controversy following his contentious claim, Maestri returned to Patagonia in 1970, this time carrying extra cameras as well as a pneumatic air compressor, a drill, and hundreds of bolts. Over several days, he and his team lodged nearly four hundred bolts into the southeast ridge of Cerro Torre and eventually reached the headwall but never the summit, because it was just too difficult. No big deal, Maestri told the world, the mushroom of ice was not part of the mountain proper, so it made no sense to scale it.

The chorus of dissent from the mountaineering world rose to a crescendo. Not only was their claim weak, but Maestri and his team were accused of desecrating the purity of the mountain with their four hundred bolts. Soon enough Maestri and his team became poster children for unethical and environmentally unsustainable climbing. Another team of Italians – Daniele Chiappa, Mario Conti, Casimiro Ferrari, and Pino Negri – made the first undisputed ascent of Cerro Torre in 1974.

But the controversy did not end there. As Cerro Torre solidified its status with the world's climbing community, the town of El Chalten began to take shape. When Terray and Detassis first attempted to reach Mount Cerro Torre in 1958, El Chalten did not exist, so it took weeks to reach the region from Rio Gallegos. Climbers had to hitch rides in mail trucks and wade rivers. But as the fame of Cerro Torre grew, and as Argentina became increasingly worried about Chilean expansion across a disputed border, El Chalten received large infrastructural investments, in 1985, from Santa Cruz governor Nestor Kirchner.

In the meantime, mountaineering culture evolved as climbers moved away from the siege-style ascents of large teams and rejected as many technologies as possible. As purist mountaineers supporting the value of free-style climbing continued to gain influence in the 2000s, American Hayden Kennedy and Canadian Jason Kruk arrived in El Chalten in January 2012 after a few days spent in the mountains. They had climbed Cerro Torre, they revealed, and to prove it, they had done something else. They'd cleared Cerro Torre of the bolts left behind by Maestri's team.

Yes, not only had they climbed the mountain, but they'd also cleaned it up. They wanted to "restore Cerro Torre back to its natural state," they told the press. A day later, they were arrested. The bolts, they were told by the authorities, were part of the mountain's heritage and local history. Townsfolk had lost their patience with foreigners showing up and doing what they pleased with the mountain.

Milena, our guide for the day, recounted the Cerro Torre story to us as we made our way toward Mount Fitz Roy on a remarkably warm and pleasant day. The wind had taken the day off, so we planned to hike as close as possible to the Paso del Viento, the Wind's Pass, with her and her boyfriend, Ben, a friendly guy from the US West Coast who had decided to join us.

Milena, a diminutive, wiry young woman who exuded calm and confidence with every step, had climbed Mount Fitz Roy three times. Modest to a fault, we learned of her accomplishments from Ben.

"So, what's Mount Fitz Roy like?" we asked her out of the blue.

She stopped and exchanged a look with Ben. "How do you know? Ben told you?"

Ben looked guilty. She admitted she'd climbed it for the first time in 2009. It's something she didn't like to brag about, so she mostly kept it to herself. Her parents didn't even know about it. She told us with a devilish grin that she hoped they wouldn't ever get a hold of this book.

Milena started climbing when she was fifteen. It's like a physical addiction, she explained, but it doesn't have to be about just climbing. It's about movement, she reflected, whether it's hiking, running, or whatever. But with climbing, it's different, "Because you are afraid, but you have to go with your mind relaxed and knowing that maybe you won't come back. The state of freedom that you feel on the summits is amazing. You feel this adrenalin. Like you've made a lot of effort, and you feel your mind clear up. And I feel very happy too."

El Chalten was a hiker's and climber's paradise. Trail after trail of relatively undeveloped country allowed both day hikers like us and serious mountaineers to explore a place that resembled the Alps before chairlifts and huts had gentrified them. The very rhythms of the town (busy and energetic at breakfast, tired but gleeful at dinner, and dead quiet at lunch) confirmed that locals and visitors weren't just there to be seen, but to see. As a result of its popularity within the mountaineering community, El Chalten had grown quickly.

"It was very different when I came here for the first time in 2008," Milena told us as we walked toward El Paso del Viento. "All the roads were gravel." Since then, summers had gotten busier. More hotels and restaurants opened each year, and the town even had two small grocery stores. It still had no hospital, but there was a school. By the time of our visit, the first ATM had opened. Despite these changes, Milena commented, the winters – from June to September – were still lonely. It was no accident that most children in town were born between March and June. "Sometimes, I go and ride my bike during winter, and I see nobody. We call it 'Death by Bike,' or 'La muerte en bicicleta.' The death is right in the bike, because if an accident happens, there's nobody around to help you."

Aside from a very spotty internet signal (which got worse on windy days, someone explained to us with a hint of philosophical resignation), the town's true problem was real estate. "The thing is," Milena explained, "we're in the national park. It's a problem because we don't have a place to live. So now we are waiting for a new deal between the state and the national park so that the National Park can surrender more land and give us land to build." She had been waiting for eleven years. In the meantime, she had to live in a bus.

We hiked slowly as we chatted. The trail wound its way through the Lenga Forest, a wooded area composed of scrubby vegetation that looked like it had been dehydrated and then beaten senseless by the dry winds. Moments after leaving the forest, the steep path reached a plain. We could see Mount Fitz Roy directly in front of us, El Chalten below us, and Viedma Lake far in the distance behind us, a speck of ice blue in a treeless, yellow-hued desert.

The trail continued to the Loma del Pliegue Tumbado, but it would have to wait for another day. We were happy to sit on the tall grass amid the wild orchids. We admired the condors flying overhead and shared a few sips of mate from Milena's *bombilla*.

"I think that 'wild' can be very deep," Milena told us as she drank some of the bitter tea. "A deep word. I can feel it with my soul. Because I feel all my instincts, as I'm a woman. I feel all the sensations in my skin. I feel very connected with nature because we are connected with the moon and with the cycles. And I also feel like I am free. I always try to follow my feelings, my instinct. If I feel like my soul is wild. This kind of life is very wild."

December had run its course. To mark the arrival of 2019, Benji suggested we do what all Argentinians do – go for some *asado*, a grilled meat extravaganza. Every single day of our stay in Argentina, we'd been presented with enough grilled meat to drown out even the faintest recollection of vegetables. We said we weren't sure how this was special. He shrugged his shoulders as if to say "When in Argentina ..."

The moment we sat down at Benji's restaurant of choice, we were presented with beef empanadas. Benji ordered grilled sausage and half a dozen different cuts of steak. He told us Patagonia doesn't exist in the minds of Argentinians the way it does in the minds of the rest of the world. "Patagonia is an invention" by the rest of the world. It's in the Global North and West that it has acquired a distinct identity as a last frontier, a place of mystery, abandonment, remoteness, and forbidding nature. For nearly all Argentinians, Patagonia is two things. If you ski, it's Bariloche in the winter. If snow isn't on your mind, then Patagonia is an uninhabited wasteland whipped by angry winds.

Benji, who had translated nearly every interview from Spanish for our benefit, recalled a few new wind-related anecdotes. During an interview, he'd been told that someone had found a kayak in their backyard the morning after a windy night. It had blown in from somewhere, when the owner couldn't be located, the person got to keep it. A runner told him she had resigned herself to doing her runs downwind and then catching a taxi home. He knifed a slab of lamb and recalled that an outfitter in El Chalten only rented bikes one way – the riders got dropped off by a company bus and rode their rental bikes downwind.

These weren't simply funny anecdotes but evidence that wildness can be found anywhere. Geographers like us use the notion of vitality to refer to aliveness, the spirited *elàn vital,* the energy with which life forces are imbued when unrestrained. Vitality is often an annoying idea to hard-nosed scientists who prefer to explain things through laws of causality. For them, the wind is caused by differences in atmospheric pressure, and that's that. To speak of vitality in the scientific world is to resort to magic or the irrational. But vitalist worldviews embrace the value of the ineffable, the unexplainable, that which exceeds causality, prediction, and mechanist relations.

A world in which wildness is imagined as a vitalist force is a world that has not lost its wonder for the power of nature. It is also a world in which the life forces exerted by all forms of life – human or nonhuman, organic or inorganic – are worthy of admiration and respect because they, too, have their stories to share. It's a world in which the vagaries of the wind defy imagination, a world in which the wind itself can act as if it possessed an imagination, as if it wanted to perform its stories with clouds, with a boundless sky as its stage.

We toasted to the arrival of 2019, and within moments the ninth round of asado landed on our plates, blood sausages. "Come on," Benji encouraged, "we haven't eaten any meat since last year."

A Snowball's Chance in Hell is a 2014 German action documentary that tells the story of a group of young men who attempted to free climb, for the first time, the southeast face of Cerro Torre. David Lama is the star of the film, which also features Juan Manuel Raselli – known to his friends as "Pipa." Pipa lived across the street from our cabin. We noticed a Deftones sticker on his car's rear bumper, which we mentioned before we exchanged greetings. He was impressed that academics could love the Deftones. Friendship was quick.

Pipa suggested we chat on a rocky cliff on the other shore of the Las Vueltas river, the side of the valley where the town hadn't yet grown. Chatting "on" – as opposed to "near" – a rocky cliff meant climbing it together. Pipa offered to lend us the necessary gear, and Autumn took him up on the offer. He assured us this would be no free climb and that he had taught young teenagers before.

Pipa was the prototypical climber dude. Young, wiry, confident, and laid-back, he was easy to talk to and fluent in English. He had travelled around the world in search of adventure and "places that had some wild within," he told us. Climbing embodied adventure, he said as he wrapped ropes around our daughter's waist, and it also meant "being able to be in permanent contact with nature."

Over time, he became a professional guide and eventually landed in El Chalten to make a living from his passion. His professionalism was obvious in everything he did. He spoke to Autumn clearly about what she needed to do. He went over the basics of the gear and ensured that she'd be calm and able to communicate as she ascended. He reassured us she'd be safe. We trusted him.

"Do you think it's a good idea for children to climb?" we asked.

"Yes, I absolutely believe that. It's another way to live, relating to the mountain since you're a child. All of these challenges that the mountain puts onto you at any level, from being able to go through a route, up to planning a trip, or an ascension." It's a great way to learn about nature and yourself, he explained while Autumn took her first step onto the bald rock.

"If there is one lesson that mountains of the world have taught you, what is it?"

"I believe that it would be to live simply. I believe that in the mountains everything reduces to that. All is so simple that at the same time it can become complicated, because we're so used to complicating things that when we have the simple answer, we refuse to accept it. But I think that when you're in the mountains, even more so in hard situations of life or death, survival is in simplicity."

Pipa had climbed Cerro Torre twice, he told us casually as he coached Autumn. From down below, we could see her grin as she surprised herself with her fast ascent.

"Untie. Right hand, Autumn."

Autumn glided even farther.

"She's doing great!" He smiled.

We smiled back, proud but nervous. Moments later, Autumn realized how far up she had gone, vastly farther than we expected her to reach. She looked down and mumbled something. We all realized that anxiety was starting to seep in, affecting her hands and feet. Pipa instructed her to come back down for a break. Seconds later, our kid's feet were back on the ground.

While Autumn rested and Benji took his turn, we chatted with Pipa. Like many others in El Chalten, he had seen the town grow. When he arrived thirteen years before, there was no internet. Now, people could book his guiding services from abroad, and he made climbing plans with them by email. El Chalten was modern in many respects, and like many modern tourist locations, it had to deal with the side effects of growth such as garbage disposal and unsustainable real estate pressures.

Pipa and Autumn watch Benji climb

Autumn looked ready to give the rock face another go. Pipa encouraged her to go higher. He set the safety rope high enough for her to have a concrete goal, and with every upward movement, she exuded greater confidence.

"Is climbing here different than in other parts of the world?"

"Technically speaking, it's about the same. Here, there is a lot less infrastructure, so it is like the Alps a hundred years ago. The approaches are very long. The forecast is not as reliable as in the Alps. That makes for interesting climbing here, more challenging."

As we had found in the Italian Alps, there was no word for "wild" in Spanish-speaking Patagonia.

"I think that the wild (*salvaje*) with regard to mountain activities is what describes Patagonia," he observed. But "salvaje" was a tricky word, evoking to some degree the same things as the word "savage" in English. "In some ways Patagonia still is *salvaje* in the sense that there is little information about what one would like to do, and climbing in Patagonia is what climbing involved from a long time ago: a lot of research on the target, the climate conditions – which are very variable – information on the routes, information on the access that have a lot of variation. In that sense, Patagonia involves the salvaje aspects of climbing, but with a certain degree of accessibility. There are still some places that are more salvaje in the world, but the climbing up here is still wild."

Autumn back on the ground for good, we bade farewell to Pipa and, soon after, El Chalten. We left without experiencing the raw power of Cerro Torre but had a new appreciation of wildness as something as ephemeral as the wind, something whose volatility felt more alive than wilderness. Wilderness is a state, a place, a scarce and finite "resource." Wildness is evanescent, an episodic force that appears in a short-lived moment marked by surprise and wonder.

Wildness manifested itself once again just a few minutes outside of El Chalten, when our bus disappeared into the infinity of the steppe landscape. Riding along a solitary road flanked by barbed-wire fencing on one side and the light cerulean waters of Viedma Lake on the other, wildness came to life as the winds howled, as a lonely guanaco watched us drift by, and the afternoon sun battled against the clouds for supremacy over the sky.

A few days after New Year's Eve, summer tourism was at its highest peak. We'd managed to find a modest but cozy cabin overlooking Lago Argentino. The sprawling town of El Calafate houses six thousand residents (twenty thousand, during peak tourist season) and countless pink flamingos at its farthest edges. Nearly every other bed in El Calafate

– from the swankiest five-star resort to the thriftiest backpacker hostel – had been booked by an eclectic mix of travellers from South and North America, Europe, and Asia.

Los Glaciares National Park was inscribed on the World Heritage List in 1981, and today it covers an area of nearly 737,000 hectares. The glaciers cover about half of the World Heritage Site. They are fed by the South Patagonian Ice Field, and they are "the most extensive South American relict of the glaciological processes of the Quaternary Period," in the language of the World Heritage Committee.

The glaciers and the region's harsh climate traditionally made agriculture difficult. The area's designation as a World Heritage Site led to increased tourism and the growth of El Calafate. The Comandante Armando Tola Airport received just over 700,000 passengers in 2016, up from 507,000 in 2010, and 383,000 in 2005.

Tourism brought to life what would have otherwise been a sleepy, remote town. Avenida del Libertador felt vibrant, busy, like it was the road to somewhere else, somewhere bigger. "It kind of feels like Banff," Autumn said at her first glance of downtown. It was nothing like El Chalten with its lonesome ATM.

Although the area within the boundaries of Los Glaciares National Park has never been inhabited, the region known today as Santa Cruz Province had long been the home of the Aónikenk people, also known as Tehuelche. Nomadic hunters, the Aónikenk moved in circuits and lived in camps known as *aik*. Their lives changed forever in 1520 when a Spanish expedition under the command of Ferdinand Magellan arrived in San Julian Bay. Surprised by the Aónikenk's tall stature, the short-statured colonizers noticed how small their own feet were in comparison, and in characteristically ethnocentric fashion, they named the land they had just reached "Patagonia," from the word Spanish word *patagones* (large-footed). Another version of the story traces the word "Patagone" to a monster described in a fourteenth-century novel.

The insult, regardless of which story is true, was nothing compared to the injuries that followed. Aónikenk people were abducted and taken back to Europe to show off as curiosities. Sometimes they were returned, sometimes not. They were eventually decimated like many Indigenous groups around the world. Today, there are just a few thousand Tehuelche left, with even fewer capable of speaking Aonekko 'a'ien. Only five small Tehuelche communities exist in Santa Cruz Province, none close to the boundaries of Los Glaciares.

If Patagonia's contemporary history is one of tourism and its modern history one of colonial violence – some of the most brutal anywhere in the world – its late modern history is one of hardship and solitude. Settlers of the region who arrived during the nineteenth or early twentieth century faced an extreme climate and the brutal loneliness of life in impossibly large and remote ranches known as *estancias*. An estancia is a large private estate dedicated to farming or raising cattle, or often both. Today, more and more estancias are welcoming guests for day tours and dining experiences or longer stays focused on agritourism.

Adolfo Santiago Jansma had stories to tell. We met Adolfo at the Estancia Nibepo Aike on a warm, clear day in early January. Estancia Nibepo Aike lies on the southern shore of Lago Roca, just southeast of Glaciar Perito Moreno, about one hour out of El Calafate. In the distance we could see the glacier, la Cordillera de los Andes, the Cerro Cervantes, and Cordón Adriana. Farther afield were continental ices and the Chilean Pacific Ocean.

Adolfo's grandfather arrived in the region in 1902, twenty-five years before the town of El Calafate began to take form. "When he came over, there was nothing at all." Adolfo's heritage was half Dutch, half Croatian. His Croatian grandpa had landed in Argentina to work, like countless European immigrants and made his way to Patagonia by horse. As it happened, other Croatians lived in nearby estancias (granted, nothing is really "nearby" in Patagonia). They told him to keep moving toward the Cordillera, and he eventually found land at the place where we found ourselves that day.

The main differences between then and now were sheep and cows, Adolfo observed. After obtaining a lease for twenty thousand hectares, Adolfo's grandpa set to work with sheep imported from the Falkland Islands – still referred to as the "Malvinas" in Argentina. He put up fifty-seven kilometres of fencing and a handful of buildings and named his estancia La Jeronima. Around five thousand kilograms of wool would

Adolfo Santiago Jansma telling stories

be produced yearly and sent to Río Gallegos (twenty days away by horse-drawn carriage) and then on to Europe.

During "one of those trips, in the year 1924, he met another Croatian, Maria Martinich, my grandmother. They ended up marrying in 1925," Adolfo recounted. One of their three daughters was Radoslava, Adolfo's mother. Adolfo's grandpa died in 1938 of tuberculosis. His grandma and her three daughters took over the estancia.

"My grandmother was left totally alone," he told us, but she soldiered on. In 1947, she bought over the estancia and renamed it Nibepo. "She had given her three daughters nicknames: Radoslava, they called her Nini; Angela, who was known as Bebe; and Maria, nicknamed Porota. NiBePo. *Aike,* in the native Tehuelche tongue, means 'the place of.' The place of Nini, Bebe, and Porota," Adolfo said proudly.

A Robert De Niro look alike, Adolfo spoke confidently and warmly. For twenty-eight years, Nibepo Aike had been operating like so many other estancias in the region as an agritourism business. The 150 sheep living there still provided wool, but they also served as a performance prop for the daily shearing show that visitors were treated to. Of course, the sheep also made their way to the asado.

"Do you think this place is wild?" April asked through Benji.

"Yes. I believe so. This place, even though it wouldn't seem so, is rural, tough."

Adolfo told us there was a unique dimension to Patagonian wildness: rurality, toughness, and the will to endure. While this is not a uniquely Patagonian quality, of all the places we had visited, Patagonia epitomized the rural, bucolic quality of wildness.

Patagonia can feel like an old soul, in many ways like the rest of Argentina. In some corners of Buenos Aires and other cities, that old spirit can take the shape of a dilapidated charm, remnants of twentieth-century grandeur. In Patagonia, that old soul manifests itself in the vastness of spaces so wide, so arid, so windswept that the place takes on an atmosphere of toughness, of old-time rurality. This is an atmosphere doused in melancholy. It's a melancholy that pervades the clothes people wear, the cars they drive, the food they eat, and the drinks they drink. Perhaps the nostalgia was shared and transmitted by generations of immigrants who left their homelands to move as far away as they could.

No single word in English can denote all this the way the Spanish word *agreste* does. To talk about wildness, most Argentinians would use words such as *naturaleza,* which is commonly used to refer to nature or to a natural landscape that appears pristine. Other words could be used too, such as *silvestre,* which seemed especially appropriate when describing a wooded area, a bush, or a wild forest. But the one that seemed to fit much of what we had seen of Patagonia (with the exception of the glaciers and the high mountains) was "agreste."

"Agreste" rang true in a place haunted by the expansiveness of its dimensions, a place where a field or cattle might have been worked by a tough old *estanciero* (cattle farmer) or *gaucho* (horseman), but a place that still retained a certain vitality to break loose of that grip and grow on its own. This was a place that remembered long-gone days and long-lost lives. But there was one more Spanish word that captured our imagination, a word and an idea that the glaciers themselves soon revealed to us.

Ruta 11 runs southwest of El Calafate, wraps around the shore of Lago Argentino, and terminates at the edge of Glaciar Perito Moreno. From there, tourists exit their coaches or cars, walk around a footpath that overlooks the glacier, take photographs, and leave. A smaller number of tourists, much smaller given the sticker price of the excursion, get much closer to the glacier. From the end of Ruta 11, they board a small vessel that shuttles them to the western shore of the lake, and from there, they begin a guided walk on the glacier itself. Those less inclined to put ice crampons on can get up close and personal with this glacier and two others via an all-day cruise that launches from Puerto Punto Bandera, not too far from El Calafate.

Neither option seemed particularly wild or salvaje, or agreste on paper, but they were interesting for ethnographic reasons, so we decided to sign up for both. Crampons on, we began walking in a single file on Glaciar Perito Moreno behind a guide. Our group consisted of about twenty people who hailed from different corners of the world. The ice was bright white, as one would expect, but it was the brilliant blue of its crevasses that stood out. We walked for about an hour feeling like small specs lost in the immensity.

We were told the glacier can speak, and it often does. It is a voice made up of cracks and breaks followed by splashes as chunks fall off and into the waters of the lake below. Those lucky enough to spend extended periods on the ice – members of glaciology research teams who are allowed to camp in the far reaches of the park – tell stories of ice groaning and murmuring, speaking with a tongue of its own.

But wildness is fleeting, and it did not come to life for us that day. We were fortunate to see large chunks of ice break off the glacier wall into the water a handful of times, but wildness was submerged by waves of tourists and their murmurs. Unfortunately, some people can't respect and honour natural spectacles deeply enough to keep quiet, even for just a few minutes.

So instead of ice cracking, we listened to chatter about what our tour companions had for supper the night before. We heard about the wines they'd consumed and how they ranked in comparison to other wines. We heard speculation about how long the trip back to Buenos Aires or Denver might be, and we got to witness them posing for selfies.

Wildness is capricious, but in a neoliberal tourist world, its aliveness is often exhausted by experiences packaged to give people not memories but "things to do" and "things to see." These are the expressions used by the tourist world and favoured by guidebooks and countless travel websites. These are the expressions of affluent people for whom the vitality of the natural world is secondary to their absolute imperative: to avoid getting bored. Wildness, in this world, is most endangered not by development or resource exploitation but by the ennui of world travellers incapable of any experience other than a moment's distraction.

Since we couldn't visit the glacier on our own, we made an appointment to enjoy it vicariously through someone who had visited more than most people in Argentina. Seventy-five-year-old Pedro Svarka was the scientific director of Glaciarium in El Calafate and one of the most highly respected glaciologists in the world. He had been working with glaciers in Argentina and Antarctica for forty years and had visited glaciers around the globe. He had experienced glaciers in a way that scientific language couldn't always capture.

"Here is one of the few, very unique places in the world where you still don't have much contamination, or where tourism has not influenced as much as in many other places on Earth, like in the Himalayas, the Alps, or Alaska," he told us. He was being truthful – the tourists were confined to a very small corner of the glacier. "And I think that UNESCO has selected this place because Glaciar Perito Moreno is the only one in the world that produces periodical damming, which is a really unique, spectacular phenomenon."

Damming occurs at regular cycles, every five or six years. The ice dams, but it is eventually weakened by the waters of Lago Argentino, which push hard to get through the ice. The waters chip away at the dam in front of the footpath where most tourists stop their cars on Ruta 11. Eventually, the ice wall collapses with a mighty thunder, releasing massive slabs of ice for everyone to admire. "It's amazing," Pedro assured us as we watched a video of the event from a few years back. He noted that video footage of chunks of the glacier falling into the water was routinely used as visual evidence of climate change. Climate change was a problem, he explained, but damming had nothing to do with it.

This was the first time in our fieldwork that climate change had come up, and it gave us pause for thought. Climate change is almost universally believed to be one of the leading causes of the loss of wilderness. The argument is simple: human activities are causing the climate to change, and that change is spoiling wild (read: previously untouched) ecosystems. But this argument is overly simplistic.

Untouched environments hardly exist. Moreover, human activities have always impacted the planet, even in its remotest corners. So rather than viewing climate change as an independent variable that affects all sorts of dependent variables, we should view climate change as the ultimate reminder that dualist views of nature and society as separate entities are and have always been faulty.

Human alteration of ecosystems, in other words, is not just an Anthropocenic event. Most of us were unprepared to notice the limits of our ideology. Climate change is a plague and the most fundamental threat our planet has ever known, but it has occurred largely as the result of the Western dualist view that humans are separate from nature and, therefore, entitled to dominate it, exhausting its vitality.

Besides climate change, there were other problems, Pedro told us: rubbish generated by numerous tourist expeditions and the unusual problem of wild cows running around the park. "The place isn't a true wilderness, because of these wild calves. And this is a big problem. Because they were imported. They are not native."

A few hundred years ago, there were farms close to the glacier. The farmers left, but some of their cows got left behind and multiplied, causing stress on the local, fragile vegetation. A group of gauchos hired by the park spend their summers hunting the cows down.

Despite this, Pedro knew the place was special. Like any good scientist, he presented us with all sorts of numerical data about the glacier, but we had an interest in something more touchy-feely, something only he could share. We asked him to share why he was so passionate about the place.

"This is the most difficult question. This is a very personal one. Well, for me, the nicest thing about these glaciers ..." He searched for the right words in English. "It's ice, green, trees, and blue. And it's unique. You are very close to the glacier. You can see the glacier almost alive."

"Almost alive? How can something be almost alive?"

"Oh, this is complicated. It is so personal, it's not ... It's subjective, I know. People ask me when I first saw the ice: an ice rupture, or the ice dam rupture. I was impressed, and I couldn't talk. They awoke me at night in my tent, and I said, 'Don't disturb me.' But then I went out, and it was just unique. When I go to the glacier, of course, I would like to not see so many people around there. And people should be silent and just watching, and not shouting, and just listen to the glacier, and watch and listen, and so they would know it's alive."

Another Spanish word to describe wild, we were told, is *indómito,* or "indomitable" in English. Indomitable is a fascinating way to describe wildness. The word refers to something that cannot be stopped, that cannot be subdued.

The glacier was indomitable, constantly advancing, moving of its own will, cracking, moaning, holding and releasing pressure, rupturing and forming impossibly beautiful sculptures of blue ice. This was the indomitable aliveness that characterized the glacier. It was an unstoppable vitality that rendered the glacier – in our imagination at least – as wild, as indomitable, as any undomesticated life.

Spanish, just like Italian and Japanese, offers no literal translation for the English word "wild" and its derivatives. This could be seen as evidence for the claim that wildness is an Anglo-Saxon invention, but that claim is unwarranted. As in Japan, the impossibility of translating wild in Patagonia yielded new insights about its meaning. We learned "wild" might mean agreste, indómito – rustic, indomitable – words that speak to qualities not often associated with wildness, words that we could now, thankfully, add to our understanding.

Our research was never intended to yield an ultimate and universal definition, something we could all agree on. Rather than a definitive and exhaustive definition, from the very beginning, our interest had been in something additive. We were driven by an interest in conjunctions – in words such as "and." For us, wildness could always be something else, and then something else, and then something else, so long as we were willing to learn what else it could be, so long as we were open-minded enough to consider what else it could be. That is the power of ethno-logical knowledge: it's not a universal knowledge but one based in place and the people who live in that place.

Patagonia, more than anywhere else in the world we had travelled, taught us that wildness could be alive, vibrant, vital. That vitality was undoubtedly ephemeral, capricious. It was a whimsy that found expres-sions in gusts of wind, in painterly clouds that erased themselves as quickly as they took form, in glacial murmurs that faded with the passing of their own echoes. It was an aliveness that could intensify suddenly, as a car engine stopped or a road became a desert. But it was also vitality exhausted by the forces of tourist distractions, compressor routes, and packaged tours.

As revealing as the Spanish language could be, it was a word that we never heard spoken that lingered in the air as we departed Patagonia. It was the name for wild used by the Aónikenk, people whom we never got to meet; people whose society, language, and culture had been decimated by Spanish-speaking colonizers; people who originally owned and occu-pied the land; people who – like countless other Indigenous groups around the world – had been silenced by a virulent form of imperialism that named them salvajes, savages, and thus exhausted their aliveness in the name of wild – in the name of God, country, empire, and other ideologies.

8

Wild Can Be Photogenic

ICELAND

IN THE YEAR 2010, travel changed profoundly. The architects of that revolution – Kevin Systrom and Mike Krieger – aren't household names, but their invention, a mobile phone app called Instagram, is now as common in the daily lives of people as the toothbrush, the electric bulb, and the microwave oven, and vastly more addictive.

Instagram was originally baptized "Burbn," and its features were similar to Foursquare, another application popular at the time. Keen on setting their invention apart from Foursquare, Systrom and Krieger decided to zero in on Burbn's photo-sharing functionality and eventually renamed their app Instagram to underline that it combined the telegram and the instant camera.

The app was downloaded by 1 million users in the first two months after its launch in 2010, but hardly anyone in those early days could fathom the consequences that Instagram would have on the experience and practice of travel and tourism. As Instagram continued to gain popularity and smartphones became more ubiquitous, it became clear that a revolution was in the making. In April 2012, Facebook acquired Instagram for US$1 billion, and by mid-2019, 1 billion people around the world had become registered Instagram users.

About half of Instagram users open the app at least once a day. They use it to stay connected with others, to show off their fashion choices and their dinner plates, as well as to lionize their cats – among other things. Many Instagrammers, 71 percent according to a Forbes study conducted in 2016, bring it along on their travels too. Moreover, as other studies have shown, Instagram users regularly draw inspiration for their travels from the photographs posted by other Instagrammers. As Lauren Bath – a marketer and Instagram user with 465,000 followers – puts it, the app is critical to the pretravel "dreaming phase."

Instagram may seem like a new technology, but its communication dynamics rely on familiar tropes. In the past, travel writers used writing, drawing, painting, and photography to tell others about their travel exploits. As it does today, travel writing in its early stages allowed readers to imagine far-flung lands and "exotic" peoples they would never be able to encounter in person. Classic travel accounts also informed and educated readers about distant cultures and societies, competing with anthropology as an educational and literary tool. Instagram draws on that time-worn tradition but, notably, it introduced two key features that travelogues never quite had: immediacy and gratification by approbation.

Like Facebook posts, Instagram posts are optimized for the accumulation of "likes" by followers. "Likes" are currency; their symbolic power bestows a gratifying aura on their recipients. Such approbation tends to be immediate and powerfully reinforcing. So, where an early twentieth-century traveller might have had to wait years to receive approbation upon publishing a book, an early twenty-first-century traveller can receive gratifying attention from friends and followers around the world in minutes.

Those "likes" and the prospect of accumulating new followers are powerful motivators. Instagrammers that have become popular for their travel images can have hundreds of thousands of followers, and some are powerful influencers. All of this makes Instagram a serious player in the world of travel and tourism. Instagram, to get to the point, commodifies both the traveller and the experiences afforded by travel destinations. Travel, in an Instagram world, is a quest for the photogenic.

There are many reasons we decided to visit Iceland as part of our journey, and Instagram is one of them. Iceland has an undeniable visual mystique. Fire, ice, infinite glaciers, odd rock formations, mighty waterfalls, desert landscapes populated by verdant mosses, and a nature unlike any other on this side of the moon make Iceland a truly unique place to share on social media. As a result, Iceland is a favourite subject of countless Instagram influencers whose images make every corner of the windswept Arctic island as impossibly beautiful as one could dream (there are over 14 million posts hashtagged "Iceland" on Instagram).

But there is another reason Iceland ended up on our itinerary: a unique park named Thingvellir. Thingvellir National Park was inscribed on the UNESCO World Heritage List for its cultural value as the assembly site of one of the world's oldest examples of parliamentary democracy. But it was also on the World Heritage Tentative List as a mixed site. A "natural wonder on a global scale," the inscription on the list reads, Thingvellir features a unique "magnificent showcase in geology and biology and an extraordinary ecosystem."

To us, Thingvellir offered a fantastic opportunity to witness natural and cultural dynamics entangling with one another in a place that was easy to access, explore, and show off on social media. Given its central location, we thought we'd make Thingvellir a basecamp of sorts to launch expeditions to the rest of the South and West Coast.

As Spring Break 2019 approached, we pulled Autumn out of school a few days early and jetted to Keflavik, Iceland's main international airport. That airport had received a record 2.3 million tourists the year before, but Iceland's growth in visitations (an increase of "only" 5.5 percent from 2017) had experienced its first slowdown in over two decades. "Iceland used to be the hottest tourist destination," a *USA Today* newspaper article noted as we arrived in the country. "What happened?"

Just days before our departure, WOW Air – a low-cost Icelandic carrier – had declared bankruptcy and shut its doors, leaving thousands of travellers stranded. As Iceland rebounded from its financial crisis, the Krona gained back against major currencies – making a very expensive country even more prohibitively expensive. There were other key economic variables at play, but the real reason for the slowdown was subtle. "We've been seeing more 'Instagrammable' remote destinations grow in popularity over the last year," Jennifer Dohm, head of PR for the Americas at Hotels.com, astutely observed in the *USA Today* article. Iceland was a fading trend.

We entered Reykjavik during a downpour of sleet. Our plan for the weeks ahead focused on the so-called Golden Circle, a road loop connecting key tourist sights. We recognized that more discerning influencers would have scoffed at our itinerary. But we weren't there to gain followers by uncovering well-kept secrets. We simply wanted to follow the well-worn tracks Instagram users had been tracing for the last decade. We wanted to see what had gone into all those square frames, to understand what Iceland was really like behind all those digital filters and how Icelanders felt about it.

To help us plan our itinerary and meet people, we reached out to a Reykjavik-based gatekeeper Thorildur Heimisdottir. Thorildur had recently completed a master's in environmental sciences at the University of Iceland, and her thesis focused on an unusual tourist attraction: volcanic eruptions. In her mid-twenties, she seemed understated and impeccably discreet on first meeting, but her quick wit and sarcasm began to shine through as we got to know her. One of the first people she introduced us to was her thesis supervisor, Anna Dóra Sæþórsdóttir. Anna Dóra greeted us with an expansive smile in her sunlit office in the Faculty of Life and Environmental Sciences, a hypermodern addition to the University of Iceland's sprawling urban campus. She was familiar with some of our writings and we with some of hers. Because she and Thorildur had been working together for the last few years, it felt a bit like a reunion among lost friends.

"Tourism has grown very fast in Iceland for the last few years," she told us. Since 2010, it had been growing at least 20 percent a year, with growth peaks between consecutive years as high as 40 percent. "So, it's a huge growth," she reflected, "far too fast in my opinion."

"Why too fast?"

"We haven't been able to keep up with our growth. We haven't been able to formulate regulations. We haven't been able to develop infrastructure or even decide what places we want to have as tourist destinations and what places we don't, and how we want to integrate tourism into society. So, when things happen that fast, we can run into troubles."

"How did it all start?"

"The big eruption in Eyjafjallajökull put Iceland on the world map of tourist destinations, and since then, there have been all kinds of marketing campaigns. People in the tourism industry were really worried after the eruption. They were worried that tourism would kind of collapse. So these big marketing campaigns started, showing how Iceland is a hip and cool destination, attracting new market groups, young people who can use social media."

The volcanic eruption grounded all air travel between North America and Europe for a week in April 2010. Attention and curiosity turned to Icelandic volcanoes and the country's remarkably unique natural landscapes. Images from Iceland inundated not only the news but also the silver screen. *Interstellar, The Secret Life of Walter Mitty, Prometheus, Oblivion, Noah, Captain America, Fast and Furious 8,* and *Game of Thrones* were just a few of the productions filmed in Iceland during the second decade of the twenty-first century. All of them cast Iceland as a mystical, other-worldly land governed by irresistible forces of nature.

Eighty percent of people who visit Iceland, Anna Dóra told us, come for nature. Young Americans are the key new market, outgrowing visitors from Continental Europe. Yet despite growth, most tourists continue to concentrate their visits on the classic destinations along the Ring Road, Iceland's main highway, which completes a circle around the island. "Those are the iconic places known on social media," Anna Dóra observed. "You can drive around this Ring Road, and you can stay in nice accommodations and kind of have adventures during the day and luxury in the evening."

Our advance planning revealed how efficient everything was, from transport and weather forecasts to accommodations and access. Anna Dóra confirmed this was part of a strategy. "Icelanders want their local nature attractions to be accessible, so tourists can go there, so they can sell accommodation or food. So they want everything to be so accessible."

But accessibility created problems. When a place is too accessible, it draws too many people, decreasing their enjoyment of the natural environment. "But it's also bad for business," Anna Dóra added, "because you want people to stay as long as possible in your community. You don't want them to hurry, because then they are out of your area, and they stay somewhere else. So you want to build hindrances for them so they have to stay long."

Yet most visitors stay in Iceland for five to seven days. So, when many of them are on a mission to check Instagrammable spots off their list, speed and accessibility matter a great deal. As a result, what many Instagram posts don't tell you is that what appears to be wilderness is often just a spot along the road, perhaps no more than a few hundred metres from a parking lot and a crowded trail.

Icelanders go elsewhere in search of domestic wildness – to the Highlands, a large region in the interior that is virtually inaccessible outside of summer. "Too bad you can't go to the Highlands at this time of year," Anna Dóra commented as we bade her farewell. "You would love it there." We would have, for sure, but searching for wild nature in the least expected places seemed more intriguing. And in Iceland, wildness could be found anywhere, any time.

Some of that wildness appeared on the front step of our cabin along the eastern shore of Lake Thingvellir the next day. It formed overnight, above us, in the shape of storm clouds. At first, the nimbostratus looked threatening but familiar. Then the clouds metamorphosed into a monstrous gargoyle that spat frozen pellets and breathed barbarian winds that swallowed the lake right before our eyes. Then the clouds engulfed the sky. Within minutes, the winds got so strong that opening our cabin door became impossible. The storm subsided a full day later. In Iceland, we soon learned, remoteness does not dictate wildness, as it may do elsewhere in the world. The weather – which happens anywhere and any time without a word of caution – is truly the spirit of all Icelandic wildness.

As soon as the roads cleared, we travelled back to Reykjavik, about an hour away, for an interview with Ari Trausti Guðmundsson, a man who wore many hats. A geologist, well-known writer and poet, documentarian, broadcaster, journalist, and mountaineer, Ari Trausti had just turned seventy, but he seemed at least ten years younger. With a modesty so typical of Nordic people, he skimmed through his list of accomplishments when we asked him to introduce himself to the camera, but we knew he had also worked as a teacher, consultant, and lecturer on earth science, environmentalism, and tourism issues. He had been a presidential candidate in 2012 and was a Green Party member of the Icelandic Parliament.

"We started to advertise Iceland as something special in the 1990s," he told us over a cup of flat white. "And then maybe we had one hundred or two hundred thousand guests per year." Still, around 2010, Iceland saw only about five hundred thousand visitors per year. "But then – some people say it has to do with the eruption of Eyjafjallajökull and Iceland being in the headlines everywhere – the campaigns that had been going on for more than a decade prior to the eruption started to pay off." By then, Icelandair had built a solid network of connections around the world. At the same time, a campaign called "Iceland Naturally" had made a significant impact on people's image of the country.

"Even I was used as a scientist, as a media person. I was sent around in Europe by the state to talk to business firms, tourist offices, agencies, and the media," Ari Trausti recounted. "I went to eight or nine countries to tell them the eruption was over, and it was okay to come. We were trying to sort of lure people back." In the next few years, hundreds of thousands of young visitors started flocking to the small island, which had only 365,000 residents.

One of those young visitors was fellow Canadian Justin Bieber. "The Biebs" – who is famous for many things, but his sense of responsibility is not one of them – shot a music video for his latest hit, "I'll Show You," in various locations in the south of the country. The social and environmental impact of his choices were starting to show.

"If you look at some of the most popular tourist destinations, they are under serious pressure," Ari Trausti said. "We have even had to close some of them – for example, one of the canyons that Bieber was sort of advertising half-naked somewhere, Fjarðárgljúfur, it's called." Bieber's fans were flocking to the spots shown in the video, causing massive soil erosion. "And then you have places like Vik in the South," he continued, "where things are too crowded. We have about 350 inhabitants who are receiving 2 to 3 million tourists per year."

Though the crowding was almost tolerable in early April, when we were there, the situation would get much worse during the summer. "You go to the Gullfoss waterfalls, you queue up, and in your photographs, you can see people from the parking lot all the way down to the waterfall, a queue of fifteen hundred to two thousand people going both ways." This caused accidents, Ari Trausti said. People had fallen off cliffs, and drownings in places like Vik's black sand beach, Reynisfjara, were becoming more and more common. When we were in Reynisfjara, we noticed many people carelessly turning their backs to the waves to capture the sea in their photographs, placing themselves at risk of getting caught in the undertow that formed right on the shore.

Autumn photographing Gullfoss

One of the newest social problems was uncontrolled growth in Airbnb accommodations. More than any other place we visited, Iceland had a high number of short-term rental properties and few hotels outside of the city. As was happening elsewhere in the world, Ari Trausti explained, the Airbnb industry was providing property owners such as farmers with a meaningful second source of income, but it was also destabilizing the countryside, turning farming and fishing families into service workers. This trend had driven up rents for residents and had led to an unequal concentration of capital as more non-resident landlords owned increasing numbers of rental units.

"The tourist industry was very important for us to recover our economy after the big crash in 2008," Ari Trausti observed, but "there are NGOs, scientists, people in the industry even, wanting us to slow down. And then there are people like Anna Dóra or myself, talking about cutting capacity limits. And this is rather new. And I'm the first member of Parliament to mention this."

Wild nature attracts tourists to Iceland's countryside, but many seek a taste of it in the immediate periphery of Reykjavik. A small city by European standards – it has a population of about 150,000 – Reykjavik is surrounded by the sea and mountains. As a result, it's easy to escape its light pollution to experience the Aurora Borealis.

But the Northern Lights can't be seen during the late spring and summer months, when Iceland basks in daylight nearly twenty-four hours a day, so many tourists keen on seeing them and showing them off on their Instagram account travel to Iceland during fall and winter. Capturing the Aurora Borealis on camera, however, is extremely difficult. First, you have to stay up at night. Second, you won't see them if the cloud cover is too thick. Third, they show up whenever they feel like it. And lastly, even if you're fortunate enough to see them with the naked eye, to capture them on camera you need serious gear and advanced knowledge of long-exposure photography techniques.

But fear not. The Northern Lights Center, one of Reykjavik's latest tourist draws, is there to give everyone a sense of the elusive solar winds whether they grace the open sky or not. The sleek multistorey interactive "museum" offers a hands-on experience of "magnificent auroral displays captured all over Iceland and projected onto a 7-meter wide screen in 4K quality." It also allows visitors to stroll through interactive exhibits to "discover history and secrets about the world's most stunning natural phenomenon."

It also offers photography workshops and tours, such as the popular Northern Lights Superjeep Tour. The excursion costs US$165 and features a guided premium tour in a warm Jeep, pickup and drop-off anywhere in Reykjavik, quality photos taken by pros, a retry in case of a nonsighting, and homemade hot chocolate.

The Northern Lights are a strong magnet for Asian tourists, we learned from YingYing, an international graduate student from China introduced to us by Thorildur. YingYing and her roommate, Michelle, a graduate student from the United States, invited us to their on-campus flat for lunch and a conversation on tourism in Iceland – the subject of their research. Both in their twenties, they knew a thing or two about being millennial visitors in Iceland, the key target audience of countless tourist marketing campaigns.

YingYing had been in Iceland for a year, she told us as we chopped veggies for a stir fry. Besides studying for a master's in tourism, she worked at a hotel in downtown Reykjavik. Before that, she'd worked at the Icelandic Embassy in Beijing for four years. The Northern Lights were bringing increasing numbers of tourists from eastern Asia, she said, many of them millennials who learned about Iceland from social media.

"Fifty-one percent of tourists in Iceland are millennials," Michelle jumped in as she made quick work of chopping a carrot. "In the past few years, there have been a lot of budget flights coming to Iceland, so it's been possible for younger people on a budget to come and travel here. They kind of do their own thing: hitchhiking, sometimes couch surfing, that sort of thing." Michelle's thesis was on millennial tourists, and she had interviewed several of them. Most of those tourists told YingYing and Michelle that their destinations were the usual ones around the South Coast.

"But it's really expensive to be here," we said. "How do people in their late twenties or early thirties cope with two-hundred-dollar restaurant meals?"

"Have you heard of Bónus?" Michelle asked, eliciting a roar of laughter from YingYing and Thorildur, who apparently also shopped at the discount grocery store chain.

"Chinese tourists have found different ways to save," YingYing added. "Most of them rent cars by pooling with strangers – other tourists from their country."

"What do you mean?"

"They've never met before. They don't really know the people that they're travelling with. They all meet online, on WeChat, for the most part. They share costs with strangers who would like to travel to the same place, and they rent one car. It's four people, one car, and then they book their accommodation on Airbnb, and they cook together." That explained why nearly every car driven by young Asians had been full.

We sat down to eat, and Michelle asked us if we had seen tourists pose for Instagram at nearby nature sights. We told her it had been a source of amusement to us. Waterfalls were especially popular, we'd noticed. It seemed to us that few people were there to enjoy a waterfall – most tourists seemed more concerned with finding the right angle to photograph their partner or fit in the frame as a couple.

"You want to get your back to the camera, and you want to be look-ing at the waterfall, and then you want a picture of yourself like that!" Michelle said. We all laughed. "Or maybe you want to hold that person's hand and have your back there!" she went on. "Or maybe you want a picture of your hand with the ring because you've just been engaged in front of the waterfall."

"Or how about finding a cliff, a promontory of sorts, and standing there contemplating the vista below you?" we added.

"It's all about the photograph," Michelle said. "People come for a few minutes, they take their photographs, they do all of that, and then they leave. I don't think people really actually absorb a site so much."

"When I was interviewing people hiking," Michelle continued, "I found that people saw pictures on Instagram, and that's why they were there. Iceland is a photogenic place. You can't take a bad picture of Iceland, wherever you are. I do think social media have a huge role in making destinations, especially for the younger demographics."

Michelle remembered that one of her research participants had told her she'd seen pictures of her ex-boyfriend and his new girlfriend hiking an Icelandic trail. "And she was, like, 'Well, if he can do that, I can do that too!' And so she booked the ticket and then hiked the same trail. There are certain places on trails where people stop and take pictures, and it is always the same place being photographed over and over. So it's almost, like, 'All right, check, I did that,' you know?"

It wasn't just trails. Justin Bieber, they told us, had turned a remote abandoned plane wreck into a major sightseeing site. Then there were the famed Icelandic horses, which every driver seemed keen on pulling over to photograph, regardless of the traffic. And, of course, they wanted pictures of the purple lupines (which, as it happens, is an invasive plant species in Iceland). These sites and sightings had become visual clichés, running jokes, but the situation was no laughing matter: there were more and more political discussions on the need to close certain popular trails to avoid further damage and erosion.

"Is there wildness in Iceland?" we asked.

"When we ask ourselves that, we have to remember the expectations and backgrounds of tourists," YingYing cautioned. Many of the Chinese tourists she researched came from big cities and, for them, it was sometimes enough to simply drive on the wild Icelandic roads. "They would be happy with the beautiful scenery, around the car, even though the car is still moving. You don't even have to be close to certain sites to enjoy the scenery."

Wildness is in the eye of the beholder, and as much as we found people constantly posing for pictures annoying, we understood that there was a cultural dynamic at play. Wild nature is mighty, undomesticated, fierce. Adventurers around the world and throughout history have always made a point of documenting their exploits in wild natural settings through writing and photography. Social media, camera phones, and GoPro's have democratized the visual documentation of adventure. And so it matters little that you walked only ten minutes to take that picture at Gulfoss. Your family, friends, and social media followers back home in Philadelphia or Shanghai don't know how convenient it was to get there and don't expect you to risk your life to chase remote waterfalls. They simply look at your photos and wish they were there. And maybe they'll get there next year and find it just as wild as you did.

Tourist photos endow people with symbolic capital. By taking and sharing your pictures, the aura of a place is bestowed upon you. You reveal yourself as someone affluent enough, knowledgeable enough, adventurous enough, hip enough to be there. But by taking and sharing aesthetically pleasing photography and video, and by sharing it on Vimeo or your travel blog, you're also telling your friends and followers back home something else – that you have artistic sensibilities, that you have the technical skills to evoke natural wonders. And in the end, that is no different than what Romantic painters and writers did as part of their travels in wild nature. They, too, craved "likes."

Wildness is a symbolic commodity – whether we like it or not. It is a commodity if you're selling IMAX theatre seats, it is a commodity if you're taking people to see the Northern Lights in warm Super Jeeps, and it is a commodity if you place yourself in the middle of it and record your presence there with your smartphone to accumulate social capital. And it's an especially valuable commodity if you're a photogenic country that doesn't have a lot of fish remaining in the ocean, or topsoil to grow crops.

Thingvellir National Park is located about forty kilometres northeast of Reykjavik. A small park – only 92.7 square kilometres – Thingvellir is cut into two distinct halves by Highway 36. The most frequently accessed area of the park, right off the highway, is a small relatively flat valley on the northern shore of Thingvallavatn Lake. It includes the park's headquarters, the famous rift valley, the church, and the lakeshore. The section of the park to the left of the highway and a couple of kilometres from the headquarters includes a small information centre with a café and a gift shop, a campground, and an infrequently accessed mountain range.

The park was established in 1930. In 2004, it was inscribed on the World Heritage List. Though the park was gazetted by the Icelandic government for its historical and geological significance, UNESCO at first recognized it only for its cultural value as the site of the Althing, Iceland's parliamentary assembly, established in 930.

"Thingvellir" is a word derived from Old Norse meaning "assembly (*Thing*) fields (*Vellir*)." The Thing or Althing wasn't just a Parliament in the modern sense: it was Iceland's central public square. At Thingvellir, chieftains met, traded, exchanged stories, and wove together a shared history and community. They travelled there from different parts of Iceland, and their journeys ranged from a day to two weeks. When they met, they formed a unique temporary community. They built dwellings out of turf and rock and stayed in them for up to two weeks. Merchants gathered to sell goods and services. Entertainers performed. People played games.

Tourists at Geysir

The Althing held its last session at Thingvellir in 1798 and eventually moved to the modern capital, Reykjavik, but it constitutes one of the earliest instances of parliamentary democracy in the world. Yet there are no ancient buildings on the site like you might see in a place such as Rome or Athens. Even the church is relatively new, as its predecessor was destroyed in a fire in the early twentieth century. Memories of the Althing are now told by interpreters, who take small groups of visitors on a short hike along the rift valley that marks the split between the North American and Eurasian tectonic plates. The rift is Thingvellir's most recognizable sight and geological wonder, a narrow alley carved between two high rock walls. One of those walls is North America, the other Europe.

Tourists typically walk the trail in the middle of the valley to a picturesque waterfall called Öxarárfoss and then walk back to head to the next destination on the Golden Circle. Visitors with more time explore the church grounds, the fissures at Silfra Lake – a popular scuba-diving site – and the interpretive centre, which features interactive displays focused on Thingvallavatn Lake's history, geology, and biodiversity. Golden Circle bus tour visitors spend on average forty-five to ninety minutes at Thingvellir before moving on to Geysir. Those with their own wheels spend a similar amount of time, or perhaps a few hours. Icelandic families camp at Thingvellir during the summer but not as frequently as they used to. There are no hotels, no resorts, no restaurants.

Knowing we had a full week at Thingvellir, Thorildur set up meetings with all staff and researchers, tour guides, and business owners and operators. On our first day on-site, we met Harald, a German expat who had come to Iceland in 2006 to complete a master's degree in environment and natural-resource management. After graduation, he got involved in research and found employment with the park, first as a ranger and then as a project manager. He understood our interest in the interconnection between nature and culture, and he planned to take us on a short hike to show us a few noteworthy sights.

But we had to wait for the snowstorm to end. "We have a few minutes before the next one starts," Harald advised. "So let's be ready, on standby." In the meantime, in the comfort of the interpretive centre, he told us that the site itself wasn't as pristine as it appeared. The venue of the assembly had seen as much clearing as the rest of the park. Trees taken for firewood had never regrown, but some non-native evergreens had been replanted in the area recently (by Thorildur's dad, among others) to beautify the park. "And this was a farming area as well," Harald added. "We had actually three farms in this area until the late eighteenth to twentieth century."

The snowstorm stopped, and we took our chance. We walked outside behind a small, orderly wave of tourist clusters who spoke American

English, Mandarin, German, Italian, Spanish, and British English. We told Harald the place was busier than we thought. This was nothing, he said. Traffic on any given summer day could be five times heavier. "Two out of three visitors come to Thingvellir," he told us. "Thingvellir in 2018 saw about a million and a half visitors."

After a short descent, the trail evened out. There was a thin layer of snow on the ground, but the unevenness of the terrain made it possible for green patches of grass and moss to break the continuity of the snowy landscape. The rock walls, as high as thirty metres on each side, were dark and blocky in appearance, and while the landscape around us wasn't spectacular, it was unmistakably and uniquely Icelandic. The country's flag, mounted on a tall flagpole, flapped in the wind. "Once, a visitor from the US," Harald said as we approached the flagpole, "complained that if there was an Icelandic flag on the Eurasian side of the rift valley, then there should be an American one on the North American tectonic plate."

Even though the weather forecast had been accurate – it cautiously called for snow, hail, freezing rain, strong winds, cloud cover, and sun breaks – many of the tourists looked woefully unprepared. Some wore flimsy shirts, Sunday church shoes, and rain jackets purchased from a convenience store. Others had gone overboard in the other direction, donning parkas, furry Arctic boots, and après-ski gear that would look more appropriate on the high streets of Aspen or Cortina. Selfie sticks were as common as rain umbrellas – both were equally cumbersome and annoying.

Harald sensed our disdain for some of the more boorish visitors. "We do run into troubles where people are getting lost on the track. We have more visitors who are here for, as I call it, an 'online pilgrimage.' They come to a place because they have seen an image, and they want to recreate it in order to diversify themselves from their friends, leaving their own online mark, basically."

Thingvellir wasn't just famous on social media. Old media had been there too. If you're a *Game of Thrones* fan, you'll recognize Thingvellir as the location of Arya's and Sandor Clegane's journey and the fight between Brienne and the Hound – among other scenes. The pass to the impregnable Eyrie was also staged there, at the rift between the tectonic plates. And if you're a Nine Inch Nails fan, take a look at the album cover of *The Fragile*. You'll see Thingvellir's famous waterfalls in the background.

We continued walking until we reached the infamous site known in the days of the Sagas and today as the "Drowning Pool." This was no fiction. It was a small pond where women were drowned for breaking marital or sexual rules. Rocks were attached to their bodies before they were thrown into the deep waters. Not too far from the Drowning Pool, there was a fissure in the ground where men had been hanged. Because of the absence of trees in the area, they were hanged underground from the cleft ground above.

"Um, we also have a burning stake and a beheading place if you're interested," Harald said, sensing our curiosity for the macabre. "It's just like a little bit below."

A mean freezing rain came out of nowhere, lashing sideways at our cameras and skin. We told Harald we'd take a rain check. Just as well, he said. He had some business to tend to anyway. We'd pick up the conversation the following day, which, the forecast promised, would have a couple of hours of sunlight.

This was far from the first time our plans had changed because of the weather. Though we'd scheduled our meetings well in advance, in typical northern European fashion, in Iceland, time was deeply entangled with weather. When the weather turned, plans shifted without much fuss. And when the promise of a good day presented itself, people jumped at the opportunity and did whatever they needed to get done.

This sense of opportunism was deeply ingrained in the national psyche, and it stemmed back to the attitude that fishing folk held toward the sea. Short-term opportunism drifted into the way business and even the national economy were run. Some had even blamed this attitude for Iceland's financial crisis, when the banks jumped at the chance for short-term gain and loss. So perhaps the temporary boom in tourism fuelled by social media was like that too – a window of good weather. People filled their nets for as long as they could and then moved on to something else when the weather changed again.

Though tourists seek Icelandic wildness wherever it can be found, from the sky to the volcanic floors and everywhere in between, the country has a specific legal definition of wilderness, rooted in the Nature Conservation Act. A wilderness in Iceland had to be 25 square kilometres, or an area large enough in size where one could enjoy solitude and the natural landscape without being disturbed by traffic or human structures. That area also had to be at least five kilometres away from human-made structures such as roads, dams, and power lines. Not only is the definition mind-numbingly precise, but it was clearly written about a precise place: the Highlands, where power lines, dams, and roads had been historically absent but were now making their threatening advance.

Aside from environmental concerns, there was something emotional and romantic in the Icelandic definition of wilderness: a feeling of solitude. Iceland is ranked as the world's fifth least densely populated country behind Mongolia, Namibia, Australia, and Suriname. With 3.6 people per square kilometre, Iceland is just a tad more densely populated than Canada, which has 4 people per square kilometre. Why was it, we wondered, that Icelanders, just like Canadians and Australians, craved solitude in the wilderness so much when solitude was common outside of officially recognized wilderness zones?

Harald thought it had to do with what he called an "emotional burden." The emotional burden, he hypothesized when we met him the next day, is based on guilt. There is a sense of guilt, he told us, that comes with the realization of our environmental sins, a sense of guilt that invests relatively untouched spaces and human dwellers with the responsibility of salvation.

"We have this romantic view of the wilderness being untamed," he explained, as "having somehow almost escaped our sins, and that's why we need to preserve it, but we also need to conquer it in order to rediscover our boundaries." He told us that Icelanders had this attitude about the Highlands, above all other places.

Anna Dóra's research into the Icelandic perception of wilderness shows that most of the areas considered wilderness are located in the central Highlands. Yet, whereas 93 percent of the Highlands were considered wilderness in 1936, by 2010, only 21 percent fell into that category.

But, as her research shows, these numbers are subjective. People attune themselves differently to human-made structures that influence the experience of solitude. However, despite individual differences, Icelanders tended to view all areas above three hundred metres of altitude as wilderness, especially if the areas had an open and homogeneous landscape marked by no human-made infrastructural landmarks such as buildings, power lines, roads, or industrial developments. Over 90 percent of her respondents considered wilderness important or very important to the country, and over two-thirds felt it was at risk.

But perhaps the biggest threat to the Icelandic wilderness, besides hydroelectric dam developments, was the infrastructure that Instagram relied on. Even the most remote spots in the country had been seen and photographed. Wildness was still in the air everywhere, but by its own definition, Iceland was witnessing its rapid decline.

As upset as we were by our inability to visit the Highlands in the springtime, we felt an odd sense of relief. After five years of travel, we welcomed not going somewhere. Not knowing, not seeing, not writing about a place, not filming it or photographing it made it feel less tame, less accessible, less welcoming, and ultimately wilder, even if only in our imagination. For all the contempt we might have toward the Instagramification of the world, in shooting a documentary video about a place, we weren't much different. It felt good to keep our digital footprints out of a place for once.

Wildness faces many threats, chiefly environmental and politico-economic. But communicative threats are also intense. When we photograph or video record a place, when we share our images and sounds with others who have not been there, we leave digital footprints that threaten the integrity of our ecological imagination. Some of the power that wildness exercises rests in our individual imaginations, in our ability to close our eyes and fantasize, and in our inability to Google every corner of our planet. But as more and more wild places become exposed by our digital thirst for documentation, we lose our fancy and our fascination with the wild. It, too, becomes just another place to tag.

It would be good if we could all rewild our imagination by recording less, by sharing less, by scrolling down less. In fact, a growing number of people around the world are starting to practise a different kind of "Leave No Trace" – a bona fide digital leave no trace. "Leave No Trace" is the mantra behind a campaign launched in 1987 by the United States Forest Service, the Bureau of Land Management, and the National Park Service. The campaign is based on a few simple principles: plan ahead and prepare, travel and camp on durable surfaces, dispose of waste properly, leave what you find, minimize the impact of campfires, respect wildlife, and be considerate of other visitors.

The digital version of this ethical campaign stresses the need to limit social media activities and be mindful of their environmental consequences. Some of the principles include thinking before you geotag, being mindful of what your images portray, being mindful of the platform you have and the people you reach when posting and commenting about the outdoors, encouraging and inspiring people to "Leave No Trace" in social media posts, and giving back to places you love.

Harpa Rún Kristjánsdóttir managed Bókakaffið in Selfoss. She let us in one hour before the business officially opened so we could talk about wildness and Thingvellir, two subjects that matter a great deal to her. With a recently completed master's degree in comparative literature in her pocket, Harpa was also a writer and farmer who helped her parents raise sheep, one cow, and some horses. She had recently published a book titled *In and Out of Sight at Thingvellir*. "In this book," as the publishers put it, "photographers Sigrún Kristjánsdóttir and Pálmi Bjarnason peer beneath the surface to capture unexpected moments beyond the beaten path, while Harpa Rún Kristjánsdóttir's lyrical prose gives voice to the unseen."

When a place is defined as a wilderness, there is the burden of determining what is absent and what is present. Determining presences and absences requires establishing with definitive proof what a place once was and what it now is. Determining absences of human development requires dissecting their traces, which, when found, are doomed as indelible. A wilderness is condemned by its own unwillingness to forget. A wilderness either is or was, with nothing in between.

We reflected with Harpa that if she and her colleagues had been tasked with writing about Thingvellir as a wilderness, they would have had to do forensic ecology to determine what was once alive and what was now dead at the site. But *In and Out of Sight* was no forensic ecology. Unconcerned with Thingvellir's status as wilderness, Harpa and her colleagues searched for wildness instead. Theirs wasn't a forensic science but an art of noticing, of becoming attuned to the whimsical. By becoming attuned and noticing, they saw that the whimsical, the unexpected, the wild was always alive there. The wild made itself known when it willed itself to do so, when someone – unpreoccupied with posing for a selfie or rushing to the next destination – paid attention.

"When I started out," Harpa told us, "I didn't know anything more than the regular Icelander knows about Thingvellir. And I felt kind of, why am I doing this? I'm not the one. But they really wanted me to do the text. So I started by reading almost anything I could get my hands on, and I wrote a bunch of just small proses. And then I went there a couple of times. First, I went at night. It was June, I think. A lot of texts came from there. We went after work on a Monday, and nobody was there. It was empty. And that's what was interesting because it's bright all night. We were there until three o'clock, and it was bright enough to write and sit there in the completely empty nature." In a place empty of tourists, but not alone, Harpa wrote while her colleagues took photographs.

"And then I went again," she continued. "It was late August, in the middle of the day, and it was crowded. And I went to the waterfall, climbed up to the rocks up there, and just sat there to watch the people, and I think one of those texts got into the book, where I was wondering, because everybody had a smartphone, and most of the people weren't even looking at the falls. They were just looking at it through their smartphones, and there I sat with a pen and paper."

The poem reads:

> Every single person that comes here
> hangs on to their phone
> pretty much the whole time.
> And here I sit with a piece of paper, covered in ink.
> Don't you understand word-pictures?

Maybe they will never be good enough,
but they are the best pictures I have,
and always special,
like the ones you keep only in your mind.

"What does wild mean to you?"

"My wilderness is the mountains," Harpa said. "I live close to Hekla, the volcano. So that's my idea of wilderness. My head goes to a different place when I go to a place like that. If I don't go there regularly, I feel that I miss it. I feel I need to go there. I need to go to a mountain just to be alone, and I don't want to see anyone. I think it's a big part of all of us."

That loneliness is sometimes misunderstood. We don't necessarily feel alone when we go to a place like that. We feel we are in the company of a mountain, a volcano, whatever more-than-human life is there. We feel a connection. Harpa worked at a hotel close to Hekla, and she knew some people went there for reasons that were less focused on connecting with the mountains and more focused on connecting with social media followers.

"We had people coming in saying, 'So where's the eruption?' And I was, like, 'There isn't any, and even if there was any, you shouldn't go there. It's not a good idea.' But tourists wanted an eruption. 'You must make one start!' Some people just thought I had a button under there. And I had some very angry guides. They'd tell me, 'I promised the group an eruption, so you're going to have to do something about that!'"

This is the challenge faced by nature in the age of Instagram travel. Nature is in and out of sight, whimsical, governed by the laws of its own will. But consumerism and the Instagramification of the planet demand a nature that is managed, predictable, at the service of people and their smartphones. This is a world that wants a nature that is always in sight, even when people are not really prepared to notice it.

"Wildness" is an odd word, Harpa reflected, "Because we always describe things from the point of view of the human. But there is a poem in the book about the dog's view of the place. I wrote a lot of stuff about the point of view from the flower, or just from the ground, or from a rock." Wild, she noted, is bigger than us humans, but wildness has a mind of its own.

Wilderness always seems to carry a burden, the burden of proving that it is uninhabited, untouched. Wildness, on the other hand, feels carefree and whimsical. Like the Northern Lights, like the weather, wildness comes and goes whenever and wherever it damn well pleases. Unconcerned with how remote, how separate, how disconnected from humans it might seem, wildness does its thing.

Whereas wilderness is burdened with the responsibility of getting away from us, wildness is empowered with the will to make a connection – flashing solar winds over our heads when the camera isn't quite ready or blowing snow at us for just long enough to bury us in our cabins.

"Wilderness" is *víðerni* or óbyggð in Icelandic, which translates in English as uninhabited. But uninhabited by whom? Certainly not by foxes, by seals, or by birds. Certainly not by fairies, winds, or volcanic spirits. Uninhabited by men and women, víðerni or *óbyggð* is an anthropocentric space, a zone defined by and in virtue of humans, regardless of other lives.

In Icelandic, "wild" is *villt,* a word that has the same Anglo-Saxon roots as "wild." Wild is will, aliveness, freedom to manifest itself by its own whims and desires.

But in 2019, wild was something else in Iceland – a photogenic wild. For about a millennium, people had travelled for days and weeks to gather at the assembly fields of Thingvellir. There, they met, traded, and exercised their various degrees of power. People still travelled across Iceland in 2019. But something had changed. People used to assemble as part of the Althing. They gathered to speak, agree, and disagree. They came together, not always peacefully, but together they came. In 2019, people simply passed by. They – most of them at least – gathered with no one but members of their own small parties. Rather than assembling with strangers, they turned their attention on themselves, and the land served as the digital-currency backdrop for their social capital. If they gathered with others, it wasn't there in the fields but rather on Facebook, Instagram, and the virtual world.

Much has been made of the world's rapid exhaustion of its wildness and wild places, and rightly so. The world needs more wild places. But much less has been said about the world's rapidly diminishing ability to understand and appreciate wildness on its own terms, not on the terms of what it can do for each of us and our status updates, or on the terms of its standing on a list of items to be checked off. The world needs more wild, but just as sorely, it needs more people to experience places in the name of wild itself, rather than its digital reproduction and symbolic trade.

9

Wildlife Can Be Us

THAILAND

THE OLD TOYOTA PICKUP had seen better days. The red light mounted on its roof had long stopped working, and the siren no longer worked. Rust ate away at its body, and its many dents had morphed together to form long crevasses above the wheels. Dust and dirt filled its bed, which contained an assortment of rucksacks and two rickety wooden benches, barely long enough to seat three bottoms each.

The benches were bolted loosely to the truck bed and spaced only three feet or so from one another. On the first row sat three soldiers dressed in green fatigues. On the back row sat a soldier on the left; our trusted gatekeeper, Supanat, in the middle; and Phillip on the right.

"Are wild elephants always so punctual?"

"Hold on, let me translate that, Doctor Phillip," Supanat offered. He leaned between the soldiers seated in front and rephrased the question in Thai. The soldiers nodded. One of them spoke for a few seconds. He raised his voice to compete with cars zooming by at eighty kilometres an hour.

"They are pretty punctual," Supanat translated. "They sleep for most of the daytime, wake up right before sunset, and come out to eat and drink around this time."

A small SUV overtook us. Two children in the back seat leaned out the window to wave. The soldiers smiled and waved back.

There was something comforting about the elephants' alleged regularity. Wild as they may be, creatures of habit felt more predictable, less threatening. That they had just woken up made them seem even less menacing. How dangerous could a large, relatively slow pachyderm be before breakfast? As sleepy as they were, could they muster enough speed to outrun the soldiers' decaying truck? Could they be aggressive at all, knowing we were there to help them? Or would they be sleepy and cuddly?

Unlike domesticated animals, wildlife is unpredictable. That is the key characteristic of their subjectivity: their unwillingness to be subdued by the human will. That is what makes them wild. We had travelled to Thailand to understand precisely this: the wildness of wildlife, and whether coexistence with humans is bound to extinguish that wildness. But we hadn't planned for this. We hadn't planned on being in high-speed pursuit of elephants jaywalking across the highway.

It happened quickly. We had spent the morning chasing butterflies at the idyllic Pala-U Waterfall. During lunch, Supanat disappeared. We knew he was on a mission. During our drive to the falls, he'd noticed a wealth of road signs cautioning drivers about elephants on Highway 3218. He went looking for intel.

We were ordering a second round of coconut ice cream when he reappeared. "I spoke to a lady working at that food stand, who told me that elephants come out at six o'clock, almost every night," he revealed.

We glanced at our watches. It wasn't even two o'clock.

"How do we know they're coming out for sure?" we asked. "And where exactly are they coming out? It's a long highway."

Supanat had an idea. We jumped on the van and after a fifteen-minute drive, we spotted a couple of soldiers chilling out at a post by the roadside. Supanat jumped out. He walked toward the soldiers and smiled.

Now imagine how this would go over in America, Europe, China, or – quite frankly – almost anywhere in the world. The soldiers would jump to their feet and read you the riot act. You'd be told, "Move along. Nothing to see here." Safety, protocol, higher-ups' order, blah, blah. And if – a big if – they were more considerate, there'd be telephone calls to make, letters to write, forms to fill out, and on and on. But this was rural Thailand, where a smile gets you further than a form. After a few minutes of chatting the soldiers up, Supanat knocked on the van's side window and gestured at us to come out. The soldiers, each with a lit cigarette dangling daintily from their lips, told us the elephants would come out around six because "that's what they do." If we were interested in joining a patrol, it could probably be arranged by asking one of the bosses.

We jumped back in the van and tracked down the right people in minutes. Smiles, bows, handshakes, introductions, jokes, and laughter went on for a while. And there's a young girl, too, they noticed. How cool. And eventually we heard the question we'd been waiting for: Would you be interested in joining a patrol today?"

With safety in mind, it was determined that Autumn would be better off in the back of a patrol SUV driven by NGO staff. April promptly agreed to keep her company. As for Supanat and Phillip, a spot could be spared on a wooden bench in the bed of the Army pickup. A few more laughs, a few jokes, some fun, and it was time to go get some elephants off the road. We drove off in a caravan formation.

"Supanat, can you ask the soldiers where their rifles are? I don't see any around here," Phillip asked. The elephants' predictability and empty stomachs, after all, were only minor reassurances of safety.

"Rifles? They have no rifles."

"No rifles? What exactly are we using to defend ourselves then?"

"Let me ask." Supanat leaned in to converse with the soldiers.

"Dr. Phillip, look."

One of the soldiers opened up a small baggy. It contained colourful balls the size and shape of a foosball. He had a few dozen in red, green, and blue.

"Our safety plan is to toss foosballs at them?"

"No, they're firecrackers. The soldiers have slingshots. They're going to scare them off the highway with firecrackers."

Elephants are sacred in Thai culture, so hurting them was unthinkable. Even though two soldiers had died over the last decade during separate patrol incidents, the military had forcefully rejected the notion of arming soldiers on the wild elephant watch. Slingshots would have to suffice. Elephants can move surprisingly fast, the soldiers explained. But they have no endurance. In case of trouble, you only have to outsprint them for one hundred metres or so. After that, you'll likely be safe if you keep running or drive away. Our thoughts drifted to how fast the old truck could accelerate.

We'd driven for over forty-five minutes. The sun began its descent and was directly in front of us above the tree-covered hills. New Year's Day 2020 was less than six hours away. While most Thais were getting ready to celebrate, we were pondering the efficiency of foosball-shaped firecrackers, the reach of slingshots, and whether smiles would be enough to calm down cranky elephants jonesing for a quick breakfast.

Highway 3218 is a paved thoroughfare wedged between the coastal city of Hua Hin to the west and Kaeng Krachan National Park's famed Pala-U Waterfall and the Myanmar border to the east. It cuts through meandering hillsides and is flanked by thick vegetation on either side. About twenty kilometres east of the waterfalls, after exiting the small town of Huai Sat Yai, the road re-enters Kaeng Krachan National Park, the home of a few families of wild elephants – about 150 in total – who need to cross the road to go about their daily business.

When they jaywalk, the elephants present a danger to motorists, but even more perilous is their tendency to loiter on the paved surface. A woman we spoke with a few days before recounted how elephants had once blocked the road late at night. One of them approached her car. Then another. She sat paralyzed with fear inside her vehicle while an elephant banged on her windshield with its trunk. She cried and prayed. Minutes felt like hours. The elephants eventually walked away. Unfortunately, other motorists aren't so lucky. Every year, a few deaths are recorded around the country. Road patrols like the one we'd joined were instrumental in keeping both wildlife and drivers safe.

We moved east at a slow speed with no elephants in sight but plenty of signs – large chunks of dung scattered on the road's shoulders and the odd fallen tree. But the vegetation was so thick, we could have missed elephants standing just steps away from the road. One of the soldiers stood in the truck bed. It seemed for a moment that a sighting had been made, but it was a false alarm. We drove with our four-way flashers on – which thankfully still worked. Vehicles passed us, and families waved to us in thanks.

We had mixed feelings about being on patrol. Not seeing wild elephants would be a let-down, for our memories and our cameras. But running into a herd of them, us armed with nothing but slingshots, didn't seem like a family-friendly way to pass New Year's Eve. The sun inched farther below the horizon. Little daylight remained. It was now or never. Seconds later, almost on cue, a driver heading west flashed his high beams and waved. He hollered something in Thai as he whizzed on by.

"Elephants on the road ahead!" Supanat translated.

"Cheeky! Cheeky!" One of the soldiers exclaimed. A second soldier pointed to a right turn in the road about 150 metres ahead. "Cheeky" was the name of the elephant they had spotted. Slowly, unperturbed by cars, Cheeky crossed the road and made his way into the bush. He wagged his tail and pranced with a relaxed demeanour.

We stopped where he headed into the bush. The soldiers hopped off the truck. Some of them were smiling and chatting; a couple of them reached for their phones. Cheeky, explained Supanat, was a well-known elephant and a much-beloved one.

Instead of disappearing completely into the forest, Cheeky had decided to stop about fifteen metres away from the road. He watched us as we watched him. Every few seconds, he broke eye contact to eat some leaves. He wagged his ears and scanned the watch party from left to right, as if to say: "I know what I'm doing. It's all good." His left ear was badly chewed up and missing pieces. That's how he'd been recognized from a distance, Supanat explained.

The quixotic standoff continued for a few minutes. Cheeky tended to linger by the road, and the soldiers were keen to get him moving because a few vehicles continued to trickle by. A soldier plucked a foosball from a baggy and loaded his slingshot. He lobbed a firecracker awkwardly into the bush.

"What kind of a throw was that?"

"Who gave this guy the slingshot?"

The laughter was louder than the explosion. A small puff of blue smoke rose into the air. Peeved, not scared or annoyed, Cheeky seemed to mumble something to himself then wobbled deeper into the bush. Despite the bad throw, our job was done.

We continued to drive in formation. The army truck led, and the SUV followed. After about a kilometre, the driver pulled onto the shoulder, and the soldiers jumped out once again. One of them sprinted ahead, and another turned his attention to oncoming traffic. Someone had spotted something. We walked up the road. The soldier who had sprinted ahead had stopped about twenty metres ahead. A family of elephants materialized out of the bush just steps away.

Huddled together like a rugby team, the elephants' legs seemed entangled. It was difficult to tell how many there were, maybe six, seven, or eight. Two stood out from the others because of their small statures. One was a juvenile, the other a baby. They crossed the road, and two more followed. The slowest one turned its head and nodded at the soldier standing no more than five metres away.

"That was an actual acknowledgment," Supanat explained. "These elephants have gotten to know the soldiers. They can recognize them." Moments later, they were gone, off to grab some breakfast.

We drove for about another half hour and saw another half dozen elephants. Then dusk gave way to near darkness. In the diminished light, we thought it would be best to leave the soldiers alone. As we bade farewell, we were told we were lucky: it was rare for so many elephants to be spotted in a single evening.

Supanat Permpoonwiwat had introduced himself with a gentle and caring smile four days before at the airport in Bangkok. We'd corresponded for weeks before our arrival, planning in detail the itinerary for our journey to Kaeng Krachan National Park, a large protected area that crossed the boundaries of Thailand's Phetchaburi, Ratchaburi, and Prachuap Khiri Khan Provinces. In his mid- to late forties and tall, confident, and extroverted but impeccably discreet, Supanat worked as the director of the Office of Promoting Politics to the People with the King Prajadhipok's Institute in Bangkok. Given that we spoke no Thai, had never spent time in the country, and had limited knowledge of how to best conduct field research in Thailand, we knew Supanat would be an invaluable asset. Little did we know how effective he would be at thinking and acting on his feet and how much our trip would change as a result.

Unlike many hot tourist destinations around the country, Kaeng Krachan National Park is visited almost exclusively by Thai nationals. As a result, the few accommodations near the park's headquarters in the town of Kaeng Krachan developed in accordance with the preferences and expectations of domestic travellers. Having a driver and staying in a resort felt extravagant and excessive. But it was cheap and practical in Thailand, Supanat argued. Vacation rentals were nonexistent around the park and "F," our driver, had a reputation for being reliable, knowledgeable, and inexpensive.

We arrived at night on December 27. Soon after the sun rose the next morning, we made our way to breakfast and got our first glimpse of Nana Resort. Part resort, part complex of small timeshare villas, part venue for family reunions, part something else that we couldn't quite sort out, Nana Resort was a meandering, sprawling complex of gardens, creeks, swimming pools, and halls that had seen better days. Yet it was comfortable and cozy in the way that a fresh coat of paint would have spoiled.

The only non-Thai guests, we walked into an expansive and lively breakfast hall to the sounds of chatter and the smell of breakfast. Supanat's notes, shared over a cup of coffee, contained our work order for the day. First item on the docket: an interview with the chief of staff at Kaeng Krachan's headquarters. Unlike our other destinations, Kaeng Krachan was not yet on UNESCO's World Heritage List. But it almost was. Why it hadn't made it yet was one of the reasons we were there.

In July 2019, the World Heritage Committee had rejected the nomination of Kaeng Krachan because of two ongoing conflicts. The first was a dispute with Myanmar over the park's boundaries. The second was the lack of participation and support from local communities. The park had failed to establish good relations with residents of nearby farming communities, largely because of the ongoing conflict between wildlife and humans.

But the residents' lack of enthusiasm was just the tip of a deeply rotten iceberg. The story begins in 2014 and includes violence and murder. Following a series of unsolved disputes between park administrators and the Karen ethnic minority over land-use rights, park staff forcibly evicted two small villages situated inside the boundaries of Kaeng

Krachan. Park Chief Chaiwat Limlikit-aksorn and his officials also arrested and accused many people of illegal activities in the park.

Among the people arrested was Porlajee Rakchongcharoen, a Karen activist known by the nickname "Billy." Billy was detained for collecting wild honey in the forest, but he viewed his arrest as retaliation for him leading a lawsuit against park staff. Billy and other villagers claimed that the park staff had torched villagers' bamboo huts and rice fields as part of their forced eviction.

Shortly after his arrest, Billy's body was found in the Kaeng Krachan dam reservoir. Just six days before our interview with the new park chief, the Department of Special Investigation had laid six charges against Chaiwat Limlikit-aksorn, including premeditated murder and concealing a body. Officials also charged him and three other staff members with unlawful detention, physical assault, robbery, and malfeasance.

All of this, of course, hampered the World Heritage inscription, so Kaeng Krachan remained for the time being on the Tentative List. Researching a park on the Tentative List was a new experience for us, one that could teach us what it takes to make the list.

Kaeng Krachan wasn't like our usual destinations for other reasons. Formed in 1981, the park is massive in size – at nearly three thousand square kilometres, it is Thailand's largest national park. But, remarkably, the park almost entirely lacks trails, as hiking is seen as too dangerous because of the elephants. Not only is hiking impossible, but so is casual sightseeing. The only road into the park – an 18.5 kilometre stretch from Bang Krang to Phanoen Thung – had recently been deemed impassable because of erosion (and reconstruction had been halted because of opposition from environmental and local groups).

Moreover, the park wasn't particularly gorgeous – at least by conventional standards. Kaeng Kra Chan Lake, the second busiest destination after Pala-U Waterfall, was pretty, but it was a reservoir for a hydroelectric dam. Undoubtedly picturesque at sunset, when the sun bathed the humidity in the air with a warm hue, the lake's shores were busy but unclean.

Regardless of its curb appeal, we decided to visit Kaeng Krachan because of the wild elephants and the existence of numerous initiatives to improve their coexistence with locals. It was also interesting to us that UNESCO kept it on the Tentative List. There can't be any sort of sustainable wildness, we knew by then, unless humans and wildlife, park agencies and local communities learn to accept each other. Supanat lined up for us a series of encounters that reconfirmed that belief and expanded our views on human-wildlife cohabitation unmeasurably.

"Best not to ask too much about the murder case," Supanat reminded us as we pulled into the park headquarters' leafy parking lot. It mattered little – after all, it was the elephants we were after. Mana Permpoon knew this, and he had prepared a presentation. He spoke formally and read from notes as he showed slides. "Wild elephants live in two parts of Kaeng Krachan National Park," he told us through Supanat's translation, "upper and lower part." Huai Kamkrit and Panuentung are the upper part. Pa Deng and Huai Sat Yai are the lower part. "We have three monitoring teams taking care of Pala-U and Pa Deng areas," he continued. "We have five teams responsible for monitoring the Nong Plub area up to Huai Mai Peang. We chase the elephants out of these five areas especially in Special Unit 7, Khoa Hup Tao, and Huai Sat Yai, where elephants usually come out to the road and in the middle of the village."

The park, Mana said, is unique in that it surrounds countless villages. A look at the park's map confirmed this: some villages sat right in the middle of the park. Others lay barely outside it, but they were enclaved into the park's boundaries, surrounded by protected areas on two or three sides.

Mana had been hired as park chief three years before, and he had the challenging task of regaining the locals' trust after Billy's case. Even though the revenues from tourist visits were low, he'd managed to assemble a mighty team of elephant patrollers. The reduction of human-elephant conflict had political value.

"There are about 150 wild elephants in this area near Huai Sat Yai," he said and moved to the next slide. "During the last two to three years, the elephants have been coming to residential areas and agriculture fields. Sometimes, they block the road and stop vehicles in order to find some fruits such as pineapples. Sometimes, they go inside the houses and eat sugar or noodles as well."

As Canadians, we were used to the notion of raccoons sneaking into the backyard to rummage through compost bins or garbage cans, but the thought of elephants barging into our kitchen to snack on noodles gave us pause for thought. Would they unwrap the packages? Would they prefer the spicy kind over the mild variety?

"It is obvious that elephants have moved out of their habitat," Mana went on, "and once they get out of their habitat, we have to take care of them safely. We have to reduce any conflict between people and wild elephants. Impacts are increasing. Sometimes, wild elephants are killed by human beings; sometimes, human beings are killed by wild elephants. Pets are killed. Agricultural products are damaged. The park has to solve these problems."

The problems ran deeper. In 1996, the government increased the conserved forest area within Kaeng Krachan. The expansion resulted in communities moving from the highlands to the lowlands; it expanded residential areas into lands that used to be part of the park's buffer zone. Elephants don't barge into someone's kitchen because they have a hankering for instant ramen. Rather, an alteration in the landscape and increased competition with humans for resources caused the elephants to range into new human settlements in search of food and water. All the authorities could do was reduce the potential for conflict.

"If the elephants come out to the community," Mana explained, almost apologetically, "we will send our staff to take care of them." The staff consisted of park personnel and members of the army who worked in collaboration with subdistrict administrative organizations, district and provincial disaster relief authorities, community leaders, and NGO staffers. For all of them, the learning curve was still steep.

"At the beginning, we didn't know the behaviours of wild elephants," Mana told us off the cuff. "So we used guns or smoke to push them back. We burned vehicle tires during the day and at nighttime. We built chili and pepper fences. We used bees, too – elephants are scared of them. We put nails on wooden planks and even tried electric fences." Mana paused, his brows furrowed. "But one tragedy happened when three elephants were killed by the electric fence."

As time went on, they learned new lessons. The current school of thought favoured a system of ditches and semipermanent fences to lead the elephants away from crops and toward human-made ponds, where they could drink and bathe. In addition, patrols like the one we would join a few days later strove to steer wayward elephants away from roads. All of this effort was accompanied by extensive monitoring and research to better understand elephant movement patterns and behaviour.

But first and foremost, the park had to work to regain the trust of locals. "In the past," Mana acknowledged, "there might have been worries of wrongdoings from park officials. Information was concealed. Now, reconciling communities and park officials can help everyone understand the problems together."

Studies show that much remains to be done. A dozen communities cope with elephants raiding crops, and many residents believe that better, more cooperative management could lead to more sustainable solutions. Advance planning could have pre-empted the problem, as human errors in land-use management had caused croplands and residential areas to expand and fracture the elephants' preferred migration routes.

Elephants are deeply revered in Thai culture and Buddhism, and they have been so for centuries. At one time, the auspicious albino elephant was even featured on the country's flag. Just as Americans might like to say that the West was won with horses, Thais might say that their country wouldn't be what it is if it weren't for the pachyderm.

Today, there are about sixty-five hundred elephants in Thailand – three thousand domesticated, the rest wild. The number of domesticated elephants was much higher in the past, however, when private possession of elephants conferred prestige and status on the owners. Elephants were also employed in traditional warfare; they fought wars alongside soldiers and defended the country from foreign invasions. The logging industry also used elephants to haul, roll, push, and lift teak logs that would have been impossible to move until the advent of modern machinery. Their work indirectly drove agricultural, residential, and ultimately industrial land development.

The deforestation caused by logging, however, led to flash floods by the late twentieth century. Through an emergency decree in January 1989, the Thai government banned logging, putting about two thousand elephants and their *mahouts* (handlers) out of work. Almost overnight, elephants – domesticated and wild alike – went from being beasts of burden to an endangered species.

In the early 1990s, news stories shed light on the plight of elephants, revealing that a few logging companies had been exploiting elephants' labour by injecting them with amphetamines and driving them to work up to 120 hours a week with little to no rest. They also revealed that elephants had been injured and had their legs amputated after stepping on landmines in war-torn territories held by ethnic minorities. And the illegal trade of ivory and live elephants was also exposed, in parallel with increasing international concern over wildlife trade. Within a matter of years, desperate and unemployed mahouts were taking their elephants into the streets of Bangkok and other cities. They panhandled and forced their elephants to perform tricks to attract tourists. A solution to the elephant problem was badly needed.

Making matters even worse, in August 1992 eight wild elephants – including babies – died in a well-publicized incident after falling down the Haew Narok Waterfall in Khao Yai National Park. Needing to act fast to ameliorate the living conditions of elephants around the country, the Thai Elephant Conservation Center (TECC) received a stronger mandate and a bigger budget and went to work.

Within a few years, TECC formed an Elephant Nursery Center, an Elephant Hospital, a Mobile Elephant Clinic, and an Elephant Adoption Project. At the same time, elephants were barred from entering cities – where they were getting hurt with increasing frequency. The organization also launched an Elephant Reproduction Project, which developed methods to facilitate natural breeding and artificial insemination under the supervision of the newly formed Elephant Breeding Center. In 1997, the Elephant Reintroduction Project was founded to solve the problem of unemployed domestic elephants and restore the genetic biodiversity of the wild elephant population in conservation areas.

With an expanded mandate, the TECC was transformed in 2002 into the National Elephant Institute under the patronage of Her Royal Highness Princess Galyani Vadhana. The NEI proceeded to draft the

Protection and Conservation of Elephants as the National Symbolic Animal Act to manage domesticated elephants. The NEI also put in place a Master Plan for National Elephant Conservation to preserve both wild and domesticated elephants and facilitate ways for them to live in harmony with forests and people while retaining their dignity as the nation's symbolic animal.

Over the next few days, following our interview with Mana, we toured fences: kilometres and kilometres of fences built around agricultural fields and the forested areas surrounding Huai Sat Yai. The hands of staff from multiple organizations and subdistricts had been put to work to build them. People took great pride in them, and most of our interviews ended with field trips to the nearest fence. Cadres of officials would accompany us for the sake of a photo-op.

Fence spotting had become a bit of a social outing. Whereas an interview elsewhere in the world might adjourn to a café or a restaurant, in Thailand, we'd stop the recorder, leap into the bed of a Toyota Hilux, and continue the conversation beside cement columns and lines of rebar. All of this unfolded just a few kilometres outside of inhabited areas, sometimes steps away from agricultural fields, where flummoxed farmers speculated about the unannounced visits of local politicians, NGO directors, army staff, and camera-wielding foreigners.

On one particularly warm afternoon, we were led by a cadre of district and subdistrict administrators down bush roads that felt more uneven than usual. We hopped on and off the trucks every few hundred metres, the administrators in casual business attire and us in sweaty T-shirts. The rhythmic ruckus temporarily halted the whir of bugs and the chirp of invisible birds.

The landscape wasn't much, but there were remarkable watering holes to be seen. Some holes were the size of swimming pools, others had the looks of ponds, and a few had the distinct shape of water reservoirs. Near all of them, in muddy ground hardened by weeks of continuous sunlight, we found elephant prints. The holes were meant for the elephants to bathe in and drink from, Supanat explained as he struggled to translate the chorus of enthusiastic officials telling their favourite elephant anecdotes. A lot of care had gone into making these holes not just efficient but practical and cozy.

A few kilometres away, down a bumpy track that cut through languid landscapes drenched by the sun in the dry season's parched sky, was the Wildlife Conservation Society's office building. It rested on the shore of a small lake called Haui Phu Sai. A bronze statue of an elephant family welcomed us at the door, moments before Manoon Pleusunoon, young and diminutive, popped his flip-flops and greeted us with a skip in his step. "You can call me Ki," he said in perfect North American English.

Ki – nicknames are very popular among Thais – was a PhD student at the University of Massachusetts, but he was in Thailand to collect data for his dissertation on elephant conservation. During his stay, he was also in charge of the Waluk Preservation Project in Kaeng Krachan National Park. Friendly, laid-back, and keen to share his knowledge, Ki explained that one of his responsibilities was to mitigate conflict between humans and wild elephants. "There are three big projects here. One is the smart patrol, which is to implement systematic patrols in the area and improve law enforcement. The second one is monitoring key wildlife species. We have to monitor how our patrol causes change or benefits them. And the last project is human-animal conflict. We try to develop mitigation techniques to minimize the impact or the conflict between humans and elephants."

The conflict was considerable. Minutes before our interview, we, Supanat, and F had stopped for a quick drink at the leafy Dusita Garden and Coffee Shop just down the road. On hearing why we were in town, the owner told us that a family of elephants had visited her the night before, causing damage to her outbuildings. Her neighbours were receiving regular visits, too, she underlined.

Ki and the Wildlife Conservation Society's greatest concern, however, was crop raiding. After trying out different techniques, Ki explained, they'd found that "the most effective one involves people." We smiled in agreement. "We started with a normal fence that could help people locate where elephants are. When elephants came, the villagers would form a team, called a collaborative mitigation, to drive the elephants back to the forest. From the information data that we have, it is very successful in one small subdistrict where we tried it. That work lowered the number of elephants because it made it harder for elephants to get access to pine-apple fields. But it's not going to work for every subdistrict."

Through their work with other subdistricts, they had come up with another idea, which they called the mobile- or night-response team. Whenever locals heard firecrackers – a sign that farmers somewhere were trying to scare off elephants – NGO staff and volunteers would rush to help the villagers drive the elephants back into the forest. This simple stratagem had reduced crop damage by 50 percent. We weren't talking about large-scale agriculture or big profits. Reducing crop damage by 50 percent could be the difference between a respectable life and going hungry.

Supanat conversing with Thai military personnel about the semipermanent fences

"Are the fences we've been seeing part of the solution?" April asked.

"Yes," Ki said. "The most recent one is called the 'semipermanent fence.'" A semipermanent fence is a cut-off fence that is not 100 percent wildlife-proof. It is built by posting concrete poles connected by metal rods. "We call it a semipermanent fence because it doesn't totally stop elephants or animals from getting through," he clarified. "Small animals can still get in and out through the fence, and the idea is just to limit the areas where elephants can get out from the forest. In the beginning, along the twenty kilometres or forty kilometres of the park boundaries, elephants could get out anywhere. But now, semipermanent fences can stop them. At the moment, there are still ten to twenty entrances where they can still get out. That helps the night team to focus on those spots." They had been working on the plan for fifteen years.

"It is very hard work," Ki reflected with a hopeful tone, "but the thing is that we found that most of the conflict comes from people's attitudes. If people could change their attitude and recognize and understand that they have to live with elephants in harmony, that is the way." Although the elephants damaged property, there were fatalities. The year before, only two people had died while walking alone at night in the forest. In previous years, the number of deaths had been even lower.

"What does 'wild' mean to you?"

"To me, 'wild' means something that is untamed and natural. It includes not just wildlife but also the habitat, forests, and the whole system."

"How do you say 'wild' in Thai?"

"'Pa,' we call it pa."

"Do you think that the park that we're in right now is a wild landscape?"

"Yes, it is. It's wilderness. Even if it's not totally wild. Like in the headquarters, you can feel that you are in the wild and living among natural habitats. You can feel the fresh air." And you could clearly feel the presence of untamed wildlife, we thought.

"Do people belong in the wilderness as well?"

"Yeah, I believe so. In terms of management, we have to include people in there because most of the consumption issues also involve humans."

"Do you think that if humans were not involved in the management, we might not have the wild elephants or the wilderness here?"

"Yes, what we believe through biology conservation is that the biodiversity crisis and other environmental issues originate from human activities. So it's our responsibility to care and provide help. Sometimes, it's not necessary to manage; sometimes, we can just leave things be. Nature has the potential to recover itself, so what we decide to manage is something that we already know that without our help is going to be gone. Elephants here, we believe that if we don't help, there's going to be a problem with them."

The newspapers were not meant for people to read. "The pineapples like newspapers," Suekrit explained, "it gives them a bit of shade." He referred to Korean, Japanese, Thai, and Chinese tabloid newspapers that related gossip and succulent stories – the language seemed not to matter. The newspapers made for a baffling landscape: pineapple crops as far as the eye could see, some of the larger fruits almost ready for picking and others much smaller in size, all wrapped in yellowing newspaper pages that detailed the latest boyfriends and girlfriends of K-pop band members.

Suekrit was the president of Bungnakorn subdistrict, an area whose remoteness and rough roads had tested the suspension of our driver's treasured sporty van. The subdistrict was surrounded by Kaeng Krachan National Park, and Suekrit and his colleagues had been working hard for years to get citizens more involved in restoring and preserving the forest. This wasn't a new job. "Elephants have a rich history in our country," he observed, "so we have had to find a way to manage wild elephants before, in a way that they could live side-by-side with humans without harming anyone."

It was midday, but the heat was tolerable. Cicadas, or at least their Thai counterparts, chirped in their usual high pitch while farmers worked quietly. Peace was in the air, and the gently rolling hills were free of development and busyness. But the peace could be breached at any moment. The crops we were standing by had witnessed plenty of elephant raids. Upon closer examination, the landscape's undulations told a clear story of strife and chaos. Elephants had a habit of hanging out in the forested hills for their shade and water and then bursting out to help themselves to pineapple, jackfruit, durian, sugar canes, mangos, and more. The terrain's undulations revealed their tracks.

A couple of farmers whose home could be seen just a few hundred metres up the dirt track joined our conversation. They confirmed that elephant families were their uneasy neighbours but said relations had improved.

Farmers gather to air their views about the administration of Kaeng Krachan Park

"As the government in this area, we try to find ways so that humans and elephants are not enemies," Suekrit said. The farmers nodded in agreement. His words were mediated by Supanat's translation, but they seemed honestly caring and were appreciated by the farmers.

"We try to protect and keep elephants in their area. Years ago, elephants would come out to eat the villagers' crops. This affected the agricultural products and the lifestyles of the families. We got notified. We had a meeting together. We tried to find a way to solve the problem with our small budget."

At first, their proposed solutions included fences, but their budgets wouldn't allow for them. Local community leaders and farmers came up with a simple but innovative alternative: making the terrain work for them. Long trenches were dug with heavy machinery anywhere the natural contour of the terrain allowed for it. It was the equivalent of digging a moat around the fields.

"We wanted to dig diagonally, with a machine that would dig three metres outwards in a slope," Suekrit explained, "so that when elephants come down, they see a slope and walk down. But by their nature, they will not walk up a steep area. Once they see the ninety-degrees angle, which comes up from the ground with rocks and dirt around six to seven metres, the elephants won't be able to go up to the other side."

We stopped to pick up a pineapple for a quick snack.

"Would you like to go see one of the trenches up close?" Suekrit asked.

We would, we told him, and hopped back on the truck. The dirt path was riddled with cracks and potholes but free of mud. We pitched and rolled along the dips and bumps and eventually reached a small patch of trees that marked the end of the field. A watchtower stood behind the trees. We were told the elephants come from the hills and the forest ahead of us.

"If the elephants come out from the mountain," Supanat said, translating from a chorus of farmers' voices, "they see the wall of dirt, but they can only drink the water that is in the hole and then walk back up the slope, back to the forest. They don't have to dig along the whole area. They just need to dig at the area where a lot of elephants come out."

The project was vastly simpler and cheaper than building fences, and rather effective. The group slowly grew in size to about eight, and we stood by the ditch and exchanged thoughts about how it all worked – what angle of steepness was ideal, how deep the trench should be, and whether it would stop elephants without endangering them, unnecessarily restrict their mobilities, or trap them at the bottom. We felt like we were in one of those impromptu crowds of passersby that form behind the fences at a construction site. The only difference was we were speculating about elephants' lives.

The shade provided by the trees gave us enough cover to converse freely while the crickets added in their own two cents. Elsewhere in the world, perhaps in the hills of Tuscany, the farm below us would have long been turned into an agritourism operation, and instead of a hole for elephants, we'd be staring at a swimming pool dug for seasonal tourists from Britain or Germany. But here, the place was shared by farmers and wildlife.

"Thai people and future generations alike have to help each other to preserve elephants, so that elephants can live alongside the history of the country," Suekrit said. "Having elephants is not a drawback, but their management must be efficient. 'To be efficient' means to be able to preserve the elephants and still have an income at the same time. Elephants have a life too. They have their own basic needs similar to humans. When they are hungry, they need to find food. We should increase their food and water sources in the forest. But many of their forests are damaged."

Many Thai recognize Ganesha as an important deity. Originally a Hindu God, Ganesha has devotees among Jains and Buddhists too. People commonly make an offering to Ganesha before a major undertaking as he is the God of new beginnings, success, and wisdom, as well as a remover of obstacles. Because Ganesha has the head of an elephant, he is recognized by people around the world who might have limited knowledge of his religious significance.

"Buddhism is a religion that believes that the soul is caring," Suekrit said. "Buddhism doesn't support killing other living beings, especially larger animals or animals that are important to the history of our country. Their life and our life are the same. We need to help each other preserve. In Buddhism, if you end a life, that is a sin."

Buddhism enjoys a delicate and not always coherent coexistence with capitalism. In the context of nature appreciation and environmental conservation, Buddhism and neoliberal capitalism are often at odds. Circus-like spectacles such as those put on by people who privately own elephants symbolize the deep fascination that Thai people have toward their beloved national animal. But those spectacles also reveal the pernicious ways that the private sector and national institutions have entered into alliances to attract domestic and global tourists. It is through arrangements like this that domesticated elephants have gradually shifted their identity over time, leaving behind their role in industrial and agricultural development and assuming a new status as players in an increasingly globalized postindustrial, neoliberal world.

But despite this, elephants' identities are not uniform. *Chang pa* (wild elephants), as opposed to *chang ban* (domesticated elephants), have their freedom acknowledged, their agency as independent beings respected, and their home habitats recognized as deserving of protection. Their wildness, somehow, bestows these rights upon them, granting them a sort of idol-like status that their domesticated counterparts lost because of their commodification.

A few days later, we spent an afternoon gazing at chang pa at Kuiburi National Park, not too far from Kaeng Krachan. Farmers and conservation agencies had restored a decayed agricultural area through reforestation and other initiatives intended to give wild elephants a home. People who had once drawn income from farming and logging now worked for the park; in the process, they realized they could not only coexist with elephants but also thrive with them.

Even though they were wild, seeing the elephants in the park did not feel nearly as wild as when we'd sighted the herd on Highway 3218. "Unnatural" or "staged" are words that come to mind. And you didn't need to be a hard-nosed academic to sense it felt more like seeing animals in the zoo. Here's what Autumn wrote in her journal:

> Today, we travelled to Kuiburi National Park with the plan of seeing wild elephants. While it was an exciting experience in itself, I felt it lacked the surprise and uncertainty that comes with suddenly encountering a wild animal. At times, I couldn't even see the elephants due to people's heads in front of me or their selfie sticks. Instead of the sound of the wind or the birds, I heard guides talking. Rather than sharing a moment with the elephants, it felt as though I was watching them from miles away.
>
> In contrast, the elephants we encountered on the highway a few days ago created a whole different experience. We went through the day like any other, not expecting to do anything out of the ordinary. But, right in the middle of the day, we suddenly found ourselves going from eating coconut ice cream to hopping on the back of a military truck to go on elephant patrol. Everything happened so quickly that I barely had the chance to realize the significance of what I was witnessing.
>
> On that day, everything felt unpredictable. Because nobody told us in advance what would happen, everything was like a surprise. When I first saw the elephants from the car, though I was at a safe distance, I felt close. The feeling of being

near an animal of that stature – something in between fear and astonishment – was one I had never experienced before. Then, I watched as the soldiers guided the wild elephants across the highway with care, as though they were friends. The way they acknowledged one another seemed surreal. It was then that I realized that my fear was unfounded because somehow the elephants were as gentle and as caring towards us as we were towards them.

Today at Kuiburi instead, everything felt predictable, for both the elephants and us, but a lot less wild.

Days before our return flight, which was scheduled for January 8, 2020, and about six months before our next and final trip – to Tanzania – a news story about a mysterious type of pneumonia started to gain traction on mainstream news channels. On December 31, 2019, the local government in Wuhan, China, confirmed that local health authorities were treating dozens of cases. Days later, amid skepticism that the newly identified virus could transmit among humans, a sixty-one-year-old man died after contracting the mysterious pneumonia in a Wuhan wet market. Although we didn't know it, when Supanat arranged our next day's interview on the evening of January 4, he was actually scheduling the last meeting of our entire project.

The next morning, we arrived at the administrative office of the Nong Plub Subdistrict and shook hands with Chainarong Namnameaung, the permanent secretary of the administrative organization. "I've arranged for other people to meet with you as well," he broke the news to us. "Follow me."

We jumped in a van and turned down a road we'd never driven down before. Fifteen minutes later, F stopped the van in the middle of a small agricultural village, where a dozen farmers and local officials awaited our arrival in a breezy open-air meeting hall or veranda.

"There's a lot of people here," Supanat said. He sounded surprised and worried. "How are we going to interview thirteen people at the same time?"

"We'll manage," we said. "Just ask them to arrange the chairs in a circle, and we'll do it town-hall meeting style." After a few introductions and furniture shifts, we took our seats.

"We've had more than thirty wild elephants that have come to eat pineapple and tomato in the Nong Plub area," Chainarong said. "The damage happened in Village Number 5, Ban Maka Si-song. Ban Lamaw and Ban Maka Si-song are seriously affected areas in the Nong Plub area. Therefore, when you contacted me to say you were coming here to speak with us, I thought this is a big problem, and I invited others to tell you about it."

Clearly, Supanat's job working for the King's Institute had somehow underlined the value of our research and our presence. It wasn't every day that the villagers felt their voices were being heard far away in the capital city or overseas.

There are ten villages in the Nong Plub Subdistrict, we learned, and after semipermanent fences had been erected in Huai Sat Yai and Bueng Nakorn, the elephants started visiting Nong Plub with greater regularity. Villages Number 8 and 5 had the most problems. Panya Chareondee Mongkol, head of Village Number 8, explained that there were 225 homes in Village Number 8, for a population of eight hundred people.

"There weren't many elephants in the past," Panya told us. "No one can do anything to elephants; therefore, they have given birth to many calves. They are living around here. There are many agricultural products which they can eat. Lately, there were about thirty elephants that came out to the agricultural area. Everything was gone! We tried to push them back, but they insisted on staying here. We used firecrackers to push them back. As a result, they separated from the group and moved to the edge of the forest. Then they came back the next day to eat again. They come every day. If they cannot come to this area, they will go to another area."

The tension in the room – though mitigated by smiles and laughter – was palpable. People took turns venting their frustrations. Jinda Pontongin, head of Village Number 5, Ban Maka Si-song, told us that they had received equipment such as firecrackers and signal devices. "However, elephants got used to those. Whenever we throw a firecracker at them, they will crunch on it."

Jinda and other villages had tried many methods to push them back, but their efforts seemed in vain. "Sometimes, I use guns or cymbals to make loud noises. I tried to push them back all night, up until four or five a.m. They will go back to the forest. They are very persistent."

It's not difficult to think of the names of countries around the world where wildlife could be shot dead for wreaking havoc on farmers' lives, but the situation was different here.

"Why are elephants so important? Why do we have to live with elephants?" Supanat asked to get to the core of the issue.

Panya replied. "An elephant is an honour of the country. We used elephants for fighting. We cannot let them die, but we cannot die either. Therefore, we cannot do anything. What we can do is to push them back to the forest. We cannot harm them."

A chorus of voices rose. "If we do not amend the law, problems will persist. We have to find solutions!"

Semipermanent fences were perceived to be effective, but unless every subdistrict had them, the elephants could simply move on to areas where they could eat whatever they pleased. In addition, the elephant population had to be managed, we were told. Fences alone can't work because a growing elephant population means their living and feeding areas decrease in size.

"Are you feeling heard by the park?" we asked. "Are you receiving support?" We might as well have thrown a firecracker on the floor.

"No!" "Never!" the villagers hollered. "The only thing they do is arrest us!" "They blamed us for ruining the forest!" "The park is careless. They just concentrate on their job." "The park does not care about the villagers." "We step on park grounds with one foot, we are guilty already."

"Are there any forums so you can talk to each other?" Supanat asked.

"They invited us to a forum once, but they didn't pay attention to the villagers." "They never implement what the villagers suggest." "The park always says that there are laws that we have to follow. The park has never invited direct stakeholders to the forum. Therefore, there are problems. If the park set up a forum in each village and listened to villagers, it would be very useful."

Compensation was another sore spot. Farmers were supposed to be compensated for damage inflicted by elephants to their crops, but sub-district administrative organizations did not have the budgets to compensate villagers. As a result, farmers' livelihoods could be seriously impacted by any elephant raid. And even though human casualties were rare, they, too, were improperly compensated. The year before our visit, a man had received only 8,000 Baht – about US$250 – after an elephant trampled his wife and killed her.

We bade farewell to the villagers knowing there was nothing we could do to ensure the park would listen to their concerns. But at least we listened to them, and that seemed to matter. The villagers taught us that people and wildlife can live together, but it's not easy. Coexistence requires fore-thought so the solutions people implement today do not become tomorrow's problems. Coexistence requires patience, but patience must be honoured by a collaborative spirit that involves stakeholders in decision making – instead of simply turning them into subjects of a distant law.

Coexistence requires respect, too, and in this regard, the Thai people we met were exemplary in honouring the rights and virtues of elephants. But coexistence has a pernicious side effect. The more people manage wildlife to solve problems and prevent conflict, the more controlled, institutionalized, and domesticated that wildlife becomes, thus blurring the boundaries between the pa and the ban – the wild and the domesticated.

Humans cohabit with animals in different ways around the world. At times, that cohabitation is superficial, like when farmers and farm animals occupy the same land but enjoy different rights to it. At times, that cohabitation is extensive but inevitable. For example, like many other British Columbians, we have deer and raccoons living on our property, and they live there whether we like it or not. Other times, cohabit-ation can be intensive. Anyone who owns and loves a domestic cat or dog will tell you that their home is their pet's as much as it is theirs.

But cohabitation is different when an animal is pa rather than ban – wild rather than domesticated – as we learned in Thailand. It's not that domestication by itself gives an animal a different status and greater rights but rather the fact that domestication puts humans and animals into a tighter relation. In virtue of that relation, an animal assumes a proper rather than a generic name, acquires a distinct identity and character, and becomes a discrete "person" – not quite a human but most certainly a companion.

Wildness, in the Western sense of the word, typically denies that nondomesticated animals can be person-like. A wild animal doesn't, in fact, have a proper name: it remains a generic member of a species. A wild animal doesn't, in fact, have an identity and character: it remains a token manifestation of broad behavioural qualities typical of a family of animals. A wild animal is wild because it is not domesticated, and it is as different as it gets from pets, farm animals, and civilized humans.

But things are completely different in Thailand. A chang pa, a wild elephant, isn't just a generic pachyderm in Thailand. It has a name, like Cheeky; it has a personality; and it has a relationship – no matter how challenging at times – with guards and with farmers. And it was in virtue of that relationship that the meaning of wildness shifted, away from "savagery," away from unfamiliarity, and toward something else entirely – recognition of rights, of individuality, of free will – toward a relation based on respect and reciprocity. Wildness can be all that without shifting into domestication, if we are willing to cultivate relations with wild beings.

Coexisting with wildlife, not just coping with it, is possible only when humans learn to see wild animals as humans. Authentic cohabitation of human beings and wildlife depends on the respect and reciprocity brought about by wild animals achieving personhood. We'd first learned this in New Zealand, where the Whanganui River had been legally granted personhood. In Thailand, personhood had been granted – socially and culturally, if not legally – to elephants. Person-like in social status, wild elephants were granted rights that allowed them to live a decent life on their land, and their wildness had not been extinguished in the process. But the park was still far from mending its relations with the Karen ethnic minority.

In July 2021, the World Heritage Committee officially recognized Kaeng Krachan as a national park, removing it from its Tentative List and adding it to its list of Natural Heritage Sites. The decision drew international condemnation by human rights groups and even UN personnel. The Karen people, whose traditional territorial rights had been continuously violated by the park administration, were also swift to condemn the decision.

In 2021, the park's harassment of the Karen people had picked up speed as Thai authorities attempted to relocate the villagers and arrested eighty who refused to leave, charging twenty-eight of them – including seven women and one child – with criminal "encroachment." The International Indigenous Peoples' Forum on World Heritage argued that adding the site to the World Heritage List was "one of the lowest points in the history of the Convention and indeed in the history of UNESCO." Francisco Cali Tzay, UN special rapporteur on the rights of Indigenous peoples, commented: "Sustainable and human rights-based conservation cannot be carried out when indigenous peoples continue to be harassed, criminalised, displaced and their land rights, traditional practices and culture are denied."

The Karen have been vocal in their opposition to the UNESCO nomination since it was first proposed. A villager from Bang Kloy, told the *Bangkok Post* on July 24: "The authorities have never explained anything to us. Most importantly, we are concerned about our livelihood. Will it affect our way of life, which is so dependent on the forest? Will such a way of life become even more challenging after its being declared a World Heritage Site? Even when it is not declared so, we have been forcibly removed from the forest, from our traditional village."

Wild Can Be Someone's Home
CANADA

THE MOST DIFFICULT PART about writing a book is making choices. You have to choose which memories to share, which individuals to present, which lessons to reflect on, which feelings to describe, and which places to reveal. You need to choose what to include and what to keep out. What you invariably omit are the less intense moments, the times when nothing magical happens, the days when your field journal barely leaves your backpack.

But dull moments aren't forgettable moments. Over time, some of those moments take on a life of their own. These "backstage" moments tie you to your travels and the people who worked and travelled with you. For us, these were often the moments between interviews, the bits of time between one appointment and the next. These were the moments spent in places where we could park ourselves to wait, space out, and ideally recharge our batteries and check email.

Even though they were spent in different places – at a café, a bakery, a picnic table in a community park, a public square – these moments had a certain mood. They were shaped by fatigue, because we had likely just finished an interview or a hike. But they were also marked by anticipation, because we likely had another engagement in an hour. They were also coloured by the feel of the place where we waited, by the smell of coffee beans, the sound of people walking in and out, the sight of a comfy chair located next to a power outlet, the taste of a latte, or the texture of cellphone screen, anxiously swiped to check the time.

Though we never gave those moments a name, we jokingly gave all the places where those moments unfolded the same name: "Da Kų." Da Kų might have been a coffee shop, a visitor's centre, a park headquarters, or an eatery. Regardless of the walls around us or the kind of roof over our head, a Da Kų, for us, was a temporary shelter, a transient place where we could kick back and unwind. Autumn chose the name "Da Kų" after we spent a few hours doing just that at the Da Kų Cultural Centre in Haines Junction (Dakwäkäda), Yukon, in the late summer of 2016.

It had been barely a month since we'd returned from the Dolomites. Kluane National Park was our first trip to a Canadian Natural World Heritage Site, the first of ten domestic journeys we took between 2016 and 2019, now covered in depth in our 2021 documentary film, *Inhabited,* and in a scholarly book, *Inhabited: Wildness and the Vitality of the Land.*

The Da Kų Cultural Centre was a new, bright, spacious cultural facility located less than a kilometre from the heart of Haines Junction. Part natural and cultural heritage centre, part museum, part gallery, and part hangout and meeting centre, Da Kų had just the right amount of foot traffic to allow us to relax and check email for free without looking like we were loitering. Our cabin was thirty minutes out of Haines Junction, but most of our interviews were in or near Haines Junction, so Da Kų quickly became a home away from home. It was physically in Yukon but by analogy everywhere.

One afternoon in early September of 2016, inside Da Kų, we chatted about the Canadian journeys covered in the domestic portion of our research grant. We planned to go to Banff National Park four months later. For 2017, we loosely scheduled trips to Joggins Fossil Cliffs in Nova Scotia, Gros Morne National Park and Mistaken Point Ecological Reserve in Newfoundland, and Wood Buffalo National Park in Alberta and Northwest Territories. We also pencilled in some trips for 2018: Waterton Lakes National Park and Dinosaur Provincial Park in Alberta and Miguasha National Park in Quebec. We set aside the Northwest Territories' Nahanni National Park Reserve for 2019. We reasoned that we'd finish our Canadian project first and then we'd end our international research in Tanzania's Serengeti in summer 2020. The two sets of trips, international and domestic, would also be separated in their outcomes: each would have its own book and documentary.

The Serengeti was supposed to be the subject of this last chapter. It was never our plan to end this book in Canada. Canada, we determined, would have a chapter somewhere in the middle of the book, but not the end. Why? There's something about wildness that calls you away from home, we reasoned, something that seduces you, that pulls you to remote places, to unfamiliar surroundings where you can't help but feel lost and unable to control the nature around you. That is what we had heard many times in interviews, when we asked people, "What's the wildest place you've ever been to"? The place always seemed to be different, but it was often far from where our interviewees lived.

"Familiarity," for many people, is the perfect antonym of "wildness." Familiarity is predictable, ordinary, habitual, all sorts of things that adventurers trade away in their quest for wildness in faraway places. We, too, fell prey to the logic, at first. We reasoned that Canada was "home," and as wild as it may have been, it felt different from the rest of our travels. Tanzania and the Serengeti felt like the farthest away we could get from Canada, so, we thought, that's where our journey should end.

Then, 2020 happened. As countries grounded planes and shut their borders, universities banned research travel and we couldn't meet face to face with interviewees. The lockdowns in the spring and fall and winter became times to write and reflect, time to question what being at home and being in wild places meant. And for that, we turned to our memories, captured in hard drives full of footage and photos, in files full of interview transcripts, and in journals full of memories, such as those from Kluane. That is how we determined that the journey should end at home, within our own borders.

We'd been at Kluane National Park for a week when we came across a brochure advertising aerial adventures over the glacial fields surrounding us high up in the mountains. The price was right, and despite our aversion to nature-based activities that ended in "-seeing," a flightseeing tour over the Lowell Glacier seemed like a reasonable chance to observe and film the vastness of a land that we couldn't explore otherwise.

There are many kinds of flightseeing. All are a rather lazy way to have an "adventure," but some are better than others. The best, in our opinion, are rides in small planes. While small planes are shaky and there's nothing but a half-inch-thick sheet of see-through plastic between you and death (that's the adventure part), they are remarkably private and free of nuisances. After sharing our sightseeing experience of Patagonian ice with a distracted group of tourists, we can confidently say that confronting vomit-inducing turbulence and near death by vertigo privately is a superior way to appreciate the wonders of glaciation.

We booked our fare without hesitation. The next day, Alex, our pilot, greeted us on the tarmac of the small Haines Junction Airport and welcomed us into his four-seater Cessna. It was a stunning crystal-clear day. We told Alex we wanted to take lots of video, sound, and pictures. "No problem," he said. He even agreed to wear a microphone so we could record our conversation through the plane's headset intercom. "And to take better shots," he added, "just pull back the little sliding glass slot in the rear left window and stick your camera outside the fuselage, but just hang on to it real tight, or it will fly away."

Lowell Glacier

After takeoff, we cruised for what felt like hours around the Lowell Glacier and Mount Logan – North America's and Canada's highest peak. The glacier looked like two massive rivers flowing into each other. Beside them, surrounding the glaciers in all directions, were countless mountains. This is an excerpt from Phillip's field journal:

The mountain beside us is reaching in. It appears to be stretching its stony limbs; as if it wanted to grab our small propeller plane by the wings and swallow it through its frozen face. Yet, it's not the one over there we truly worry about, but the one beside it. It stands farther but it's bigger, stronger, sharper, hungrier. Its edges are protruding further and its walls are prohibitively more precipitous. Our flimsy four-seater is flying too close not to be engulfed by it. The sudden quiet of our voices has drowned the headset intercom in loud static noise.

April, sitting next to Alex, looks like she's about to start crying with anxiety. She gingerly turns around with a ghastly look on her face, quivering. Her eyes intersect with mine. I am seated in the very back row. She smiles and mouths a four-letter word. I acknowledge with a nervous grin. The plane drones on, reaching deeper into the St. Elias mountains. April turns back toward the front, bringing her right hand to her forehead.

Autumn – incongruously calm and somehow looking ready for an afternoon nap – smiles at her with sympathy. April's eyes seem struggling to glance away from what lays outside, aching to shut, yet still wanting to still take in the awe-inspiring beauty of the expanse outside.

I resume work, staring into the camera viewfinder, knowing that by keeping busy I won't be perturbed by thoughts of terror. Once more I stick the camera lens outside of the plane and press the record button. Holding the camera steady as it gets battered by airspeed I manage to keep a grip on the world. But it's an illusion. We have no control. The mountains and the glaciers have surrounded us. They can snatch us any time they wish.

In the unpressurized cabin of a small Cessna the atmosphere that the mountains breathe is the atmosphere you breathe. You can feel the indomitable power of space above and beside you. You can feel the peaks belittling you. You can feel the immense power of nature below you, in the channels of glacial ice bending toward infinite space and in the icebergs floating freely in seemingly unpeopled lakes. But you can also feel a wildness that lives in excess of this. It is in something around you, something inaudible and unsayable, something invisible yet present in the air. You can feel this land has stories to tell.

Countless people around the world told us the wildest place they've ever visited was Canada's North. We believed them. But as we travelled there, we realized that it was no wilderness, if by "wilderness" we mean an uninhabited place. This was and is a land with stories, with ancestral presences, with resident lives enmeshed in a deep kinship that binds animals, plants, and humans. It is Land with a capital "L," a being with personhood and a life of its own.

Our plane reached farther into the world's largest nonpolar ice field and eventually approached Mount Logan. The day before, in Haines Junction, we'd met a man who'd climbed the mountain. Ron Chambers told us he might be the first First Nations man to have reached the summit. The expedition took him eighteen days. As incredible as that was, it was one of the responses he got on his return that made the story stand out. When he got back to town, one of the Elder ladies of the community saw him in the grocery store.

"Oh, I hear you climbed that big mountain there."

"Yeah."

"Any sheep there?"

"No."

"Goats there?"

"No, no goats either."

Puzzled, she looked him in the eye. "So what did you go there for?"

Ron told us other stories. He told us that his father used to trap in Kluane National Park, before it became a national park and before the

Yukon Territorial Government evicted him and other residents from their land to turn the place into a protected wilderness. There's a lake just above Kathleen Lake called Louise Lake. It was named after Ron's grandmother. He also had an aunt by the name of Kluane, his older sister's name is Kluane, and his eldest daughter's middle name is Kluane. There might not be goats or people, but as Ron told us, "This isn't a people-free wilderness. It is our home." The land was part of his family.

If you choose to listen to its many voices, the place isn't empty or quiet. In 2007, anthropologist Julie Cruikshank wrote that the glaciers in the area could listen. She was taught by Tlingit people that glaciers are sensitive beings, contrary to what most people think. She was told that stories dwell there and that a profound kinship exists there, one that blurs the lines between what is conventionally believed to be animate and inanimate. The mountains, the glaciers, the lakes are all alive with these stories and the spirits of those who inhabited the place, and still do.

Indigenous people, gold diggers, trappers, berry pickers, those seeking copper and obsidian, mountaineers, bush plane pilots, and geologists whose family names are still scattered amid the mountains all have their stories. Indigenous people were first, and they are still here; their stories are still alive and inscribed upon Land. Above all, there are ancestors living here, and their lives confound the threshold between presence and memory, the human and nonhuman, spirituality and ecology. You wouldn't know any of this if you simply flew over the place to "flightsee," or if you drove by on the Alaska Highway in a rush. But you would know it if you, too, did what the glaciers do: if you took the time to listen.

People often call a place a wilderness when they have no stories for that place. The World Heritage inscription, for example, has no stories for the glaciers of Kluane National Park. "Healthy terrestrial and marine fish and wildlife populations of key species endemic to the northwest of the North American continent are well-represented within the property," the UNESCO language reads. "Ecological processes are functioning naturally within intact ecosystems, and the property as a whole retains its wilderness values and character, and its scenic beauty." There are no stories in this scientific classification system. There are listed values for a "property," tokens representing a species, processes, and functions. This is a piece of real estate enriched by a mathematical nature imagined and studied as a variable independent from its culture, an ecosystem isolated from its human inhabitants and their ways of life.

But whose perspective is this? Who is it, more broadly, that can call a place a wilderness? For the foreigner, the settler, the colonizer, the bureaucrat managing from a distance, the visitor unable or unwilling to listen to the stories of the land, a place such as Kluane can easily appear as nobody's land, an uninhabited wilderness. But to the traditional and rightful Indigenous inhabitant, that place is something different. "It's home," as Ron told us, "and it will always be home."

A few days after meeting Ron, we took a trip one hundred kilometres north to Burwash Landing to continue the conversation with members of the Kluane First Nation. Mary Jane was a member of the Lhù' ààn Mân Ku Dań (Kluane Lake people), also known as the Kluane First Nation, the traditional inhabitants of Ä́sía Keyi (Grandfather's Country), an area that envelops the shores of Kluane Lake and the Ruby and Nisling Mountain Ranges to the northeast and the Saint Elias Mountains to the southwest. Residing mostly in and around the small community of Burwash Landing, most members of the Kluane First Nation identify as descendants of the Southern Tutchone. Two Clans, the Khanjet (Crow Clan) and Ägunda (Wolf Clan), make up the nation's dominant matriarchal moiety system, though other members of the Kluane have other origins, such as Tlingit, Upper Tanana, and Northern Tutchone.

"Holy mackerel," Mary Jane Johnson exploded and nearly jumped out of her seat when we asked her whether Kluane National Park was a wilderness. "It's a good thing my uncle is not alive to tell you something different. He'd say, 'Where the heck do you get this word "wilderness"?' He'd say, 'There is not one place in this world that has not been touched by a human at some point or another.'"

Mary Jane paused. We were silent. She wasn't angry, but she had a lesson to teach us.

"My family is from all of this area that you're talking about, down from Fort Selkirk, all throughout this country, down through to Alsek, down in the coast toward Haines, Alaska, and over through to Skagway." Not too long ago, she continued, "We were way the heck back up on the glacier, and then they found a bear hide, a grizzly bear hide, way back up there, and it would take you a full day of skiing up over on top of the icefields to get there, and they found a bear hide, and it was human-modified because of the slits and the ties that were on there, and how in the heck it got up there on the glacier?" She paused, long enough for April to ask a big question.

"So, is there a problem with the word 'wilderness'?"

"When you say 'wilderness,' why are we excluded from that idea of wilderness? People are part of the wilderness; people are part of the land. My body does not survive day to day without being part of that land or without being part of that water. And find me one person on this earth who is not part of this land or part of that water where they live. And why are we putting ourselves outside of the idea of wilderness? 'Wilderness' is just a goofy word for somebody that lived in a concrete block for twenty years and came out and saw the wild leaves for the first time or a moose or a bear for the first time. No, we're not above this land and we're not below the water. We are part of it."

Mary Jane was the heritage manager for the Kluane First Nation. She seemed tough, someone experienced in all matters of things and not afraid to tell it like it is. She had a lesson for UNESCO too. "The idea of cultural heritage and the way that UNESCO has defined it is based on the history of built structures and the history of man's place on this earth and their creations to make a place special to themselves. Natural heritage is a hard thing to define because many people on this earth do not have built structures. They do not have structures that are seven hundred to one thousand years old. Here, we've got maybe one or two *njals* that are still standing, little wooden teepee structures. We don't have monuments of stone." The warm September sun bathed the sunflowers planted in the garden behind her.

"But when I go down the river, I see some of the old fish traps on the Nisling. I see old njals that are along some of the rivers or some of the lakes, and if you look at that kind of use of the land or use of the waters, you see that we have had an influence on how the land has changed. By us building rock ways in the river to get salmon and by hunting sheep in different areas, by building hunting blinds up in the mountain to hunt sheep, we've influenced land change."

Initially, Parks Canada did not understand any of this. When the park was gazetted in 1976, all Indigenous inhabitants were evicted, kicked out of their homeland. The colonizers had imagined the place as a wilderness, and they thought it had to be protected that way. People's presence was seen as a hindrance to preserving the place in the name of wild. But the place wasn't a wilderness. It wasn't an unpeopled, untouched, virginal nature that needed to be conserved. The place could only be thought of as a wilderness by people, by a distant colonizing government, whose home was not there, people who did not know the stories the land had to tell.

The notion of wildness as something disconnected from people's lives rests in lack of knowledge. This ignorance can generate a dangerous attitude: the attitude of someone who comes to a place unaware of that land's stories; someone who confuses their foreignness with the foreignness of the place; someone who mistakes that place's naturalness with their own unwillingness to listen to the stories of the land and its inhabitants; someone who is unprepared to recognize their status as outsider, visitor, and colonizer; someone who is unprepared to recognize residents as the rightful inhabitants of the place. This is how wilderness and wild places end up becoming the opposite of home. This is how wildness gets confused with remoteness.

Binary oppositions between wilderness and home, between uninhabited and inhabited, and between nature and culture rely on another, deeper, opposition: the opposition between us and them. This has happened throughout the environmental history of the world. Our own travel itinerary was full of examples of lands subject to colonization, of places becoming "wild" only after settlers showed up. The Galápagos and Ecuador had been colonized by Spaniards. Canada, Australia, and New Zealand had been colonized by the British Empire. South Tyrol had been colonized by the Italian government and Mussolini. Belize had been known as British Honduras until a few decades ago. The Ogasawara Islands had been colonized by Americans and Europeans and then the

Japanese, who came from the main island. Patagonia's Indigenous inhabitants had been exterminated by Spanish settlers. Iceland had been settled by the Norse and the Celts.

The idea of wilderness has a dangerous colonial legacy, and few people realize that colonialism has been justified in the name of developing, controlling, taming, and civilizing the wild. For example, few people outside of Canada (and arguably few even inside Canada) know what the word "Canada" means. "Canada" is an adaptation of a Huron-Iroquois word *kanata*. As the story goes, the word was first heard in 1535 by French explorer Jacques Cartier. He was trying to find his way when two kids from the village of Stadacona (today's Quebec City) told him kanata was nearby. "Kanata" was their word for their village, their home.

In the following centuries, under the Doctrine of Discovery, settlers claimed the vast so-called wilderness for their heads of state, and in the name of civilization, they proceeded to colonize the "wild" inhabitants of the land and settle so-called wild landscapes.

The heritage displays at Da Ku̧ told similar stories but with a more modern twist. Da Ku̧ rested on the Traditional Territory of the Shadhäla Äshèyi yè Kwädän (Champagne and Aishihik First Nations). The Shadhäla Äshèyi yè Kwädän homeland is a land of *kwata* (forests), *dhal* (mountains), *taga* (rivers), *man* (lakes), and *tan shi̧* (glaciers). The place isn't a wilderness. Since time immemorial the Land has offered *mbat* (food), *ur* (clothing), and *ku̧* (house, shelter) to the Champagne and Aishihik's ancestors.

"Da Ku̧" simply means "our house." Learning this was a profound realization. Their house, and more broadly speaking their land, had been turned into a park during the twentieth century so that wilderness could be protected and depeopled. The doctrine of discovery hadn't gone away – it had simply been adapted for the sake of furthering conservation policy, for the sake of protecting a land from its people in the name of wild.

Alberta contains four of Canada's UNESCO Natural World Heritage Sites. Most international visitors gravitate to the Rockies and Banff National Park. Fewer visit the other three: Wood Buffalo National Park, Dinosaur Provincial Park, and Waterton Lakes National Park. Wood

Buffalo National Park feels like a country of its own, impossibly expansive and remote. Dinosaur Provincial Park feels like its own planet, an intermediate stop between an earthly desert and petrified stratosphere where gods and dinosaurs once played with sandcastles.

Waterton Lakes National Park is where prairies meet the Rockies, Parks Canada says. The meeting really takes place about twenty klicks south of ranch land towns such as Twin Butte and thirty klicks west of Cardston, where flatlands and mountains bump into each other. A small park, Waterton Lakes is recognized by UNESCO as a single site with Montana's Glacier National Park "because of their superlative mountain scenery, their high topographic relief, glacial landforms and abundant diversity of wildlife and wildflowers."

The park was formed in 1895 and is Canada's fourth-oldest National Park. Head to Parks Canada's website, click on the "Culture" tab, and you'll get the story of how it was formed. The story begins in the 1890s (presumably the place was a *terra nullius* until then). It was then that a Pincher Creek rancher by the name of F. W. Godsal first proposed turning the area into a park because it had been deemed useless for ranching or farming. The park was named after Squire Charles Waterton (1782–1865), a British naturalist who never set foot in the place.

None of this sat well with the rightful inhabitants of the place, Mike Bruised Head told us in Fort MacLeod, ninety kilometres away from Waterton Lakes National Park. We met Mike and Elder Charlie Crowchief to learn about the First Nations history that Parks Canada wasn't making public. Mike welcomed the opportunity to share with us insights from his ongoing PhD dissertation research at the nearby University of Lethbridge in cultural, social, and political thought. "'Knowing from Place: The Colonial Impact of Blackfoot Names Removed in the Mountains Geographically Located in Waterton National Park.' That's my dissertation's full title," he told us in nearly a single breath.

"Before the settlers and the colonizers arrived, that was our territory. We've been taken out of the equation as Blackfoot people," Mike explained, part of a "calculated manoeuvre to attempt to remove us from our association with the mountains and Waterton and the waters." Mike didn't mince words, and he was right. Back in the late 1800s, Lieutenant

Thomas Blakiston, a member of the Palliser Expedition, decided to call a chain of lakes in the area "Waterton" after the naturalist he most admired. "Blakiston then named a mountain after himself, a creek, a little waterway, and then changed a valley to his name, Blakiston Valley. But all those mountains and passes had names before."

This was not just an Alberta-wide practice. Colonizers all over Canada viewed the vast expanses of land before their eyes as terra nullius, nobody's land, and named them after themselves. "But we were Indigenous to that area," Mike told us. "And, to us, Waterton is a sacred place. You just heard about vision quests from Elder Charlie. You heard about hunting and gathering and Buffalo jumps. Those have been there long before colonizers stepped in and started renaming the area, and the mappers and early surveyors started naming mountains and geographical points of interest in Waterton, putting their label on it, their name."

The park was protected in the name of wild, but "that protection was kind of misleading; it didn't protect us," Mike stated. "And so, imagine. Thousands of years, we've maintained the conservation and environmental best practices of all times, of all humanity, and Waterton was held as a special place. We didn't need any European legislation or acts of law to protect it. We had a duty, a real Indigenous stewardship of the land. And so, when we were pushed away, it marginalized our people. It alienated us from the actual continued occupancy, settlement, hunting, and gathering of our medicines and our spiritual affiliation to Waterton. A protected area is okay. But it's not okay when the very lands some people were actually born in, the mountains where they had their sacred birth grounds, were all removed. That was our land. And it would still be the same environmentally protected area, but according to us. We held it special, we held it sacred, and we did not abuse it. And so, today, we feel like foreigners in our own land."

Australian philosopher Val Plumwood would agree with that viewpoint. Plumwood argued in a 1998 essay titled "Wilderness Skepticism and Wilderness Dualism" that Indigenous people and their lands all over the world have been victimized by a "virulently imperial form of culture, one that held them to be nature, not fully inhabitants of a space empty of culture." European colonizers, Plumwood continued, "did not begin to comprehend the mutual nourishment of the land and the people that made up the country."

It is for these reasons, we believe, that early protection policies put in place in the name of wild must be rethought. Environmental protection is of the utmost importance, make no mistake, but it must recognize the mistakes of the past. It must come to terms with the fact that it, too, has often functioned as a form of colonization. It must seek new collaborative ways of fully incorporating Indigenous knowledge into policies and practices. And it must be informed by an authentic spirit of reconciliation that recognizes Indigenous people's right to manage their unceded lands.

These are, of course, high-level political manoeuvres that we do not have much power over. But we, and you, can do something else: we can change what goes on in the name of wild. We can start by being critical readers and viewers. We can call out authors and producers on their ignorance whenever they act like modern-day colonists. We can do the same for outfitters and tour operators whenever they hastily pronounce somebody's land a wilderness. And we can resist not only industrial and commercial schemes to develop wild lands but also conservation policies that exclude, marginalize, and evict their Indigenous occupants.

We want to see wild environments protected and expanded. But we think there are innovative ways to do this, ways that begin with rethinking what wildness means. Rethinking wildness should begin by recognizing the complexities of the political and cultural relations between people and the land. That recognition must start with a reflection on who we are, who you are in relation to the land you call home and the lands you call wild.

For the three of us, that relation is clear. We and our ancestors came to this land from somewhere else, from Europe. We are settlers, and we are visitors (the kind that stay over forever). And so are many of the people we interviewed for this book. And so are many of you, our readers. As settlers, we must recognize our relationship with the lands we live in, the lands we visit, and all their stories and relations.

Ask yourself where your ancestors came from, where their lands were. And then ask yourself whose Traditional Territory your current home rests on. Who are you in relation to the land you occupy? Who are you in relation to the land where you travel for leisure or vacation? Who are you in relation to the places you call wild?

We – Autumn, April, and Phillip – are Canadians. As Canadians, we must recognize our relations with the Indigenous peoples who have lived on these lands long before we or our ancestors did. We must come to terms with difficult subjects, difficult positions, and difficult issues and make challenging choices and decisions every day about our relations with this land. As Emma Battell Lowman and Adam Barker write in their book *Settler,* by recognizing our identity as settlers, we take on an uncomfortable, personal position. Yet this is a position that forces us to understand things differently and act differently. "Settler" is an uncomfortable identity that forces us "to confront the fundamental problems and injustices" in all settler-colonial societies worldwide.

When we recognize who we are as settlers, we become aware of the colonial history of our countries and how the legacies of colonial history still inform official policies and culture. When we recognize who we are as settlers, we also become more keenly aware of the meaning of the words we use, words such as "wild."

When we, as settlers, call a place wild, we call into question our history with that place, our relations with it. If we call that place wild because we believe it to be empty of culture, empty of human history, free of modifications put in place by humans, free of ancestors' spirits, then we are likely ignorant. We are likely blind to the many traces of human inhabitation. We are likely deaf to the presence of the ancestors' spirits, and we are likely uneducated about that place's history and its kinships with Indigenous and non-Indigenous inhabitants. When we recognize who we are as settlers, we realize that "wild" often names something else, something we probably never thought of before, something we should be careful about naming.

When we name a place "wild," perhaps we could name something else, something new and different. As Valerie Plumwood writes, we must overcome the notion of wildness as something cordoned off from the rest of the social world and confined "to pristine situations which entirely lack, or have rendered invisible, cultural influence." If we change what we mean in the name of wild, we can "reclaim the ground of continuity, to recognize both the culture which has been denied in the sphere conceived as pure nature, and to recognize the nature which has been denied in the sphere conceived as pure culture," as Plumwood puts it. We don't need to throw away the word "wild," but if we decide to change what we name with it, to reclaim the word, to reconceive it, what, exactly, should we call wild?

Banff National Park is Canada's oldest park and the world's fourth-oldest national park. Like many other early protected areas in North America and around the world, Banff National Park was initially built on the principle of exclusion. As tourists began to arrive by train at the turn of the twentieth century, the Indigenous peoples of the region were barred from hunting and eventually excluded from areas they had long called home. This was no eviction in the name of wilderness preservation, however. Attracting leisure hunters and their money was the end goal, and game conservation was the means. First Nations who had relied on the bison hunt were simply kicked out, their cultural rituals eradicated (save for those they could perform for tourists).

To learn about that history and the evolution of those policies, we met with a group of seven Stoney Nakoda First Nation members in January 2017. Bill Snow began by telling us how the Stoneys were run out of Banff back in the early 1900s. By then, the bison had become so scarce that the Stoney Nakoda and other First Nations living in the area could no longer subsist on bison meat. But the bison was not simply a source of food. The bison also provided clothing and tools and played a key role in culture and spirituality.

With the bison all but destroyed, it became easy for the federal government to confine the Stoney and the other Treaty 7 nations to reserves. The simultaneous objectives of annihilating the bison and Indigenous peoples had been achieved. "I am not at all sorry that this has happened," Canada's prime minister, John A. Macdonald, commented in the House of Commons. "So long as there was a hope that buffalo would come into the country, there was no means of inducing the Indians to settle down on their reserves."

Members of the Stoney Nakoda First Nation. Standing, left to right: Bill Snow, Duane Wesley, Chris Clarke, and Chris Goodstoney. Seated, left to right: Charles Powderface, Charlie Rabbit, and Jackson Wesley

Over time, attitudes changed. Today, First Nations and conservation organizations such as Bison Belong have been successful in reintroducing bison to Banff National Park. It's not only a symbolic achievement but also an important ecological success story. Wild bison, we were told at our meeting with the Stoney Nakoda, perform important functions on the landscape: "They are very important keystone species," Bill told us. "And they have to have room to do all of those functions that they do on landscapes, because they help wildlife, birds, reptiles, ungulates, other predators, other forms of life out there. So, they contribute so much not only to the ecosystem but to other forms of wildlife. When they come back to an area, they really make a big impact."

In addition, bison perform an essential affective role in the psychological, social, and cultural health of Indigenous groups such as the Stoney Nakoda. Charles Powderface told us that Stoney Nakoda "truly honour the bison because it saved us. Way back, it fed us. We didn't go hungry. We relied on the bison, and when they signed the treaty after, there were restrictions about hunting bison. But still to this day, we still rely on the bison spiritually. We pray and we rely on the buffalo spirit."

Scholars agree that the bison is not simply a keystone species in relation to the biological functioning of an ecosystem but also a cultural keystone species. Bringing the bison back to Banff National Park can, therefore, restore ways of life central to the survival of both animals and humans. This was "a story of restoration and reconciliation," in the words of Marie-Eve Marchand, one of the leaders of Bison Belong and one of the many people we spoke with in Banff.

Bringing the bison back also marked a key moment in the evolution of Parks Canada. Earlier in the twentieth century, parks had often been formed after First Nations had been evicted in utter disregard of their human rights and in ignorance of the role they played in the ecosystem. But over time, Parks Canada had begun to consult and then, more meaningfully, to collaborate and comanage protected areas with First Nations.

A lot of work remains to be done, but there are signs of progress. The year we visited Banff, for example, UNESCO approved Canada's nomination of Manitoba's Pimachiowin Aki as a mixed Natural-Cultural Heritage Site. Pimachiowin Aki (The Land That Gives Life) is recognized as "part of the ancestral home of the Anishinaabeg, an Indigenous people living from fishing, hunting and gathering" and as "an exceptional example of the cultural tradition of Ji-ganawendamang Gidakiiminaan ('keeping the land'), which consists of honouring the gifts of the Creator, respecting all forms of life, and maintaining harmonious relations with others." This is quite different from protecting a land for its wilderness qualities.

"Wild, to us, means peace," we were told at our meeting with the Stoney Nakoda. Other people around the world had told us that the experience of wildness felt peaceful, but there was something different about what the Stoney Nakoda were teaching us. This wasn't so much the kind of peace that you feel when you disconnect with noise, with the city, with people, or technology. This was a spiritual and deeply political peace, a sense of belonging in an ecosystem and on one's land, together in harmony with other species and other spirits. Bringing back the bison was a key ecological and political move in restoring that connection and that peace.

The Stoney Nakoda taught us that bison and humans are related through an ancestral heritage that does not make binary classificatory distinctions. Bill Snow told us that Western science is based on binary oppositions, distinctions, and categories, but for the Stoney Nakoda – like so many other Indigenous groups in Canada – knowledge is based on systems of relations and interconnections. Wildness in the Western sense is based on classifications such as "domesticated and undomesticated," "developed and undeveloped," "proximate and remote," "cultural and natural," and "spoiled and pristine." From an Indigenous knowledge perspective, things are quite different and based on reciprocity, harmony, peace, and respect.

During our meeting with the Stoney Nakoda, Christ Goodstoney explained to us that "in a wild forest, for our people, there's nothing wild or dangerous. It's a peaceful environment where our people can be at peace with the animals, especially the protectors, the Grizzly, the Wolf. You go in there with respect, and then nature respects you." Reciprocity is essential, and reciprocity is based on the idea that humans and other species are not different from each other. They are kin.

Métis/otipemisiw scholar Zoe Todd teaches us that if we humans thought of ourselves as coconstituted with the lifeworlds that we share with nonhumans – as opposed to thinking of ourselves as different and removed from them – we would learn to view ourselves as being in kinship with all beings. This notion of kinship is central in many Indigenous worldviews.

For example, anthropologist Enrique Salmón tells us that a Rarámuri worldview does not differentiate between human and nonhuman. He calls this a kincentric ecology. In kincentric ecology, everything is related and interconnected. In kincentric ecology, there is no need for categories of thought that separate wildlife from humanity. No longer strangers to each other, humans and wild animals form a harmonious kinship. Indigenous bodies of knowledge and kincentric ecological perspectives can help us to reimagine what "wild" means.

Wild matters. Wild needs to be honoured, respected, and protected. But we need to be careful about what we name wild, why we do so, and how we act toward it. As Val Plumwood writes, "We need to create new, non-colonizing understandings" of wildness and situate them within the context of a renewed, radical ecology committed to healing the nature/ culture split and ending the war on the Other," whether Indigenous, animal, or abiotic. Doing so, she reflects, will entail viewing wildness not as a sign *of* absence – absence of human traces, of human history, culture, social organization, or inhabitation. Rather, wild places can be understood and appreciated as places inhabited by the presence of the Other, the "presence of the long-evolving biotic communities and animal species which reside there, the presence of ancient biospheric forces and of the unique combination of them which has shaped that particular, unique place." It is then, and only then, that the rest of us settler colonials will be able to walk into an environment and feel the peace that true wildness brings.

It's January 2021. There will be no more journeys to World Heritage Sites or national parks for a long while. We're being asked to stay within our communities, to stay at home as much as possible, to not meet with one another. While we sit on our couch, read over our field journals, and edit drafts of our chapters, the last seven years of borderless travel and shaking hands with strangers feels like a dream. As we share memories of our most vivid experiences of wildness, Autumn decides to put hers on paper to close the final chapter of her journal:

> "What does the word 'wild' mean to you?" I've heard that
> question countless times throughout the last eight years of my
> life. I've heard it asked in different languages, and answered by
> hundreds of different people in twenty parts of the world.
> However, interestingly enough, I've never heard the exact same
> answer twice.
>   Throughout the years I've spent travelling with my parents,
> I've often imagined how I would answer this question myself.
> What exactly does the word "wild" mean to me? How would I
> define it? After pondering over answers for quite some time, I've
> finally thought of one. It comes with a short story.
>   It was the fourth day of our hike on the Hollyford Track. We
> had already spent the whole day hiking along the dreaded

"Demon's Trail" and we were still walking, aimlessly – it felt like. It had been several hours since we'd seen another person, and our bodies were limp due to the rocky terrain. Saying we were exhausted would be an understatement. It felt like forever since we'd seen a trail sign, which – due to our nearly useless map – was our primary source of navigation. We kept trekking blindly *towards* our destination, a hut which seemed days away. As we walked quietly, by then too tired to talk, the only noises came from the forest surrounding us and our shoes meeting the ground underneath.

But despite our exhaustion, everything was strangely peaceful. It felt as though we were completely alone in this vast forest. Alone *with* the forest. This moment was one of my most intense experiences of wildness. When I think of the word "wild," I imagine the feeling of being completely isolated in a landscape. This feeling doesn't necessarily always have to be peaceful; being in the wild comes with a lot of uncertainty as well, which is typically what makes it more intense and memorable.

Then suddenly, my dad pointed to something on the trail ahead of us. I followed his finger with my gaze and in the thick vegetation I spotted a trail sign indicating that the next hut was nearby. Along with my parents, I started running. As my dad hooted and hollered like a little kid I ran with excitement *towards* the hut. Once we got there, all three of us collapsed upon the grassy field, thankful to have finally arrived.

With extra time to read and think, we pore over every detail of our interview transcripts. We play back recordings and listen to spoken words even more closely than we did in person. Images and sounds transport us back to people we met a long time ago. Interviews from years back reveal insights that suddenly make more sense.

We pause on the words of Peter Adams, an American expat we met in Tasmania. "We tend to think of wilderness as separate from humankind," he told us in early January 2016. "We tend to think that to walk into wilderness is to leave behind all of humanity's structures and houses and camps. But what is true wilderness? In our definition, it's where there is no human impact, and I don't believe in that. Because then you deny all that Aboriginal ancestry of any place, their legitimate connection to that land." Wildness is something else, he reflected. "Maybe it's there if you listen. Do you feel the energy? And maybe that has come about through all this ancestral energy that's been flowing through the years."

Then, with a few clicks of a mouse, we skip ahead four years and thousands of miles. We land in Fort Simpson, just outside Nahanni National Park. As we browse our folders, we find transcripts of an interview with Kristen Tanche. "My mother is Kathy Tanche, and my father is Gunnar Paulson. I'm part of the Dehcho First Nations," the young woman introduces herself on the tape. "From what I've heard from Elders and cultural Knowledge Holders and people of the areas, people would come here to gather, to meet each other, to have celebrations, to do drum dances. We all have ties to all sorts of different parts of the land. We're a nomadic people traditionally. So we would be everywhere. We'd be following the trails of our ancestors. A lot of our connections are very holistic. We're not just connected to one piece of land. We're connected to the Nahanni National Park. We're connected to the falls. We're connected to this entire region."

The rain picks up outside our living-room window. Kristen's recorded words go on and grow in intensity in tandem with the rainfall on our roof: "Not every single area on earth, but a lot of them, have been frequented by people, by animals. There's traces of people or their footprints on all, and everywhere, especially here. So it's not untouched. There's been people here. 'They've lived here since time immemorial' is what our people say. So is there really a wild place? This place, I wouldn't necessarily call it wild," she concludes. "I'd call it powerful."

Wildness is power. The power of wildness is ineffable, indomitable. It wants to escape an ultimate definition. It wants to be something else, and then something more, and then something more. It is alive, powerful, and has a will of its own.

West Coast winter rains grow harder around us, and in the long dark days, we dig deeper into our transcripts. We read the words of Gerald

Antoine, Dene National Chief, who thinks that "wildness" means aliveness. "We have a unique spiritual connection with a place that we call home." What the Dene call home, countless other people who visit Nahanni National Park call wilderness. "The word *Dene* is connected to two things: one is the river, and the other one is about the land. So there is this relationship that we have." That idea pops up again: wildness not as disconnection and separation but as connectedness and relation.

When people from all over the world come to visit Nahanni, Gerald explains, they are excited because they think they are going into the wild. "Out here, everything is alive, and this is something that is really special for visitors. And it helps them to reconnect themselves with the things that they need to connect with, and it varies depending on where they come from and what they're looking for. And where they come from, they see that as something really wild. And for us, as Dene people, we don't necessarily look at it as wild. We look at it as something very special and very sacred."

Wildness is a sacred relation. A relation is an existing connection, a kinship. A relation demands commitment. It demands respect and reciprocity. Being in a relationship with a wild place, a wild life, or a wild thing demands we understand its past and present because it is alive, because it demands we care for it and that we safeguard its future. Wildness asks us to listen to it and honour its presence. With its every act, it reminds us that we are not in control. With its indomitable power, which goes beyond us, wildness tells us that we will never fully capture its essence or harness its force. A relation with wildness is special and sacred.

To say that wildness is relational is not the same as saying that wildness is relative. When we say that wildness is relative, we recognize that anyone has the right to call a place wild or not wild. But it can't work that way. If wildness was relative, you'd be free to name whatever you want wild, regardless of whose land it is. And you'd be also free to turn a blind eye to the sacredness and relationality of the land and call a place a resource, a wasteland, an empty land and do whatever you want with it. No, wildness isn't relative, and it isn't subjective. Wildness is a relationship and a bond.

As a relation, wildness makes demands on us. It gives us duties and obligations. Wildness is life, it is aliveness itself, but it also demands from us that we do not exhaust it, that we let it live. Wildness gives us time to get away, but it also asks for our time, time to listen to its stories and to feel its presence. Wildness gives us a chance to uncover other forms of life, but it also asks us to recognize their rights. Wildness gives us humans kinship with nonhumans, but it also asks us to enact policies that further extend that kinship.

That relation makes another demand. It asks us to understand what truly is in the name of wild. Not separation but connection. Not absence but presence. Not domination but respect. Not domestication, control, and exploitation but a willingness to coexist. Not emptiness but sacredness. Not the pristine or the untouched or the virginal but kinship, interdependence, and commitment. Not an object but a subject, one that is enlivened, spirited, and deserving of care. Not fear or danger but personhood and aliveness. Across different individuals, societies, languages, and cultures, let this be what we mean when we say "wild."

Acknowledgments

This book was written at our home in British Columbia between 2014 and 2021. Our home is situated on a small island in the Salish Sea, unceded Traditional Territory of the Snuneymuxw First Nation. But our book comes from stories, experiences, and perspectives we gathered around Canada and the world as we travelled far away from home. To all those who gave us hospitality, who taught us the places we wanted to learn about, who opened the doors of their home, who walked with us, who showed us the way, who donated their time to us, who shared their thoughts and experiences, we wish to say "thank you." None of what we know, none of the material included in this book, could be shared if it weren't for you, for your generosity with your time and your knowledge.

We are also unmeasurably thankful to the many gatekeepers who helped us with planning our journeys, connecting with people, translating interviews, adapting ideas, mediating relations, establishing and maintaining rapport, navigating intercultural communication, and staying safe. To Marisa MacArthur, Wiebke Finkler, Emanuel Valentin, Lyra Spang, Yosuke Washiya, Benji Juarez, Thorildur Heimisdottir, Supanat Permpoonwiwat, thank you, dilan, grazie, danke, arigato gozaimashita, gracias, Þakka þér fyrir, ขอขอบคุณ.

We wish to acknowledge three individuals whose work was foundational. Tobi Elliott's research assistance with interviews in Nahanni National Park, Jules Molloy's tireless work on the interactive documentary, and David Phu's patient and accurate transcriptions were priceless sources of help. David alone transcribed about 1.5 million words in about four thousand single-spaced pages of interviews. Others who helped with transcription include Angela Sasso, Yuki Soekawa, Supanat Permpoonwiwat, Emanuel Valentin, Christine Duggan, and Erin Booker. We cannot thank them enough for their work.

A book comes to life only after many people are involved in various stages of the publishing process. To that effect, we are infinitely grateful to our agent, Louise Rebelle, our editor Lesley Erickson, and to the staff at On Point Press/UBC Press. We are also thankful to Royal Roads University, the Canada Research Chair program, and the Social Sciences and Humanities Research Council of Canada, whose funding made this work possible.

Many of the ideas presented in this book were initially elaborated as part of scholarly writings, and to our peer reviewers and editors we are very indebted. Within Royal Roads University, Deborah Zornes offered support that went above and beyond her call of duty, and we will always be grateful to her for everything she did.

Lastly, we would like to thank the numerous park agencies that permitted us to do research and film, often giving us significantly discounted prices on permits and even enabling our research by spending time with us, teaching us, and helping us establish relations on site.